EXCESS
IN FOOD
DRINK
AND SEX

Other books by Charles Neilson Gattey

The Bloomer Girls (*Femina*)
Gauguin's Astonishing Grandmother (*Constable*)
A Bird of Curious Plumage (*Leslie Frewin*)
They Saw Tomorrow (*Harrap*)
Queens of Song (*Barrie and Jenkins*)
The Elephant That Swallowed A Nightingale (*Hutchinson*)
Foie Gras and Trumpets (*Constable*)
Great Dining Disasters (*Columbus*)

EXCESS
IN FOOD, DRINK AND SEX

CHARLES NEILSON GATTEY

HARRAP
LONDON

FOR EDWARD A. MURPHY

First published in Great Britain 1986
by HARRAP LTD

© Charles Neilson Gattey 1986

ISBN 0 245-54397-X

Designed by Linda Wade

Printed and bound in Great Britain
by Biddles Ltd, Guildford

CONTENTS

I	'Moderation is a Bore'	7
II	The Ancient World	10
III	From The Wife of Bath to Ninon de Lenclos	35
IV	Drunken Parliaments and The King of Rakes	51
V	The 'Secret History of Clubs'	60
VI	Gluttony and Gin	68
VII	Port and Passion	81
VIII	Louis XV and His Seraglio	107
IX	Roistering in Russia — and Phallic Gods	112

X   Coffee, Chocolate, Tea — and
         Cocktails   123

XI   George IV and French Cuisine   132

XII   Victorian Vice and
         The 'Demon Drink'   144

XIII   The Reign of The Courtesans   156

XIV   Gluttony in The Guildhall   164

XV   Edwardian Voluptuaries   170

XVI   'Yama The Pit' and 'Dead Souls'   178

XVII   Abandon in America   187

XVIII   Some Twentieth Century
         Sybarites   195

XIX   Abnormal Appetites and
         Aphrodisiacs   220

XX   The New Permissiveness   231

Select Bibliography   235

Index   239

I

'MODERATION IS A BORE'

Moderation is a bore, millionairess Barbara Hutton once said, and 'Maigret' author, Georges Simenon, boasted at the age of eighty-two that he had slept with some 10,000 women during his lifetime. Puccini, on the other hand, later regretted having had so many love affairs, pointing out that he might have written more operas had he not spent so much time in a horizontal position. Excess can be expensive — and it can exterminate, too. King Canute did not die from a chill through getting his feet wet but from over-eating at a wedding feast, and his son, Hardecanute, passed days and nights carousing and perished after a drunken orgy. Henry I dropped dead after stuffing himself with lampreys, and the *White Ship* sank drowning his heir through the crew being the worse for liquor. It has been claimed that if King John had not held at Christmas 1199 the most costly banquet, lasting several days, ever to have been given in England, the offended barons he failed to invite would not have rebelled and forced him to sign Magna Carta. John's demise was caused by eating peaches with too much new cider, and a violent fever aggravated by eating too many peacocks, some said, felled Edward IV. There are various versions as to how the Duke of Clarence came to be found lifeless in a butt of malmsey. One is that, sorrowing over the fate of his wife, he drank too much and tumbled inside. Thanks to modern surgery, Edward VII, known as Tum Tum, suffered only his Coronation's postponement through getting acute appendicitis.

In France, Louis XVI was denounced as a glutton by the Revolutionaries. Camille Desmoulins taught the populace in Paris to believe that the King would have escaped from the country and Madame Guillotine had he not tarried at Varennes to gorge at the inn on pigs' trotters. In more recent times, another monarch, Farouk, died when still in his forties after a night of eating too much at his favourite restaurant in Rome, whilst in Hollywood Errol Flynn, who boasted that he had devoted nearly 14,000 nights to making love, had a fatal massive heart attack after drinking-bouts lasting a week.

Some writers claim that wars have had a considerable influence on national drinking habits, and that these in turn have affected the course of history. A French authority on wine maintained that the onslaught of the Gauls on Rome in 309 BC, when the geese gave the famous warning, was caused by their craving for Italian fine wines. Morton Shand suggests that the Crusaders pillaging Gallia in the thirteenth century were animated as much by a ravenous thirst as by religious zeal. Five centuries later, in August 1792, when Prussian soldiers plundered the vineyards of Champagne, the unripe grapes they gorged proved their undoing. So many became ill with colic that they were defeated at Valmy by the French revolutionary army.

Warnings of the dire consequences of excess are more often than not ignored by those obsessed with their fixed ideas, and they are sometimes encouraged by the *laissez-faire* attitude of modern society. Sir Alexander Korda whenever he gave a nephew a fiver would say: 'Don't spend it — waste it.' Somerset Maugham once remarked in favour of adultery that it had provided him with absorbing material for his writings, and he added: 'You know, of course, that the Tasmanians, who never committed adultery, are now extinct.'

There are those who become excessively intolerant of what they regard as excesses in others, such as the Nosy Parkers who called on John Strachan, first Anglican Bishop of Toronto, to ask him to warn their pastor about the bad example he was setting his flock through having so many empty whisky bottles in his dustbin every week. 'Whisky bottles!' exclaimed the hard-headed Scot disapprovingly. 'Yes, indeed, I must speak to him. Bottles — that's very extravagant. I buy my whisky by the keg.'

II

THE ANCIENT WORLD

'Nothing succeeds like excess' may have been some roué's riposte to 'Nothing to excess' the maxim carved on a column in the temple at Delphi and one observed by many Greeks. There were exceptions such as Geta, who made his cooks provide for him at every meal as many courses as there were letters in the alphabet, and as many dishes as could be found the names of which began with every letter. According to Pindar, Hercules was so fond of beef that he ate at one meal the grilled carcass of a bull together with the still-glowing coals stuck to it. Ulysses's voracity is mentioned in the *Odyssey,* and the renowned athlete, Milo of Crotona, after carrying a four-year-old bull on his shoulder round the stadium at Olympia, consumed it, watched by his admirers.

Asked where the Acropolis is to be found, the cultured will reply — Athens. The same question put to a modern rake might well receive the answer — Paris. Just before the last war an earthly heaven for sybarites opened near the Opéra. Facing them as they entered the principal salon and covering a whole wall was a painting of the famed Athenian citadel, and grouped around its rocky base were provocatively dressed Greek *hetaerae.* The décor was Graeco-Roman and the dance floor of jade and illuminated glass, surrounded by colonnaded galleries. Under the arches at tables sat the male customers, wealthy pillars of industry, stage and film personalities, sex-starved politicians, drinking champagne with bevies of beauties in diaphanous shifts and looking as though they had'stepped out of the fresco.

Everything was extremely chic and costly. If you preferred a Chinese, Persian, or Turkish setting, there were salons in those styles with girls to match. Homesick Arabs could have sex in the Desert Room lying on oriental rugs in a tent that had an opening providing views of shimmering sands and radiant skies with a caravan gliding past on the horizon — all on a diorama. For those who wanted to get extra kicks out of horizontal jogging there was a Chamber of Mirrors that multiplied embraces and couplings a hundred times. Less pleasant was a medieval castle's torture chamber catering for either masochists or sadists.

At the other end of the social ladder there was the *Moulin Galant*, where sixty girls, known as hustlers, stood in one line on becoming free and the men in the other had to take whoever happened to be standing next to them when they reached madam at the cash register.

It was Corinth and not Athens which had the reputation of being the most immoral of all cities in ancient Greece, and there its temple dedicated to the Goddess of Love, Aphrodite, was the abode of a thousand young women known as the *hieroduli*, who were really *hetaerae* or harlots. They debased the religious festival of the Aphrodisia into licentious revelry and would come out at night in search of men, their chief customers being sailors or, every fourth year, athletes passing through the city on their way to and from the Olympics. On account of this married women were not permitted to go to the games.

The cult of hedonism, of course, originated with the Greeks, whose festivities served as outlets for sexual vigour, following which the majority would calm down and accept the restraints of every-day life. The Romans in

11

contrast beneath a veneer of culture were in many cases barbarians who made their main aim in life unbridled sensual gratification. They took over the Greek god of wine after the second Punic War and held Bacchanalia as a celebration after the grape harvest. At first conducted much on the same lines as the Greek Dionysia, the proceedings soon degenerated into sexual orgies.

According to legend, Dionysus first came to be worshipped in Greece when Pegasus brought some of the god's images to Athens where these were treated with disrespect by its people. To punish them for this affront the god afflicted all the men with a calamitous complaint in their sexual organs which no doctor could cure. When an oracle was consulted for guidance, the reply received was that all would have their virility restored if the deity's images were given proper reverence. This led to the rejoicings known as the Dionysia with the participants bearing wooden phalluses tied to the thyrsi. The legend closely resembles one involving Priapus and the Lampsacenians, in whose temples orgies took place, full of all kinds of perversions.

Erected everywhere by the wayside in ancient Greece were stone statues of Hermes, the god of the roads, with enormous male organs, similar to those raised elsewhere to Priapus. Yearly festivals, called Hermae, took place chiefly in Athens and also elsewhere in the country, which were the scenes of phallic rites and excesses, resembling those common at the Dionysia.

Cooking, as an art, originated in Greece and spread from there to Rome, where the oldest known book on the subject, in which are collected the best Greek recipes, was published by a gourmet, Marcus Gavius Apicius, in the Emperor Tiberius's reign. Having spent 60 million sesterces on the food he ate and, finding himself left with 10 million, the prospect of no longer being able to enjoy such a life so depressed him that he committed suicide. But it was a general, Lucullus (110–56 BC), whom Athenaeus blamed for introducing luxurious living into Roman society. He spent two hundred thousand sesterces feasting

Pompey and Cicero. His villa seemed to consist of only dining-halls in which he entertained guests in graduating degrees of extravagance, according to their importance. At reckless expense, he had a large hill near his summer residence flattened and a canal dug leading to the sea and admitting its water to a huge pond at the rear of his property, and this he stocked with the fish he preferred.

Lucullus's contemporary, Aulus Hirtius, who deputized for Julius Caesar in Gaul, also had a reservoir built which was filled with thousands of lampreys for the great banquets honouring his victories. According to early biographers, Caesar was completely amoral. Sent as a young man on a mission to King Nicomedes of Bithynia, he had a homosexual affair with him, then, on returning to Rome, he married Pompeia and also commenced a life-long liaison with Servilia, whilst at the same time sleeping in turn with any woman who could further his career. Curio called him 'the wife of all men and the husband of all women'. So it is not surprising that he readily accepted Cleopatra as a mistress after she had gone to the trouble of smuggling herself, disguised into his presence — some say rolled up in a carpet.

Cleopatra has been the subject of so many stories that it is impossible to distinguish between fact and fiction. She has been accused of orgies lasting for weeks and of fellating a hundred Roman officers in one night. Later, in Antony she found a lover who was the most extravagant of epicures, travelling everywhere with his complete gold dining-service. Once a visitor, discovering that eight wild boars were being roasted, asked the cook if many guests had been invited. Only a dozen, the man answered, but, as his employer was a perfectionist, if any dish were not up to his exactingly high standards, back it went to the kitchen, so replacements had to be readily available. Cooks who excelled were generously rewarded. Antony gave one a large town as a tip.

An often told anecdote of Antony and Cleopatra is that they engaged in a culinary contest, each striving to outshine the other in *outré* fare, and that Cleopatra was judged the winner when she removed a priceless pearl ear-drop, dissolved it in lemon juice, and drank the potion, saying: 'My toast to Anthony shall exceed in value the whole banquet.' The drinking excesses of the Romans themselves were less imaginative — mainly contests to see who could swallow the most without stopping or win bouts lasting a number of days. A physician unexpectedly won on one occasion through finding that almonds eaten beforehand prevented intoxication.

Julius Caesar's great-nephew, Augustus, the first Roman Emperor, was neither a drunkard nor a glutton, but, according to his contemporaries, he was so oversexed that at banquets he would leave the table between the courses and lie on a couch in an anteroom with whatever woman he suddenly desired, even his friends' wives. It was noticed that he did not trouble to put right his clothes before returning.

Augustus's successor, the second Roman Emperor, was such a heavy wine drinker as a young soldier that he was called Tiberius. He celebrated the start of his reign by spending a whole night and two days feasting, with naked girls serving him at table. He appointed an outsider to the post of Questor in preference to better qualified candidates, because, in toasting the Emperor's health, he drank an amphora full of wine at a single draught. Asellius Sabinus received 200,000 sesterces from Tiberius for writing a dialogue about a truffle and a figpecker disputing with an oyster and a thrush, and he created a new office for 'the originating of unfamiliar carnal pleasures'.

According to Suetonius, the Emperor in his retreat at Capri kept a room furnished with many couches and 'adapted to the purpose of secret wantonness, where he entertained companies of girls and catamites, and assembled from all quarters dancers of monstrous lewdness whom he called Spiritriae . . . He had many bedchambers hung with pictures and statues representing figures in the most lascivious attitudes and furnished with the books of Elephantis, that none might want a pattern for the execution of any filthy project that was prescribed him. He arranged in the woods and groves, here and there, recesses for the gratification of lust, where, within caves and hollow rocks, young persons of both sexes indulged their passions in the disguise of little Pans and nymphs.' On account of this, the Emperor was nicknamed 'Caprineus', for the word, Capri, has a double meaning, one of them being 'a goat'.

Suetonius continues that Tiberius taught 'fine boys the tenderest and daintiest that might be had (whom he termed his little fishes) to converse and play between his thighs as he was swimming and prettily with tongue and teeth seem to nibble at his secret parts . . . It is also reported that during a sacrifice, he took such an ardent fancy to the beautiful face and form of a youth who held a censer, that, before the religious rites were well over, he took him aside and abused his body; as also a brother of his who had been playing the flute; and soon afterwards broke the legs of both of them for upbraiding one another with their shame.'

The next Emperor was Caligula, that most vicious sadist with the hairless head and the hairy body, who, Suetonius tells us 'in riotous and extraordinary expenditure surpassed the wits and inventions of all the people that ever lived; devising a new kind of bath, with strong dishes and suppers, washing in precious unguents, both warm and cold, drinking pearls of immense value dissolved in vinegar, and serving up for his guests loaves of bread and other foods made out of gold.' He had 'an unnatural passion for Marcus Lepidus Mnester, an actor, and for certain hostages, and engaged with them in the practice of mutual pollution. Valerius Catullus, a young man of a consular family, complained aloud in public that he had been exhausted by them in that abominable commerce. Besides Caligula's incest with his sister and his passion for Pyrallis, a common prostitute, there was hardly any lady of

15

distinction whom he did not force to have sex with him.' Compared with all this, the costly dinner that he had served in honour of his horse, Incitatus, must be regarded as a minor aberration — even though he wanted the animal installed as the supreme magistrate, the Consul.

Claudius the lame, who succeeded Caligula, gave sumptuous banquets whenever he could, peppering his drinks with powdered pearls and ordering that a gem be added to the contents of every dish placed before him. Often, he entertained some six hundred guests and his appetite for meat and drink was such that he was ready to partake of it at any time or in any place. Once, when presiding in a law court, he smelt the dinner that was being prepared for the Leaping Priests in the adjoining temple and, leaving the tribunal, went to share their meal. On another occasion, after paying no attention to the arguments of the litigants, he interrupted them with the profound statement: 'Those meat pies were marvellous. We shall have them again for dinner.' He hardly ever left the table until he had crammed himself with food and drunk to intoxication. Then he would fall asleep, lying upon his back with his mouth open. While in this state, a feather would usually be put down his throat to make him throw up the contents of his stomach, so that he could start all over again on awakening. He doted on mushrooms and died from eating a dishful poisoned by his wife, Agrippina.

Claudius's wife before Agrippina was the infamous Messalina, who was thirty-two years younger than he, and, who, judging from contemporary accounts was no beauty, having 'a flat head, a florid face, and a malformed chest', but that did not prevent her from netting an estimated 156 lovers — a total reached, says Juvenal, through insinuating herself, disguised, into brothels and taking on all customers she could.

Messalina's sexual record was similar to that of Julia's, wife to the Emperor Tiberius, who was her third husband and who must have been aware of her nymphomania and drunkenness when he married her. Later, after they had parted, she became so promiscuous that she would station herself with the prostitutes by the statue of Marsyas at night, and, if trade were slack, she would prowl around the streets, seizing hold of men and pulling them, if bashful, into some convenient dark corner, where the coupling could be quickly accomplished so that she might lose no time in catching further prey.

Very similar in behaviour, 500 years later, was Theodora, the actress and courtesan, who married Justinian I, Roman Emperor of the East. According to her contemporary, Procopius, she did not wait 'to be asked by anyone she met, but on the contrary with inviting jests or coarse flaunting of her skirts tempted all men who passed by, especially those who were adolescent'.

Much has been written about the Emperor after Claudius, Nero, and how his vices worsened as he grew older. Banquets lengthened until they lasted from noon until midnight. He frequently supped in public and employed common prostitutes to wait upon him. He ran the gamut of sexual perversions: boys — married women — raped a vestal virgin — had Sporus castrated, wed him, and treated him as his Empress — at the same time he married Doryphorus, called him 'my husband', and in bed, says Suetonius, 'counterfeited the noise and cries of maidens when they are deflowered' — and, according to the same authority, 'devised a new kind of sport; that being disguised in a wild beast's skin and let loose from a cage, he would attack the private parts of both men and women while they stood tied to stakes'.

Rumour had it that Nero had Rome set on fire because he wanted to found a new city to be called after himself. After the disaster, only four of its fourteen districts had not been destroyed and he took advantage of this to build his Golden Palace with its circular Imperial Banqueting Hall that revolved 'perpetually, both day and night, in the manner of the celestial bodies' and on the walls of which were painted life-size pictures of nudes in various positions having sex.

One might have thought that with such depraved tastes in sex, Nero would have relished the culinary grotesque, but his favourite food was leeks which he ate regularly to improve his voice. What Nero enjoyed most about feasting was the *mise-en-scène* and the opportunities it provided for debauchery of all kinds. Tacitus wrote in his *Annals* that in AD 64:

> Nero gave feasts in public places as if the whole city were his own house. But the most prodigal and notorious banquet was given by Tigellinus [joint commander of the Praetorian Guard who gained great influence over him]. To avoid repetitious accounts of extravagance, I shall describe it as a model of its kind. The entertainment took place on a raft constructed on Marcus Agrippa's lake. It was towed about by other vessels with gold and ivory fittings. Their rowers were degenerate, assorted according to age and vice. Tigellinus had also collected birds and animals from remote countries, and even the produce of the ocean. On the quays were brothels stocked with high-ranking ladies. Opposite them would be seen naked prostitutes, indecently posturing and gesturing. At nightfall, the woods and houses nearby echoed with singing and blazed with lights. Nero was already corrupted by every lust, natural and unnatural, but he now refuted any surmises that no further degradation was possible for him. For a few days later, he went through a formal wedding ceremony with one of the perverted gang....

Galba, the next Emperor, was overthrown and slain after seven months. He was a glutton and, wrote Suetonius, 'given to an unnatural lust for the male sex and such of them, too, as were old . . . when Icelus, an old catamite of his, brought him the news of Nero's death, he not only kissed him tenderly in the sight of all but entreated him to remove all impediments and then took him aside into a private apartment'.

Galba's wild and riotous successor, Otho, deposed after 95 days, committed suicide. Then came Vitellius, whose life was one continuous meal — going from one friend to the other, eating on arrival, leaving when he had finished, and able to vomit at will. When his brother entertained him at a banquet, no less than 2,000 choice fishes and 7,000 birds were served. But even this feast was surpassed in sumptuousness by one he gave himself to launch a new dish especially made for him, and which, on account of its extraordinary size, he called *The Shield of Minerva*. It consisted of a mixture of the brains of peacocks and pheasants, the livers of parrot-fish, the tongues of flamingos and the entrails of lampreys. Vitellius, however, was by no means an epicure. Even when at last he left a banquet, any scrap of food he noticed, whether it was in a beggar's hand or on an altar as a sacrifice to the gods, he would seize and devour as though he had not fed for weeks.

The next two Emperors, Vespasian and Titus, were both tremendous trenchermen; then came Domitian (AD 81–96) who to check drunkenness in Britain ordered the destruction of half the vineyards there. He divorced his wife, so that his handsome lover, the pantomimist Paris, could live with him, and had a strange hobby. He used to retire into a secret place for one hour every day and do nothing but catch flies and stick them through the body with a sharp pin. When a visitor therefore inquired whether any one was with Domitian, an aide replied: 'No, not so much as a fly.' On one occasion he summoned his ministers to come at once to his villa to advise him on a matter of the greatest importance. After being kept waiting for a long while, they were admitted to his presence and were told that he had bought a rare fish too large to be put into any of his dishes. Would they consider the problem carefully and advise whether he should buy another dish or have the fish minced?

Imperial excesses reached a new peak with Heliogabalus (AD 218–22) whose banquets never cost less than a

100,000 sesterces and who would eat the brains of 600 ostriches for supper. He was always urging his cooks to invent new sauces, but, if what was offered to him proved not to his liking, he forced the man to feed on nothing else until he had prepared another sauce that appealed to his master. Heliogabalus was proud of his own recipe for lobster rissoles, preferred fish somewhat stale, had a passion for pies full of tongues and brains of song-birds, and stifled pigs served in sows' wombs. He never tired of practical jokes, such as leather couches filled with air, which were deflated when elderly guests sat on them so that they fell off. Drunks who passed out awoke to find themselves in bedrooms with tigers and leopards. Not knowing that these were tame, some had fatal heart-attacks. During Heliogabalus's short reign, Rome witnessed an appalling exhibition of licentiousness from him and his entourage. Within three years, he married and divorced no fewer than five wives, including one of the vestal virgins.

The later Roman Emperors were obsessed with building larger and larger baths fed by hot springs where those who had wrecked their health could disport themselves. Marcus Aurelius Caracalla thought he had reached the limit with one a mile in circumference that could accommodate 1,600 bathers but Diocletian some eighty years later far outshone him by employing slave labour to construct a mammoth affair with room for 3,000 persons. The majority of these were not genuinely sick, but libertines seeking to sweat away the toxic effects of dissipation so that they could resume their debauchery. Cynics jested that if this went on, Rome would become a city within a bath.

In order to excuse their excesses the Romans might have been tempted to enlarge their dynasty of deities with a god of gluttony, but they left that to the Sicilians in whose island a temple to Vocacitas was erected and the cult later gained followers in other parts of the Mediterranean. Dionysius the Younger, ruler of Sicily, has been called the worst drunkard of all times, for he was often intoxicated for as long as six months. Right from the earliest times, excessive drinking led to profiteers adulterating wines, forcing them with egg whites, bitter almonds, or isinglass, using hepatic aloes to give the semblance of age, and even mixing sand or powdered marble with inferior ones. Salt water, too, was often added to cleanse and prevent deterioration. This was discovered through a Roman slave in charge of a cask of wine sampling some and then trying to hide his theft. When his employer tasted the doctored contents, he found them far superior to the wine of the same growth in the other casks.

Status-seeking Roman vulgarians vied with one another in these ways to make their feasts more talked about than anybody else's. They and their Emperors with the plunder obtained from conquered countries were able to spend huge sums, while the populace went hungry if the corn shipped from Alexandria failed to reach them. Tacitus says: 'The extravagance of the table was passionately maintained for a hundred years from the battle of Actium up to the coming of Galba.' The Emperors, by their example, were responsible for causing the consumption of meat and pork, in particular, to soar among their affluent citizens. Pliny tells us that the first Roman to serve a whole boar at table was Servilius Rullus — 'a luxury which today has become general, for now we consume two or three boars at a time, and for the first course only'. Quintus Hortensius, the orator, watered his plane trees with wine and left ten thousand pipes of it in his cellars for his heir.

The rich gorged on fish, too, mullet being especially prized. Seneca in his *Naturales Questiones* wrote:

The fish swim in the banqueting hall. They are seized under the table to reappear above a moment later, for the mullet is not considered to be fresh unless it has expired in the hands of a guest. They are exposed in a glass bowl where can be observed the various nuances of colour through which they successively pass in their slow and painful agony. At other times, they are doomed to perish in brine where they are pickled alive. What can be more lovely, they say, than an expiring mullet! The palate of our gourmets has become so delicate that they cannot taste the fish unless they have seen it swimming about in the midst of the feast. Such fruitfulness of invention to resuscitate the surfeited stomach!

In order to cater for the rich Romans' lust for new kinds of food, merchants searched far and wide, those produced in Italy being regarded as fit only for plebeians, so ships imported peacocks from Samos, grouse and turkeys from Phrygia, cranes from Melos, Ambracian kids, Tarentine oysters, tunny-fish from Chalcedon, muraenas from Gades, sturgeon from Rhodes, crabs from Chios, Tatian nuts, Egyptian dates, and Iberian nuts. Before the Third Punic War began, the Roman Senate could not agree whether to attempt the conquest of Carthage. Then, Cato the Elder held out a handful of African figs and demanded if it were not worth many battles, however hardly fought, to own a country where such superb fruit could be obtained in abundance. All doubts dispelled, the Senate voted for war; and, as a result of their eventual victory, the Romans also gained for themselves plentiful supplies of coarse-ribbed melons grown at Cantalupo.

There were, too, Romans with abnormal palates like Vedius Pollio, who fattened his lampreys upon the flesh of his slaves. Further afield in Asia Minor, Cambis, King of Lydia, was reported to have eaten his wife. Cantibaris of Persia consumed so much over such lengths of time that his jaws tired before his stomach was full, so he made his servants push the food into his mouth and then work his jaws up and down until all had disappeared down his throat.

To display their artistry, cooks served food that was not what it appeared to be. Roasts of meat and poultry would turn out to be made of almond paste — and cakes of minced pork. Surprise pies, when opened, released blackbirds and thrushes, which, alas, were then caught and eaten later on.

Seneca disapproved of gastronomic excess and he also wrote: 'Ever since a thousand seasonings have been invented for the sole purpose of exciting gluttony, what was once food for the appetite has become a burden for the stomach.' He listed the illnesses caused by greed at the table, branding them as 'the just punishment for our luxuriousness'. He adds: 'Men eat to vomit and vomit to eat, their dishes are fetched from every corner of the earth, and then they do not even deign to digest them.'

The Roman Senate did attempt to curb excess by a law imposing a ceiling on the amount that might be spent on a banquet, but no notice was taken of it. Instead, the gluttons complained why had not the gods given them gullets like swans' necks so that they could taste for a longer space of time what they ate — and why had the gods not equipped them with much larger stomachs?

All this excess lent itself to satire. Horace, for example, fabricates a dinner party held by Nasidienus, a *nouveau riche*, who tells his guests that the first dish served, a Lucanian boar, was captured 'when the south wind was softly blowing' and that the next, a lamprey, was caught before spawning as its meat is best then. Horace continues in this vein, making Nasidienus describe at length the innumerable ingredients — roe from the Spanish mackerel, vinegar made from fermenting Lesbian wine, unwashed sea-urchins, etc. — that are needed for the shrimp sauce.

Gaius Petronius was a contemporary of Nero's and in his celebrated *Satyricon* he, too, ridicules the follies then prevalent in Rome. The story is told by Encolpius, a young, well-educated, sexually ambivalent anti-hero. Circe's maid tells him:

> You say you're just a poor slave, but this is just what is exciting my mistress's desire to boiling-point. Some

women get het-up about absolute scum and can't feel any passion unless they see slaves or bare-legged messengers. The arena sets some of them on heat, or a mule-driver covered with dust, or actors displayed on the stage. She's one of those — jumps across the first fourteen seats from the orchestra and hunts for something to love among the lowest of the low.

The maid herself is quick to add that she is just the opposite. 'I have never been to bed with a slave. Even though I'm a servant, I've never sat anywhere except in the lap of knights.' She would not demean herself to have sex with any one of lower rank.

The best of the satiric episodes is the *Cena Trimalchionis*. It pillories an obnoxious freedman who has amassed a fortune through shady practices and who strives to eclipse all his rivals in sparing no expense on entertaining. Those who accept his hospitality are mostly spongers. They glut themselves with his food and wine and make fun of him behind his back. Trimalchio is such an upstart that he makes his guests wait at table for him to appear, but they themselves are too ill-mannered to do so and by the time he does arrive they are busily eating the hors-d'oeuvre, consisting of dormice sprinkled with honey and poppy-seed, black damsons from Damascus, and other gourmet delicacies.

Suddenly, Trimalchio makes what is intended to be an impressive entrance. Slaves carry him in to the sound of music and set him down on a huge pile of gaudily coloured cushions. He looks so absurd that his guests cannot help laughing. His cropped head sticks out from a scarlet coat and his scraggy neck is well muffled up. Round it hangs a napkin with broad purple stripes from which dangle fancy tassels. He is picking his teeth with a silver toothpick. As the orchestra goes on playing, two slaves bear in a tray on which is a wooden hen sitting on straw in a basket. They pull out what resemble eggs and distribute them. The shells prove to be made of rich pastry covering figpeckers rolled up in spiced yolk of egg.

Singing slaves wash the guests' hands in *vin ordinaire*. Then, carefully sealed wine bottles are brought in, labelled: 'FALERNIAN CONSUL OPIMUS — ONE HUNDRED YEARS OLD'. While they are inspecting these inscriptions, Trimalchio says with a sigh: 'Wine has a longer life than us poor folks. I'm giving you real Opimus. I didn't put out such fine liquor yesterday, though the company was much better class.' The guests retaliate by pointing out how small their glasses are and demand larger ones, which they receive. Meanwhile, they are entertained in a macabre way by a slave jerking the wires holding together a silver skeleton and making it perform a grotesque dance, as Trimalchio declaims:

> Man's life, alas is but a span,
> So let us live it while we can,
> We'll be like this when dead.

The next course is set out on a deep circular dish the edge of which is adorned with the signs of the Zodiac, and on each sign is laid what Trimalchio considers proper to it: over the Ram, butter beans — the Bull, a piece of beef — the Heavenly Twins, testicles and kidneys — the Crab, a garland — the Lion, an African fig — the Virgin, a young sow's udder — the Scales, a muffin in one pan and a cake in the other — over Scorpio, a lobster — over Sagittarius the Archer, a bull's eye — and so on.

Trimalchio explains: 'We've got to have some culture at my dinner. I know everything as that dish bears witness. Look now, these here heavens. First, there is the Ram — whoever is born under that sign will have a lot of herds and wool and a hard head with a sharp horn as well.' He goes on interpreting what he regards as the characteristics of those born under the various signs. The faces of the others fall as they anticipate being served with the mostly unappetizing food appropriate to their dates of birth.

Then, suddenly, to more music four slaves dance in and remove the cover over the centre part of the great dish

revealing plump fowls, sows' udders, and a hare with
wings attached to look like Pegasus, together with fish
swimming in a peppery wine sauce. In astonished delight,
they all applaud. Next, the slaves drape embroidered
cloths displaying hunting scenes over the couches and a
pack of hounds bound in, followed by servants tottering
under the weight of a dish bearing a wild boar with a
freedman's cap on its head. Baskets full of the best dates
hang from the creature's tusks and it is surrounded by
piglets made of baked dough, placed as if at suck. A
bearded giant lunges furiously at the boar with a hunting
knife and out flies a flock of thrushes, which are then
caught and taken away for cooking and serving as an extra
course later.

After the company have stuffed themselves with wild
boar, Trimalchio goes to the toilet and the diners seize the
opportunity to drink up all the wine and obtain more. On
returning, he says:

> Excuse my leaving you, dear friends, but my insides
> have been on strike for several days now. The doctors
> are puzzled, but some pomegranate rind and resin in
> vinegar has done me good. I hope now my stomach will
> behave. Otherwise, it rumbles like a bull. So, if any of
> you wants to leave the room, there's no need to be
> embarrassed. . . .Believe me, if the wind goes to your
> brain, it starts flooding your whole body, too. I've
> known a lot of people die from this because they
> wouldn't be honest with themselves.

Three pigs of varying sizes, muzzled and decked out with
bells, are now brought into the dining-room and Trimalchio summons his chef and orders him to kill the largest
and serve it next. Then, with a lordly leer, Trimalchio
says: 'If you don't like the wine, I'll have it changed. I don't
buy it. I have an enormous cellar — all comes from an
estate I haven't seen yet. It is said to adjoin my other
estates at Tarracina and Tarentum. [Two hundred miles

apart!] What I'd like to do is to add Sicily to my little bit of land, so that when I want to go to Africa, I could sail there without leaving my own property.' He is still droning on when, to the others' amazement, the pig already roasted is carried in. It is clearly another animal substituted to impress them with the chef's skill.

But the feast, it seems, has hardly begun. After acrobats sing and dance and jump through blazing hoops, a calf boiled whole and wearing a helmet is borne in on a monstrously heavy plate by tottering slaves dressed like Homeric heroes. 'Ajax' follows, dashes furiously at it with a sword, slices it up and distributes the flesh among the guests. Before they can eat any of it, the whole room shakes and a gap appears in the ceiling and jars of toilet preparations are lowered as presents.

Dessert comes in the form of a Priapus fashioned in pastry and standing on a table, holding up every kind of fruit in his wide apron. Around him are piled buns which, when seized by the diners, spurt saffron in their faces. Further horseplay follows and they all become very drunk. Trimalchio tells them how he made his money and about his marital problems. He reads aloud his will, makes them all have a bath, then leads them into a second dining-room shouting: 'Let us whet our throttles and not stop eating till dawn.' No sooner has he said this than a cock crows. A bad omen. It must be caught and cooked. Everybody lurches about ineffectually. Trimalchio anoints himself and, putting on his shroud, summons the cornet players. 'Imagine I'm dead and play something touching,' he demands. They strike up a funeral march and one of them, a slave belonging to the undertaker, blows so loudly that he rouses the whole neighbourhood and the fire brigade, assuming that the house is alight, tear in and drench them all with water.

This derisive description of a fictitious social climber's behaviour was not so far removed from reality. At some feasts, class distinctions affected what you were given to eat. Calling Virro a low-born upstart, Juvenal relates how he was served by his slaves with a huge lobster, garnished with asparagus, a marvellous mullet, the finest lamprey, an outsize capon, a boar 'piping hot worthy of Meleager's steel', truffles, mushrooms, and 'apples whose scent would be worth a feast'. But humble guests had to be content with coarse wine, bits of hard bread turned mouldy, sickly greens cooked in rancid oil, an eel first cousin to a water snake, toadstools, and rotten apples.

In Babylonia, then commonly know as Chaldea, in the tenth century BC, no girl on reaching puberty could marry until she had gone into the Temple of Mylitta and had sex with any man who would pay for it by placing a fixed sum of money on the altar of the goddess for the benefit of the priests. The beautiful and the bewitching were seized as they entered. The plain but rich had to purchase their freedom by paying men to do the necessary. The poor and ugly waited often as long as three years before a man took pity on them.

One learns from the works of Athenaeus, Macrobius, and Plutarch of the orgies that took place as the early Persians celebrated in honour of their goddess of love, Mittira, when erotic music and dancing and wine excited their senses, causing all manner of sexual perversions to take place. Egypt was notorious for its courtesans right back to the days of the Pharaohs. Girls married at ten, and the men were so ruttish that, according to Herodotus, no attractive young woman's body would be taken to the embalmer's for several days following her death, due to a degenerate's having been caught violating the corpse of a virgin.

The French novelist, Pierre Louÿs, spent three years of research in Egypt before he wrote his colourful evocation of Alexandria in Cleopatra's time, *Aphrodite*. The Temple of the Great Goddess, the inviolable Astarteion, he says, was a colossal edifice. Its gold doors were guarded by twelve hermaphrodite slaves who symbolized the two objects of love and the twelve hours of the night. The architrave was supported by eighty-six columns, tinted deep red from the base to the centre and the upper halves stood out from these crimson sheaths with striking whiteness like the loins of standing women.

Between the epistyle and the coronis stretched the long zophorus with its ornamentation depicting sexual excess.

There were centauresses mounted by stallions, she-goats joined with slender satyrs, virgins coupled with monstrous bulls, naiads covered by stags, bacchantes penetrated by tigers, lionesses gripped by griffins. The multitude of creatures surged on, driven by the irresistible divine passion. The male thrust forward, the female opened . . . Leda guided the swan between her young yielding thighs. Further on, the insatiable siren was exhausting the expiring Glaucus; the god Pan was possessing, standing, a dishevelled hama-dryad; the Sphinx was raising her croup to the level of the horse Pegasus.

Later, Pierre Louÿs describes with vivid touches a banquet. The table was covered with wreaths, foliage, goblets and pitchers. Slaves carried in snow-white bread in woven baskets, followed by fat eels sprinkled with seasonings, wax-coloured aphestes and sacred beauty-fish upon platters of painted earthenware. Then was served a pompilos, a purple fish said to have been born of the same foam as Aphrodite, boops, smelts, a surmullet flanked by squids, and multi-coloured scorpion fish. So that they could be eaten burning hot, slices of fat tunny fish and octopi with tender tentacles were served in little casseroles. Next, the belly of a white torpedo, 'round as a beautiful woman's'. Such was the first course of which the guests ate the best pieces and left the rest for the slaves.

For the second course, there were pheasants, sand-grouse, a magnificent red and blue sultana-bird and a swan bearing all its feathers which had been carefully cooked for forty-eight hours so as not to scorch its wings.

Upon curved platters lay water-plants, pelicans and a white peacock, which seemed to have just hatched, roast snipes stuffed with pork — in fact, there was so much that a hundred persons could easily have been well-fed with what was left. But all this was nothing beside the last dish, a masterpiece, for nothing like it had been seen in Alexandria for years. It was a young pig, half of which had been roasted and the other half stewed in bouillon.

The animal was stuffed with quails, the breasts of fowls and larks, slices of vulva, minced meat and succulent sauces. General cries of admiration greeted its appearance. Seven rare wines accompanied all this and as a result of excessive drinking as well we learn that the conversation 'degenerated' as the feast proceeded.

Louÿs states that there were some fifteen courtesans working in Alexandria at that time but even that number was insufficient to cope with the demand for their services from over-sexed males.

'Ah, beneficent courtesans!' exclaimed Philodemos. 'We ought to sing their everlasting praises with incense and golden verse!. . . They save us from long waiting in the rain, rickety ladders, secret doors, interrupted meetings, intercepted letters and misunderstood signals. Oh, how I love you, dear women! With you, there's no need to lay a siege: for a few little coins you give us skilfully what other women would give us badly and as a special favour, after making us wait the usual three weeks. The money we give you doesn't buy your precious affections: it's merely fair payment for the charming and varied luxury which you kindly consent to maintain, and in the midst of which you gratify our voluptuous demands every night.'

In *Salammbô*, Gustave Flaubert brings ancient Carthage vigorously back to life. The book opens in the gardens of

Hamilcar at Megara where the soldiers that the general led in Sicily are holding a feast to celebrate the Battle of Eryx. As he is absent, the men of all nationalities there are able to indulge in a veritable orgy. His own kitchens being inadequate for the purpose, the Council had sent slaves, utensils, and couches, and on monstrous blazing fires oxen were roasting.

Around baskets of gold filigree bright with flowers were ranged loaves of bread flavoured with aniseed, cheeses heavier than discuses, bowls overflowing with wine and flagons of water. All eyes shone with anticipation at the thought of being able at last to gorge and gorge without restraint, and singing had begun.

First, they were served with birds and green sauce . . . then with every kind of shell-fish that can be gathered on the Punic coasts, wheaten porridge, beans, barley, and snails dressed with cummin on dishes of amber. Then the tables were covered with meats: antelopes with their horns, peacocks with their feathers, whole sheep boiled in sweet wine, haunches of she-camels and of buffaloes, hedgehogs with garum, fried grasshoppers and preserved dormice. Large pieces of fat floated amid saffron in bowls of wood from Tamrapanni. Everything was running over with wine, truffles and asafoetida. Pyramids of fruit tottered upon honeycombs, and the purveyors had even included among the fare a Carthaginian dish held in abhorrence by other nations, a few small plump-bellied little dogs with red silky hair and fattened on olive orts.

Surprise at the novel fare roused the lust of appetite. Long-haired Gauls snatched the water-melons and lemons and crunched them up, rind and all. Negroes, who had never seen a lobster, tore their faces with the long spines. Shaven Greeks, whiter than marble, threw the leavings on their plates over their shoulders, while the herdsmen from Brutium, clad in wolf-skins, ate in greedy silence with their faces in the food.

Night fell. The awning stretched above the cypress avenue was drawn back and torches were lit. . . . They gulped down all the Greek wines in their leathern bottles, the Campanian wines in jars, the Cantabrian wines brought in casks, and the wines made from the jujube tree, from cinnamon and from the lotus. Pools of wine spilt on the ground made it slippery. The reek of viands mingled with hot human breath rose into the foliage. . . . And as the men became increasingly intoxicated, they voiced more and more their anger with the injustice of Carthage.

Wine was unknown in England before its conquest by the Romans, and, for the three centuries they were in occupation, the beverage was imported for consumption by their forces, who, to reconcile themselves to living in an inclement climate, indulged in excessive drinking. It was recorded of one general that he was such a drunkard that when he committed suicide after his defeat in AD 281, the soldiers jested — there hung a tankard and not a man.

When at the end of the fifth century the Saxons under Hengist invaded southern England, he proposed to ratify a peace treaty with the British King, Vortigern, by a feast to which he invited him and some 300 of his nobles; then, when they were all drunk, his men slew them except for Vortigern, who was held to ransom until he ceded Essex, Sussex, and Middlesex. One of the most important surviving fragments of Cymric literature, *The Gododin*, a sixth-century poem, describes the fighting between the Britons and the Teutonic invaders of the area between the Tees and the Forth. It dwells on how the Britons were routed at Cattraeth. The warriors marched there 'full of mead' which gave them temporary pleasure:

For the sweetness of mead,
In the day of our need,
Is our bitterness; blunts all our arms for the strife,

Is a friend to the lip and a foe to the life.
I drank the Mordei's wine and mead,
I drank, and now for that I bleed.

Among the Anglo-Saxons themselves, drinking and eating became almost their entire occupation from mid-day until late into the night. The Christian Church constantly condemned intemperance, but with little success and many ecclesiastics set bad examples. The Venerable Bede in the eighth century wrote to Egbert, Archbishop of York:

> It is commonly reported of certain bishops that the way they serve Christ is this. They have no one near them of any religious spirit or continence, but only such as are given to laughter, jokes, amusing stories, feasting, drunkenness and the other snares of a sensual life — men who feed their belly with meats, rather than their souls with the heavenly sacrifice.

There does not appear to have been much improvement as a result of Bede's criticisms, for about fifty years later Boniface, Archbishop of the Germans, wrote to Cuthbert, Archbishop of York:

> It is reported that in your dioceses the vice of drunkenness is too frequent; so that not only certain bishops do not hinder it, but they themselves indulge in excess of drink, and force others to drink till they are intoxicated.

In the tenth century, King Edgar, prompted by Archbishop Dunstan, tried to bring about restraint by decreeing that pegs should be fixed into all drinking-cups at prescribed distances to prevent people imbibing beyond these marks. This well-meant regulation unfortunately had the adverse effect to what Dunstan intended, as revellers used the pegs for scoring who could drink the most. The following century the English were to pay dearly for this when it has been claimed they lost the Battle of Hastings through having spent the previous night carousing while the Normans fasted and prayed.

III

FROM THE WIFE OF BATH TO NINON DE LENCLOS

In Chaucer's *Canterbury Tales*, the Pardoner, referring to Eve and the apple, cries: 'O gluttony, full of cursedness . . . O original of our damnation!' and among the other pilgrims we have the lusty Wife of Bath, who, having had five husbands, seeks a sixth, and the Prioress, who is an excellent example of those excessively bound at table by the rules of etiquette. This Madam Eglantine lets no morsel fall from lips, wets but her finger-tips in the sauce, and wipes her upper lips so thoroughly that no trace of grease is to be found in her cup after she has drunk. Very dainty is she in reaching for her food and takes pains to model herself on those at court. Her small dogs, too, are obviously carefully brought up and she feeds them upon roasted meat, milk and the finest wheaten bread.

The Monk was not pale like a wasted ghost, but believed in keeping his belly full and of viands loved most a fat roasted swan. The Begging Friar forgave any sins with an easy penance, if given a good dinner. But it is the Franklin who is the most memorable of Chaucer's food-lovers. Ruddy of face and sanguine of temper, he enjoyed a sop of cake in wine of a morning and delighted in all the pleasures of the table. He was Epicurus's true son, kept open house and all he served was of the finest quality.

Never were a man's wine-cellars better stocked. Huge pasties of fish and of meat were available all day and night in his house where it snowed meat and drink and every dainty that a man could dream of. According to the seasons of the year, he varied his menus. Many a fat partridge were in his coops and innumerable bream and pike in his ponds. Woe to his cook unless his sauces were pungent and sharp, and he was ready to cook anything at all hours.

The pilgrims also had a cook in attendance for the journey to boil chickens with the marrow-bones, and who could roast, fry, broil, stew, make dainty pottage, and bake as well. He had an unquenchable thirst for London ale.

The Sompnour or Ecclesiastical Apparitor had a thirst for wine and, in return for a quart of it, would countenance the worst of sins. He had a fire-red face and was as lecherous as a sparrow:

> Well loved he garlike, onion, and lekes
> And for to drinke strong win as rede as blood.
> Than wolde he speke, and crie as he were wood.
> And when that he wel drunken had the win,
> Then would he speken no word but Latin.

In medieval times, spiced possets, supposed to have aphrodisiac qualities, were given a newly-married couple to drink when they retired for the night. As Chaucer wrote:

> He drinkyth ipocras, clarret and veinage,
> Of spyces hote, t'encreasen his corage.

First thing in the morning, a bridesmaid would take in more posset to revive the pair's vigour, and this continued for between a week and ten days following the wedding.

Typical of the banquets given by the nobility was that of the Earl of Warwick in 1470. Sixty-two cooks with five hundred and fifteen assistants prepared the meal and as the castle kitchens were insufficiently large many of the dishes were cooked in others throughout the town. Of drink alone, there were 104 tuns of wine and 300 of ale; whilst 6 bulls, 1,004 wethers, 3,000 calves, 10 fat oxen, 300 pigs with the same number of hogs, and 4,000 deer provided meat for the occasion, together with 2,000 chickens, 300 capons, 4,000 ducks, 4,000 pigeons, about a 1,000 game of all kinds, a 100 peacocks, 4,000 rabbits, over that number of pike and other fish. The feast ended with 1,000 dishes of jellies, 400 tarts and 2,000 hot custards.

A fourteenth-century poet described such a banquet thus:

The boar's head shall be brought with bays aloft.
Bucktails full broad in broths therewithal,
Venison with the fruments, and pheasants full rich,
Baked meats near by, on the board well set,
Chewets of chopped flesh, and chickens grilled,
Each several guest has six men's share.
Were this not enough, another course follows,
Roast with rich sauces and royal spice,
Kids cleft in the back, quartered swans . . .

Spices were added to almost everything — cinnamon, ginger, nutmeg, saffron, pepper — even to wine; just as salt later became essential to cooking. Recipes of the period resemble those of the Middle East, which was partly due to those returning from the Crusades having acquired a taste for such piquant flavours, and partly because of the need to hide the fact that food was going off as it could not be refrigerated. Beatrice, Duchess of Milan, wrote to Isabella, Duchess of Mantua, in March 1491: 'I have had a whole field of garlic planted for your benefit, so that when you come, we may be able to have plenty of your favourite dishes!'

This excess of food and drink called for pauses during such marathons to build up the appetite, so main courses would be preceded by the serving of confectionery appropriately called 'warners', fancifully shaped as birds and beasts and consisting of jelly and sugar. The practice also arose of having intervals when some entertainment would be performed by minstrels, clowns, jugglers, strolling players, rope dancers and the like. The spectacles staged needed to be startlingly unusual to hold the attention of the company already getting comatose. For example, in 1237 at the marriage of Robert, Comte d'Artois, during one interlude in the banquet, a horseman crossed the hall by making his mount walk along a rope extended above the heads of the guests while at the ends of the table were musicians seated on oxen and, also, astride goats, were monkeys waving harps.

As might be expected, royal feasts were even more spectacular affairs. Stowe tells us that William Rufus 'prodigally spent in great banquetting and sumptuous apparel, for he would neither eate, drinke or weare anything, but that it cost unmeasurably deere'. Profligate Richard II kept a sumptuous table employing over 300 servants in the kitchen. His chief chef called him 'the best and royallest viander of all Christian Kynges'. Walsingham in his chronicles describes how for Richard's Coronation the conduits in the City ran with wine for three hours.

> In the upper end of the Cheap was erected a castle with four towers, on two sides of which ran forth wine abundantly. In the towers were placed four beautiful girls dressed in white, who, on the King's approach, blew in his face leaves of gold, and filling cups of gold with wine at the spouts of the castle, presented them to the King and his nobles.

At his Court, Richard provided food for up to 10,000 people daily. Christmas was always celebrated with showy extravagance. In 1398, when he spent it at Lichfield, 200 tuns of wine were drunk and 2,000 oxen slaughtered. Henry IV's bridal feast lasted several days and Froissart observed that there were seven fountains running with red and white wine along the route the King and his Queen passed in the City. Another chronicler, Matthew Paris, stated that it would take him a day to describe the hospitality received by those attending in 1243 the nuptials of Richard, Earl of Cornwall, Henry III's brother, and Sanchia, the Comte de Provence's daughter, in London when over 30,000 dishes were set before the company at the marriage banquet.

The higher clergy competed with the Court in such banqueting squander-mania. To celebrate the enthrone-ment of George Nevill, Archbishop of York in 1464, some 5,000 oxen, wild bulls, sheep, pigs, geese, capons, swans, peacocks, quails, and fish of various kinds were delivered to sixty-two cooks in the kitchens for the feast — together with 300 tuns of ale, 100 of wine, and one pipe of hippocras. For an earlier Archbishop's enthronement in 1295, the fish provided consisted of 300 ling, 600 cod, 40 fresh salmon, 7 barrels of salt salmon, 14 of white herrings, 20 of red herrings, 5 of salt sturgeon, 2 of salt eels, 60 fresh eels, 8,000 whelks, 100 pike, 400 tench, 100 carp, 800 bream, 80 fresh large Severn lampreys, 1,400 small lampreys, 124 salt conger eels, 200 large roach, as well as porpoises and seals. The amount of wine drunk was enormous — some 80 tuns annually were emptied in the household of Archbishop Booth, Nevill's predecessor.

Excesses among the clergy were widespread elsewhere in Europe. In the tenth century the Bishop of Sens had the monks evicted from the *Abbaye de Saint-Pierre* so that he could use it as a harem for his many concubines, whilst in the next century Cardinal Pierleone took one with him on his travels and had children by his sister. The notorious Borgia Pope, Alexander VI, has been accused of innumer-able excesses. After attending one of his banquets, Burchard, Bishop of Ostia wrote in his *Diarium Romanum* that fifty reputable whores 'not common but the kind called courtesans' were present and 'after supper they danced about with the servants and others in that place, first in their clothes and then nude . . . candelabra with lighted candles were set on the floor and chestnuts were strewn about and the naked courtesans on hands and knees gathered them up, wriggling in and out among the candelabra . . . . Then all those present in the hall were carnally treated in public.' Alexander, Cesare and Lucrezia gave prizes to the men who copulated most with the courtesans.

Holinshed in his *Chronicles* includes an amusing anecdote about Pope Julius III, an egregious gourmet who enjoyed eating peacocks best of all. Once at dinner, he pointed at a peacock which he had left and said: 'Keep that cold bird for my supper which I shall take in the garden as I am expecting guests.' Holinshed wrote: 'So when supper came and amongst the hot peacocks he saw not his cold one brought to table, the Pope, after his wonted manner fell into an extreme rage. Whereupon one of his Cardinals, sitting by him, said: "Let not your Holiness, I pray you, be so moved with a matter of so small weight." ' To this, the Pope retorted: 'What! If God were so angry for one apple that he cast our first parents out of Paradise for the sin, why may I not, being his vicar, be angry over the loss of a peacock which is greater than an apple?'

With such Papal examples a fifteenth-century bishop can hardly be blamed for sitting at his dining-table almost continually for three years. He rose only to answer the calls of nature, and claimed even to have slept at the table, but he did say prayers before and after every course.

Such indulgence was minor compared with that of the privileged laity. Peter the Hermit, responsible for making the upper classes take part in the First Crusade, was scathing about how some set out for the Holy Land. He wrote in a letter:

> You see their baggage horses loaded, not with iron but wine, not with lances but cheeses, not with swords but bottles, not with spears but spits. You would imagine they were going to prepare a great feast rather than to make war.

Lust ran amok as the court cases bear witness. Many knights were not 'parfit gentil' but lechers. Burgo Partridge in his *History of Orgies* states that 'to judge from contemporary poems and romances, the first thought of every knight on finding a lady unprotected, was to do her violence . . . and Gawain, the alleged paragon of knightly chivalry, raped Gran de Lis, despite her screams and struggles, when she refused to sleep with him'.

And, even at King Arthur's Court they committed that other deadly sin, gluttony; according to Malory, they feasted at Christmas for twelve whole days, and the cooks must have toiled during the nights as well, preparing the 30,000 dishes that were served.

During the long war with France in Edward III's reign, a statute was passed by Parliament against excessive eating and making it an offence for any man to be served at dinner or supper with more than two courses, except upon certain specified holidays, on which three courses were permitted. However, these restrictions were mostly ignored. When wine was scarce during these hostilities, rogues foisted on simple folk vile concoctions prepared from wine dregs, vinegar or oil of vitriol, and coloured with blackberry juice or a dye called tournesole, while the more sophisticated were sometimes conned into paying high prices for cheap light wines made to appear full-bodied by the addition of gum or starch.

The large quantities of wine drunk by royalty and the nobility would have no doubt been somewhat less if their servants had not abused prior assay. This was originally intended, of course, as a guard against poison being added. Watched by the marshal, the butler had to drink part of the contents of every vessel before it was taken to the high table. The marshal, if he felt like it, would try the wine or other liquor, too, before covering the vessel and entrusting it to the lord's cupbearer who was forbidden to raise the lid before reaching the table. There he would pour some of the fluid into the inverted lid and taste it before handing the cup to his master who, thus reassured, could drink without fear.

Rabelais's great works, *Gargantua* (1535) and *Pantagruel* (1533), are an allegorical skit on the extravagance of princes and their excesses. Grangousier or Great Gullet, Gargantua's father, drinks deeper than any other man on earth and devours every kind of salted meat so as to rouse his thirst. His wife, Garganelle, eats too much tripe at a banquet and gives birth to a boy who bawls: 'Drink, drink, drink!' Father exclaims: *'Que grand tu as le gousier!'* ('What a great gullet you have!') — and all present chorus that the child should be called *'Grand tu as'* which became 'Gargantua'.

Although the infant drew from his mother's breasts 2,103 hogsheads and 19 pints of milk at one time, this was not sufficient to satisfy him, so 17,913 cows were recruited to supply the extra quantities he demanded. At twenty-two months, he had eighteen chins and used an elephant's tusk as a toothpick. It was then that Grangousier ordered clothes to be made for him. 'The tailoring of Gargantua's codpiece required 16¼ ells of the finest white broadcloth,' Rabelais wrote. 'In shape, it resembled a buttress.' Two emeralds, each the size of an orange, adorned this, as the gem was believed to exert 'a highly creative and bracing influence upon the genitals'.

Gargantua has a son, Pantagruel, meaning 'All Athirst', who had to drink almost continually to quench 'the coals of fire' in his throat and goes on 'the quest of the oracle of the Holy Bottle'. He visits a country ruled by Gaster or 'Belly' who is served by the Gastrolaters or stomach worshippers. Pantagruel compares him to the gigantic Cyclops Polyphemus who, according to Euripedes, declared: 'I sacrifice to myself alone, not to the gods. This, my belly, is the greatest of all gods.'

Pantagruel watched the Gastrolaters feeding for hours their 'ventripotent god', led by a pot-bellied youth bearing on top of a richly gilded staff, the idol Gluttony. Rabelais wrote:

Plautus, Juvenal and Pompeius Festus have described it; at Lyons, in Carnival time, it is called Gnaw-crust.

The Gastrolaters named theirs, Manduce. This monstrous figure has eyes bigger than its belly and its head larger than all the rest of its body, . . . having wide, terrifying jaws lined with teeth which, by means of wires concealed within the hollow staff, were made to rattle menacingly together.

Rabelais's contemporary, King Henry VIII, had a huge appetite and he must have thought more highly of his cook than of his chaplain, for the Christmas 1510 court accounts read: 'Paid to the preacher in reward, 6s.; paid to the cook, 15s.' An Italian attending one of the royal banquets at Greenwich for 1,000 guests wrote that they remained at the tables for seven hours and that the removal and replacing of dishes were incessant. In the summer of 1533, when Henry celebrated the coronation of his second wife, Anne Boleyn, fountains and conduits ran all day with free wine for the populace. Cardinal Wolsey, whose downfall Anne caused, once became so drunk at a fair when Rector of Lymington that he was put in the stocks.

Nearly half a century later, Camden, the historian, wrote that the English were once 'of all the northern nations the most commended for their sobriety' and that 'they first learnt in their wars in the Netherlands to drown themselves with immoderate drinking'. Tom Nash, who also lived in Elizabeth I's reign, agreed: 'Superfluity of drink is a sin that ever since we have mixed ourselves with the Low Countries is counted honourable, but, before we knew their lingering wars, was held in the highest degree of hatred that might be.' Then, in 1604, the year after the Queen's death, when *Othello* was first produced, Shakespeare made Iago say: 'In England... they are most potent in potting: your Dane, your German, and your swag-bellied Hollander... are nothing to your English.'

Certainly, as from Elizabeth's accession in 1558, drunkenness at the table became far more common in England, though she herself was abstemious, and it was largely caused by the introduction of spirits from abroad. The Queen, also, never over-ate, except for sweets, finding anything composed of marchpane (marzipan) irresistible, but she disapproved of the City banquets where venison was served as plentifully as though it were rabbit. Lord Burghley conveyed her displeasure to the Lord Mayor and his Aldermen and they agreed to forbid the holding of venison feasts. There had already been complaints during the reign of her step-sister, Mary I, regarding the prodigality of the City magistrates, and, as a result, many prominent citizens retired into the country rather than, by holding public office, have to pay for the lavish entertainment that would be expected of them.

William Harrison, in his *Description of England* in 1577, wrote that all who could afford it were gross meat and fish eaters as well as of 'such diversity of wild and tame fowls as are either bred in our island or brought over unto us from other countries of the main'. If one dined with an English lord and helped oneself from every dish before one it could result in 'the speedy suppression of natural health'.

In Scotland, Harrison had found that the well-to-do far exceeded the English 'in over much and distempered gourmandise and so ingross their bodies that divers of them do oft become unapt to any other purpose than to spend their time in large tabling and belly cheer'. This had been caused through King James I of Scotland having been captured as a boy by the English and kept prisoner by them for nineteen years. On returning to his home country, he had brought some English friends with him and the eating habits at court and of the nobility and gentry had completely changed as a result of their influence. The simple frugal meals of the past had been replaced by gluttonous feasting which led to Henry Wardlow, Bishop of St Andrews, vehemently denouncing such over-indulgence in open Parliament held at Perth in 1433 before the three estates.

Parliament was swayed by the Bishop's arguments and a law was passed 'for the restraint of superfluous diet', and baked meats, unknown at Scottish tables before James I introduced such dishes, could no longer be eaten by anyone 'under the degree of a gentleman, and then only on high and festival days'. Harrison adds: 'But, alas, it was soon forgotten!' Calls from the belly proved louder than thunder from the pulpit even when supported by the big guns of the law.

In France, according to Pierre de l'Estoile's entry in his journal for 19 June 1576, Queen Catherine de Médicis, a glutton for cockscombs and livers, ate so many at a banquet, together with artichoke bottoms, that she almost burst and was extremely ill. Twenty-three years later, Thomas Platter wrote that every day the people of Paris consumed 200 oxen, 2,000 sheep, 1,000 calves and 70,000 fowls and pigeons. 'Moreover, on fish days so much of it is eaten, both sea fish and freshwater fish, that it would be impossible to compute the number.'

The year that Elizabeth I became Queen of England, the Emperor Charles V of Germany died. He had some odd tastes in food, for his favourite dishes were cats in jelly, lizard soup, roast horse, and fried frogs. Asked to create something unusual for him to eat, his cook suggested a compôte of watches, as he knew that the monarch had a passion for collecting them. For breakfast, Charles liked potted capons, prepared with sugar, milk and spices, washed down with iced beer, whilst with other meals he preferred Rhine wine, amazing strangers present by the ease with which he would drink a quart of it without stopping.

In 1606, King James I and his brother-in-law, Christian IV of Denmark, were the guests of the chief Minister, the Earl of Salisbury, at his seat, Theobalds. Taking advantage of the absence of his wife, James — whom Macaulay characterized as 'His Sowship' — became extremely drunk and so did most of the company. Sir John Harrington described what he witnessed thus:

> Those whom I never could get to taste good liquor now wallow in beastly delights. The ladies abandon sobriety,

and are seen to roll about in intoxication. After dinner, the representation of Solomon, his temple, and the coming of the Queen of Sheba was made, or, as I may better say, was meant to have been made . . . The lady who did play the Queen's part did carry most precious gifts to both their Majesties, but, forgetting the steppes . . . overset her casket in his Danish Majesty's lap, and fell at his feet, though I rather think it was on his face. Much was the hurry and confusion — cloths and napkins were at hand to make all clean. His Majesty then got up and would dance with the Queen of Sheba, but he fell down and tumbled himself before her and was carried to his inner chamber. The entertainment and show went forward, and most of the presenters went backward or fell down, wine did so occupy their upper chambers.

Robert Burton in his *Anatomy of Melancholy*, published in 1621, castigated his fellow-countrymen for the 'immoderate drinking in every place' that had occurred during King James's reign. 'How they flock to the tavern as if they were born to no other end but to eat and drink. . . . No disparagement now to stagger in the streets, reel, rave, etc., but much to his renown. . . . How they love a man that will be drunk, crown him and honour him for it. . . .'

Probably the champion English glutton of the seventeenth century was the subject of the poet John Taylor's brief life published in 1630, *The Great Eater of Kent or Part of the Admirable Teeth and Stomach Exploits of Nicholas Wood of Harrison in the County of Kent*. We learn that:

he hath eaten a whole sheep of sixteen shillings price, raw at one meal (pardon me) I think he left the skin, the wool, the horns, and bones: but what talk I of a sheep, when it is apparently known that he hath at one repast, and with one dish, feasted his carcase with all manner of meats. Two loins of mutton and one loin of veal were but as three sprats to him; once at Sir

Warham Saint Ledger's house, and at Sir William Sydleye's, he shewed himself so valiant of teeth, and stomach, that he ate as much as would well have served and sufficed thirty men, so that his belly was like to turn bankrupt and break, but that the serving-man turned him to the fire, and anointed his paunch with grease and butter, to make it stretch and hold; and afterwards being laid in bed, he slept eight hours, and fasted all the while. . . .

Taylor continues his saga of a singular stomach:

Our Nick the Great (in his own person) without the help or aid of any person . . . devoured in one week, as much as would have sufficed a reasonable and sufficient Army in a day, for he hath at one meal made an assault upon seven dozen of good rabbits at the Lord Wotton's in Kent. . . . His mouth is a mill of perpetual motion, for let the wind or the water rise or fall, yet his teeth will ever be grinding.

His biographer says that this prodigy kept to an English diet and would eat any kind of regional fare — 'the bag-puddings of Gloucestershire, the black-puddings of Worcestershire, the pan-puddings of Shropshire, the white-puddings of Somerset, the hasty-puddings of Hampshire, and the pudding-pies of any shire, all is one to him, nothing comes amiss . . . he is no puling meacock, nor in all his life time the queasyness of his stomach needed any saucy spur or switch of sour verjuice or acute vinegar. . . . His eyes are sunk inward, as if he looked into the insides of his entrails, to note what customed or uncustomed goods he took in whilst his belly (like a mainsail in a cabin) hangs ruffled and wrinkled (in folds and wrathes) flat to the mast of his carcase, till the storm of abundance fills it, and violently drives it into the full sea of satisfaction.'

French society in the sixteenth and seventeenth centuries

experienced a widespread decline in moral standards largely due to the bad example set by the monarchy. Marguerite de Valois, known as *La Reine Margot*, had four lovers before she married Henry IV, who eventually divorced her and who, in later life, boasted that he had scored fifty-six in mistresses. But this was nothing compared with the Parisian, Ninon de Lenclos (1620-1705), who became a legend in the annals of easy virtue, and who, it was alleged, slept with nearly 5,000 men — a tenth of these being monks and other ecclesiastics — during her long life. Her father, who was an experienced lady-killer, told her before he died: 'You probably have many years to live. Make full use of them. Have no scruples as to the number of your pleasures, but be fastidious in your choice.' Once she was financially secure, Ninon took that advice and, with one exception, her liaisons were short, never lasting more than three months. She alienated the strait-laced with her disregard of the conventions and her lively supper parties in the Rue des Trois-Pavillons frequented by literary lions and important courtiers. Her opponents persuaded the Queen, Anne of Austria, to order her to be shut up in a convent, but she was allowed to select which one.

Ninon replied: 'The Queen is very kind. I choose the convent of the Grand Cordeliers. I think, perhaps, I shall be welcome there.' It was an impudent response as the place was notorious for the licentiousness of its inmates, but, when Ninon's supporters in court circles pleaded her cause, the Queen was persuaded to withdraw the order. The Marquis de Villarceaux, accomplished man of the world and the capital's most successful seducer, fell deeply in love with Ninon and induced her to live with him in his country château where she bore him three children. But he became so jealously possessive that after some years she left him and went back to Paris where she installed herself in the Rue des Tournelles. All her old admirers and an ever-growing number of new ones gathered there, deriding marriage and morality. The clergy and holier-than-thou ladies denounced her and she was compelled to enter a convent for repentant wantons run by the *Madelonnettes* in the Quartier Saint-Martin-des-Champs, but the nuns were so pestered by men trying to gain admittance to her that she was moved to Lagny where she was permitted to see friends.

Queen Christina of Sweden held similar opinions to Ninon on love. She had already had many lovers and believed in gratifying one's senses. After staying at the French Court she was making for Italy when her escort, a former flame of Ninon's, the Maréchal d'Albret, suggested that the Queen should call on the controversial Mlle de Lenclos, which she did, spending nearly half-a-day with her. Christina was so impressed that she used her influence with Cardinal Mazarin to have Ninon released and allowed to return to the Rue des Tournelles.

Ninon in her old age was kept busy teaching young men, who could have been her grandsons, how to make love with finesse and the utmost satisfaction. She had the added advantage of being arguably the most cultured of courtesans, whom poets like Scarron and writers like Molière and Saint-Evremond regarded as their intellectual equal and who became her close friends. She told the latter: 'Love looks as if it were always the same thing, over and over again, but, in reality, it is perfectly new and different each time, which is just what makes it so delightful.' To the end, she maintained that 'the secret of love lies in the avoidance of marriage'. When eighty, she had her last affair, which was, appropriately, with a cleric, the Abbé Geduyn.

Ninon also believed that a carefully thought out gourmet meal makes the perfect prelude to a night of love. Still esteemed by gastronomes is her recipe for a soup, *Crème de Ninon de Lenclos*, a blend of purée of peas with consommé, a drop or two of lemon juice, a tot of dry sherry — then, added at the last minute, frothy whipped cream and a quart of champagne.

Francis I (1494-1547) was the first King of France to

introduce excessive pomp and snobbery into his banquets. Everything was in luxuriant style and for maximum effect, regardless of expense. The company was graded, according to rank, and grandiloquent new names given to the various functionaries. There was a table of the great chamberlain, another for the chamberlain, one for his gentlemen, one for the gentlemen's servants, and so on.

Louis XIV was the next to make his feasts dazzlingly brilliant assemblies of top people where, in his case, all was orchestrated to contribute to his prestige as the Sun King. When his natural daughter, Mlle de Blois, married the Prince of Conti, 160 dishes were served with each of the three courses, and the ortolans alone cost 16,000 francs. Louis himself was a greedy eater who preferred to dine alone and a favourite menu of his consisted of five different soups, roast veal, a fricassée of half-a-dozen chickens, a couple of turkeys, several roasted chickens, minced partridge, sweetmeats, and two baskets of fruit.

This was a snack compared with the voracity of the Swiss porter feeding at the servants' board of Marshal Villars who once asked him how many sirloins of beef he could eat at one sitting. 'Not many, my Lord. Five or six at the most,' the giant replied.

'And how many legs of mutton?'
'Perhaps a dozen.'
'Pigeons?'
'Fifty — if they are plump.'
'Then I expect you'd want two or three hundred larks.'
'Oh, no, my lord. Why I could eat larks for ever!'

IV

DRUNKEN PARLIAMENTS
AND THE KING OF RAKES

It is often assumed that Puritan restraint was rigorously enforced during the Commonwealth but as regards intoxicants this was not the case. In 1657, Reeve complained in his *Plea for Nineveh*: 'We seem to be steeped in liquors, or to be the dizzy island. We drink as if we were nothing but sponges . . . or had tunnels in our mouth.' Then, with the Restoration of King Charles II, all restrictions were swept away. The 'Everlasting Club', begun during the Civil War, thrived. They sat night and day drinking, one party relieving another. The fire was never allowed to go out, and they sang old catches to encourage one another to drink more. It was said that by the end of the century the Club had smoked 50 tons of tobacco and drunk 30,000 butts of ale, 1,000 hogsheads of red port, 200 barrels of brandy, and a kilderkin of small beer.

The first Scottish Parliament at Edinburgh after the Restoration was known as the 'Drunken Parliament'. Burnet commented later: 'It was a mad, warring time, full of extravagance; and no wonder it was so, when the men of affairs were almost perpetually drunk.' Charles II himself warned in a speech at the close of the 1661-62 English Parliament at Westminster:

The whole nation seems to be a little corrupted in their excess of living; all men spend much more on their clothes, on their diet and all other expenses than they have been used to do. I hope it has been only the excess of joy after so much long suffering that has transported us to these other excesses, but let us take heed that the continuance of them does not indeed corrupt our natures. I do believe I have been faulty myself. I promise you I will reform and if you will join with me in your several capacities, we shall by our example do more good both in city and country than any new laws would do.

But the Merry Monarch made no attempt to put such precepts into practice, and soon John Evelyn was complaining in his diary that 'jolly blades racing, dancing, feasting and revelling' were making life at court resemble more 'a luxurious and abandoned rout than a Christian one', and he wrote to a friend that great ladies were frequenting taverns 'where a courtesan in other cities would scarcely vouchsafe to be entertained, but you will be more astonished when I tell you that they drink their crowned cups roundly, strain healths through their smocks, dance after the fiddle, kiss freely and esteem it an honourable treat!'

The French Ambassador, De Comminges, in a despatch reported in similar fashion that 'excesses in taverns and brothels pass among people of note merely for gallantries and even women of good condition do not refuse a gallant to accompany him to drink Spanish wine'.

At the English court itself, despite the King's speech, there was no moderation. Between eighty and ninety tables would be prepared in the banqueting hall every day. In the first decade of the reign the average annual supplies to the kitchens were 10,400 oxen, calves, sheep, lambs, and pigs, 3,800 dozen fowl, 364,000 bushels of wheat, 150,200 gallons of wine, and 428,400 gallons of beer.

The knowledge that Charles was squandering on his own pleasures the subsidies voted by Parliament for the war with the Dutch led to his opponents parodying his speeches. One broadside went: 'I must speak freely to you. . . . Besides my harlots in service, my reformed concubines lie heavy on me. I have a passable good estate, I confess, but God's fish I have a great charge upon it. . . . All the money designed for next summer's guards must of necessity be applied to the next year's cradles and swaddling clothes.'

Most outrageous of Restoration rakes was John Wilmot, second Earl of Rochester, who specialized in rapes and riots, and regarded water as dangerous except for bathing. 'He told me,' wrote Burnet, 'for five years together he was continuously drunk; not all the while under the visible effects of it, but his blood was so inflamed that he was not in all that time cool enough to be perfectly master of himself. This led him to say and do many unaccountable things.' Rochester coined the famous mock epigram on the King and was the author of a controversial play for, as he put it, 'the Royal Company of Whoremasters' entitled *Sodom; or The Quintessence of Debauchery*, a savage satire on Charles's entourage, depicting the excesses of libertinage gone berserk.

By 1668 the immorality rife at Court had spread. Pepys complained in his diary for 30 May that year after visiting Vauxhall Gardens: 'What a loose company it was there tonight, one need only go there once to perceive the kind of doings there are.' And after another visit on 27 July, he adds: 'Observed how coarse some young gallants from the town were. They go into the arbors where there is no man and ravish the women there, and the audacity of vice in our time enraged me.' Though Pepys himself had love affairs, he believed that they should be discreet. He did not approve of what went on at Court either. There was so much of 'the vices of drinking, swearing and loose amours' that he did not know what would be the end of it 'but confusion'. When a child was dropped by one of the ladies in dancing, he was shocked — 'nobody knew who, it being taken up by somebody in their handkerchief'. It was said that the scientifically minded King dissected the body in his laboratory.

The London apprentices, cradled in the Commonwealth with its Puritan outlook, rebelled and destroyed the brothels in Moorfields, and eight were hanged, defiantly regretting that they had not wrecked the Merry Monarch's personal seraglio. Cynical hacks circulated such broadsides as *The Poor Whores' Petition to the Most Splendid, Illustrious, Serene and Eminent Lady of Pleasure, the Countess of Castlemaine*, pretending this was sent by the 'undone company of poor distressed whores, bawds, pimps and panders' seeking her help against persecution for 'a trade wherein Your Ladyship hath great experience and for your diligence therein have arrived to high and eminent advancement'. In due course, there was hawked around *The Gracious Answer of the Most Illustrious Lady of Pleasure, the Countess of Castlemaine, to the Poor Whores' Petition* advising them to give no entertainment without ready money — 'For had we not been careful in that particular we had neither gained honour nor reward.' This was 'Given at our Closet in King Street, Westminster, *Die Veneris*, April 24 1668'.

Lady Castlemaine reaped a fine harvest of titles for her sexual services to King Charles. He created her Baroness Nonsuch, Countess of Southampton, and Duchess of Cleveland, whilst his French mistress, Louise Kéroual, not to be left in the shade, became Baroness Petersfield, Countess of Fareham, and Duchess of Portsmouth. Charles, nicknamed 'Old Rowley' some alleged after a lecherous goat in the Privy Garden, indulged in excess till the end. John Evelyn wrote in his diary how he was present at Court the night before the King's death.

> I shall never forget the inexpressible luxury and profaneness, gaming and all dissoluteness ... to which I was witness; the King sitting toying with his concubines, Portsmouth, Cleveland, Mazarin, etc. A French boy

singing love songs in that glorious gallery whilst about twenty of the great courtiers and other dissolute persons were at basset round a large table, a bank of at least £2,000 in gold before them, upon which two gentlemen who were with me made reflections with astonishment.

And how did that watchdog for the people, Parliament, behave? Pepys in his journal for 19 December 1666, states:

Among other things Sir R. Ford did make me understand how the House of Commons is a beast not to be understood, it being impossible to know beforehand the success almost of any small plain thing. . . . He did tell me, and so did Sir W. Batten, how Sir Allen Brodericke and Sir Allen Apsly did come drunk the other day into the House and did both speak for half an hour together and could not be either laughed, or pulled, or bid to sit down and hold their peace, to the great contempt of the king's servants and cause.

Outside Parliament others disgraced themselves in drinking bouts. Charles Sackville, Earl of Dorset, together with two rakes, Sir Charles Sedley, and Sir Thomas Ogle, became so intoxicated at the Cock in Bow Street, Covent Garden, that Sedley, urged on by the others, swaggered on to the first-floor balcony and exhibited himself naked to the passers-by. According to Pepys, Sedley acted 'all the postures of lust and buggery that could be imagined, and abusing of Scripture . . . preached a mountebank sermon from that pulpit, saying that there he hath to sell such a powder as should make all the cunts run after him — a thousand people standing underneath to see and hear him. And that being done he took a glass of wine and drank the King's health.' When the trio urinated on the crowd, a riot broke out. Brought before the Lord Chief Justice, Sedley, Ogle and the Earl were each fined £2,000.

The intemperance of the period depicted in stage

comedies sometimes affected the cast themselves. When *The Wary Widow or Sir Noisy Parrot*, for example, was put on in 1693, the author had contrived so much drinking of punch into the plot that the actors all became so intoxicated that they were unable to continue and the curtain was brought down half-way through the play and the audience left.

In the Church of England, wine consumption was high, the parish having to pay not only for that used in communions but also for drinking in the vestry. Entries in the Darlington registers read:

> 1639. For Mr Thomson that presided the forenoon and afternoon, for a quart of sack, 14*d*. 1650. For six quarts of sack to the minister that preached when we had not a minister, 9*s*. 1666. For one quart of sack bestowed on Mr Gillet when he preached, 2*s*.4*d*. 1691. For a pint of brandy, when Mr George Ball preached here, 1*s*.4*d*. When the Dean of Durban preached here, spent in a treat with him, 3*s*.6*d*.

In Lancashire during a service, the pulpit pedestal once exploded. Inside it was a secret cupboard where the verger had put his elderberry wine to ferment.

Jorevin de Rochefort in his book, published in Paris in 1672, relates how when in Cambridge he was visited by a clergyman 'during which it was necessary to drink two or three pots of beer during our party, for no kind of business is transacted in England without the intervention of pots of beer'. This was then the most popular of drinks. In 1667, 1,522,781 barrels of beer were brewed in the city of London. Lecky, the historian, wrote that by 1688 no less than 12,400,000 barrels were brewed in England in a single year, though the entire population was little more than five million.

Seeking information for conditions north of the Border, we find Andrew Fletcher of Saltoun complaining in his *Second Discourse on the Affairs of Scotland*:

Many thousands of beggars meet in the mountains, where they feast and riot for many days, and at country weddings, markets, burials, and the like public occasions, they are to be seen, both men and women, perpetually drunk, blaspheming, and fighting together.

Some in the Royal Navy feasted aboard their ships in gargantuan style in the reign of King Charles II, judging from the lively journals of the Revd Henry Teonge, who served as Chaplain on the *Assistance, Bristol* and *Royal Oak.* Off Lisbon, for example, the noble Captain regaled the officers of his small squadron with 'four dishes of meat, viz. four excellent hens and a piece of pork boiled, in a dish; a gigot of excellent mutton and turnips; a piece of beef of eight ribs, well seasoned and roasted; and a couple of very fat green geese; last of all, a great Cheshire cheese'. They drank 'Canary, Sherry, Rhenish, Claret, white wine, cyder, ale, beer, all of the best sort, and punch as plentiful as ditch water'.

When the English Consul at Scanderoon entertained the officers to a 'prince-like' dinner, following each toast, every guest broke the glass he drank in so that by the end they had destroyed 'a whole chest of pure Venice glass'. Teonge describes as 'a treat' the dinner given them by the Consul at Assera on 9 May 1676. It was 'such a one as I never saw before' and he not only names the thirty-six dishes but also includes a diagram showing how they were set out on the table. Then, a few days later, the Chaplain and his fellow officers attended a farewell dinner party given by a Captain Brown 'the greatest that ever I saw'. There were over a hundred 'princely dishes, besides cheese, and other small dishes of rare kinds of sweetmeats'.

On shore, when fresh eggs could be obtained, enterprising cooks spent hours preparing for a feast the egg 'bigger than a man's head' from the original recipe by the Neapolitan, Baptista Porta, which Charles II's chef, Giles Rose, had reproduced in his *Perfect School of Instructions for*

Officers of the Mouth. This reads:

> If you would have an egge so bigge, there is an art, how it may cover other eggs in it, and be not known from a natural egge. You shall part fifty or more yelks of eggs and whites, one from the other; mingle the yelks gently, and put them into a bladder, and bind it round as you can; put it into a pot full of water, and when you see it bubble, or when they are grown hard, take them out and add the whites to them, so filling the yelks that they stand in the middle, and boil them again; so shall you have an egge made without a shell, which you shall frame thus. Powder the white egg-shells, clean washed, that they may fly into fine dust, steep this in strong or distilled vinegar, till they grow soft; for if an egge be long in vinegar the shell will dissolve, and grow tender, that it may be easily passed through the small mouth of a glass; when it is thrust in with fair water it will come to its former hardness, that you will wonder at it; when the shells are dissolved like an unguent, with a pencil make a shell about your egg that is boiled, and let it harden in clear water, so you shall have a natural egge.

This, Rose adds, is not so much as a 'creature for man's comfort' as a 'curious adornment and spectacle'. The marvel was often served on aristocratic supper tables in the seventeenth century.

Another noted chef of the period, Robert May, also excelled in inventing banquet novelties. His masterpiece was the one devised as prelude to a Court supper on Twelfth Night, which he describes in his book, *The Accomplished Cook, or the Art and Mystery of Cookery*, giving full details for anyone sufficiently adept to try and copy him. Having modelled a ship out of pasteboard, he mounted on it toy guns coated with sugar and pastry, decorated it with flags and streamers, and fixed it firmly in the centre of a charger surrounded by eggshells filled with rosewater. On another platter, he erected a paste stag, containing claret and with an arrow in its side serving as a cork, and flanked by two hollow pies made of coarse paste, gilded in spots, and confining, the one, live birds and, the other, live frogs. On a third platter, he stood a pasteboard castle, strongly fortified and with practical guns at the ready.

When all the guests were seated, some of the ladies would be asked to pull the arrow away from the stag causing the wine to run out like blood from a wound. This would be the signal for the guns on the ship and the castle to start firing at each other, when to 'sweeten the stink of the powder', the ladies would pick up the eggshells filled with rosewater and throw them at one another.

All dangers being seemingly over, by this time you may suppose they will desire to see what is in the pyes; when lifting first the lid off one pye, out skip some frogs, which make the ladies to skip and shreek; next after the other pye, when come out the birds, who by a natural instinct flying into the lights, will put out the candles, so that what with the flying birds and the skipping frogs, the ones above, the others beneath, will cause much delight and pleasure.

V

THE 'SECRET HISTORY OF CLUBS'

With the Revolution of 1688 a new era began that for the next century was to see excesses widespread in the country on a scale never before experienced. Daniel Defoe wrote: ' "Jack," said a gentleman of very high quality, when, after the debate in the House of Lords, King William was voted into the vacant throne, "Jack, go home to your lady, and tell her we have got a Protestant king and queen, and go and make a bonfire as big as a house, and bid the butler make ye all drunk, ye dog." ' When William was the guest of Lord Brooke at Warwick Castle, a cistern containing 120 gallons of punch was drained dry by the company many times, so often did they drink the King's health. Some drank healths upon their knees; others put their own blood into their drink and then toasted William. Since the Restoration, a craze for toasting had come over the country. Two students in love with a belle at Oxford engaged in a contest to prove the strength of their devotion. One drank soot mixed with his wine and the other ink neat.

Possibly the largest punch bowl ever prepared was when one of William's supporters, Admiral Edward Russell, entertained at Alicante. A marble fountain was turned into a huge bowl into which were poured one pipe of Malaga; 4

hogsheads of brandy, 29 jars of lime juice, 2,500 lemons, 13 cwt of sugar, 5 lb grated nutmeg, and 8 hogsheads of water.

For vivid but vulgar impressions of low life in the last years of the seventeenth century one can turn to *The London Spy*, the precursor of today's *Private Eye*, published and written by Ned Ward, the Cockney tavern-keeper, who revelled in eating. He was also the author of a *Secret History of Clubs*, which he described as some satirical reflections on bizarre ones that were in vogue at the time. Of all those, he wrote, that took pains to make themselves 'stink in the nostrils of the public' surely 'no ridiculous Community' ever rivalled the Farting Club which was founded by 'a parcel of empty Sparks about Thirty years since at a Publick House in Cripple-Gate Parish' where they met once a week and were 'so vain in their Ambition to out Fart one another, that they us'd to Diet themselves against their Club-Nights, with Cabbage, Onions, and Pease-porridge that every one's Bum-fiddle might be the better qualify'd to sound forth its Emulation'.

Stewards were selected once a quarter as judges of the quality of the sounds emitted. New ale and juniper water were drunk by the members 'till every one was swell'd like a blown Bag-Pipe, and then they began to Thunder out whole Volleys like a Regiment of Trainbands in a vigorous Attack. . . .'

When a toast was drunk, it would be accompanied by the 'Windy compliment of a Gun from the Stern' and with as much formality as in a Royal Navy mess, 'every Member's affection to the Person nam'd being measur'd by the strength and loudness of the Stinking Report with which he crown'd his Bumper'.

A far more salubrious Club was that of the Florists, and here Ned Ward ridiculed the way in which they over-charged their stomachs. The first dish served when he ate with them was 'a side of Salmon very palatably dress'd with shrimps and Oysters, insomuch that one of the Members, who had a Body like an Elephant, a Stomach like a Tyger, and a Mouth like an Alligator, as he sat shov'ling in the Fish, as a Scavenger does Soil into his Dirty Vehicle, happen'd to be highly commending the excellency of the Sauce'. But his enjoyment vanished when 'a merry Fellow' sitting opposite him remarked: 'Don't you know one of the Stewards is a Kitchen Gardener, and the Rogue to save some Charges has put in Worms instead of Shrimps, and Snails in the Room of Oysters?' This checked the glutton's voracity and he took as much time over swallowing the morsel in his mouth 'as a Cow does her Cud, or an Ass a Thistle'.

Another of the many strange Clubs was the Smokers. Sam Scott kept a shop at the Temple-Gate where he sold harps and fiddles and in order to ingratiate himself with his customers who liked to relax with 'Bottle Adventures and merry Midnight Revellings' he started such a Club consisting of a dancing-master, four other musicians and himself. They acquired 'such an expeditious way of consuming a Pipe of Tobacco' that, when they met, a pound of it would vanish in a hour, driving out with clouds of smoke all the other customers of the taverns visited and for this reason they became unpopular and were constantly having to move on.

There was a hostelry behind St Clement's where the liquor was so excellent that Sam Scott and his bosom companions were reluctant to leave it despite mine host's requests, so one evening when they arrived with a pound of tobacco and he realized that all his rooms were to be filled with smoke 'like a Yarmouth herring-house' he hurried out and, calling on the beadle, who lived near by, ordered him to bring 'the Parish Engine with two or three Buckets of Water in it, and to place it right against his Door'. The publican then confided his plan to the other customers so that none should leave when the alarm was given. Once the equipment was stationed in position then all in the know roared out: 'Fire!' The smokers jumped up, threw down their pipes 'as if the Father of everlasting Fire had been at the heels of them and in a hurry tumbled over one another down the stairs and just as they were in the middle of the Entry, striving who should squeeze out first, the Beadle, according to Direction, let fly the Engine into the House, and made them as wet as so many Water-Lane Divers drag'd thro' a Horse-Pond'. Scott and his friends fled into the night, then later they ventured to return and, finding no visible signs of any damage by fire, cautiously climbed upstairs. Above, they were greeted with tumultuous laughter, and the landlord asked where they had been to come back in such 'a dripping pickle'.

Scott replied that he and his friends had run out to discover where the fire was when some 'rogue or other' had slapped a bucket of water in their faces. 'Bless me, Gentlemen,' answered the Landlord, 'some of my officious Neighbours seeing such a terrible Smoak gush out of the Window of your Club Room ran, in a Consternation, and fetch'd the Parish Engine and the Buckets, and here they have done me I know not what Damage in playing into my House, believing 'twas on fire'.

To this Sam Scott returns coolly: 'Come, come, it's well it is no worse. Prithee, bring us some Pipes that we may sit and Smoak-dry ourselves a little.' A response that provoked the other to retort: 'By my soul, Gentlemen, if you fall again to Smoaking, my Neighbours will run again for the Parish Engine and the Buckets.' So Scott and his friends had no option but to leave 'and the Victualler by Stratagem got finally quit of their fumiferous Company'. When the news spread among their 'Rakish Acquaintances', they found it impossible to settle in any tavern for long lest some practical joke be played on them, so were forced to frequent coffee houses where they were unknown. There they made 'such a damnable Smother' that no one could read a newspaper in peace 'unless he was able to live in Soot and Smoak, like a Brew-House Stoker or a Chimney-Sweeper, for no sooner were their Pipes well-lighted than there would commence a coughing concert as if in Church in winter'.

When the Fog began to spread, up would rise an Old

'Shrivel'd Shop-Keeper, who, straining his Sides with a violent Fit of Barking, would be forc'd to leave half his Liquor behind him, and run Head foremost out of the Coffee Room to suck in a little Street Air.... after him, perhaps, an Old Asthmatical Counsellor, who would fall, of a sudden, into such a Fit of Wheezing, as if a Pauper Client was asking his Advice without an answerable Fee, and that he had suddenly Counterfeited a Fit of the Asthma, to get rid of his Impertinence, crying out, 'Ah, Smoak, Smoak, more Air for God's sake'.

In this manner, Scott and his smokers would clear a Coffee House of its clientele within half an hour.

This Sort of Trade the extravagant Fumigators drove for a few Years, till they had stupify'd their Senses by the Narcottick Fumes of the Mundungus Weed, dry'd their Skins to Parchment; bak'd their Intrails to Cinders; exhausted all their radical Moisture, and made themselves such irrecoverable Sots, by excessive Smoaking and Drinking, the Want of regular Eating and sensible Rest that they all drop'd off in the Prime of their Days . . . and went out of the World as well dry'd as Yarmouth Herrings, Yorkshire Hung-Beef, or West Phalia Bacon, as if they meant whilst Living, to be their own Embalmers.

Ned Ward also showered with his satiric barbs those who drank too much in his chapter on the Market Women's Club. There were several, who, as soon as business was over, sped for refreshment to the nearest taverns, and one of these in Clare Market was typical. A certain vintner in Cheapside made an offer for a parcel of wines, but the merchant would not accept the bid. They talked about other things and touched on the subject of hard drinking. The vintner said that women were just as prone to it as men and proposed a contest to settle the price of the wines. If the merchant provided a hogshead of claret, he would bring along three women he believed to be capable of drinking it all at one sitting without falling asleep or spewing. In the event of their succeeding, the merchant would then have to accept his bid, whilst, if they failed, the vintner promised to pay the higher price. Believing it impossible for women to be found capable of accomplishing such a feat, the seller accepted the challenge.

The vintner, having had personal experience of the drinking capabilities of the women in Clare Market, visited their stalls, spent some money, presented some of those who had 'the best Stowage with a liberal morning's Draught, and told them what he planned'. They agreed to take part in the test. 'When the time came, the Hogshead being elevated up one pair of Stairs into a commodious Room, and two Thirty Gallon Tubs for Chamber-Pots, placed behind a Curtain in a convenient Corner, the Female Undertakers of the Grand Exploit' made a punctual appearance and found the two men 'with a Dish of Tongues before them' seated ready.

' "Prithee, Mr Flowere," says Bess Gundy to the Vintner, "fill that Monteith there that I may taste the liquor, for we will not poison ourselves for e'er a Pimp in England." ' So the hogshead was broached and the Monteith filled and she swiftly swallowed the two gallons it contained in three or four gulps without breathing. ' "Good Tipple, girls," cries the Dame to her Mess-mates. So the other two confiding in the Judgment of her Palate, pledg'd their Tun-belly'd Sister in the like Quantity, without winking, all agreeing 'twas as good a Tub of Tipple as they could desire.'

When the merchant saw how quickly they drank the wine and with so little trouble, he despaired of winning and thought it wise to acknowledge he had lost to save the claret remaining in the hogshead. This suggestion angered the women and, calling him a 'sneaking cuckold', they swore that they had come for 'a Bellifull and a Bellifull they would have; and that they would see the last of it, were it a Mile to the bottom'. As they went on imbibing, the trio told tales of drinking achievements; one how her grandmother finished a butt of beer in twenty-four hours and 'never pissed but thrice till she came to the bottom', the second boasted that she drank twenty pitchers of wort out of the tun when she was but sixteen years old, and that it never gave her the 'wild-Squirt', and the third claimed that the first time she tried her strength before she was married was at Uxbridge Fair, and that she drank nineteen quarts of sack and sugar 'to oblige young Squire Cuddle, and afterwards Rid Home a Straddle, three miles, upon her Father's Mare without falling'.

The women went on relating similar stories, and now and then in turn would step behind the curtain 'to imitate the roaring of London Bridge'. When by five in the morning they finished the hogshead, each called for a quart of mulled white wine to settle her stomach, drank it more quickly than 'a grave Citizen does a sober Dish of Coffee; thank'd the Merchant for his kind entertainment, and away they jog'd by six . . . so far from being Drunk that they march'd very steadily down to Clare Market, to meet their Horses and their Drudges, who were to bring in their Commodities, being dog'd by the Merchant, who expected their Walking, together with the Air, would have put the Wine upon a Ferment. But he could not observe anything that look'd whimsical or frolicksome, till they came into Lincoln Inn Fields where they join'd Paws, took a short Dance round, and sung "Three merry Wives are we". Then disjoining their hands, Mother Gundy advanc'd foremost, crying, "Come, come, Girls, Drunk or Sober, always mind your Business". Thus they all went off fairly without Staggering or Spewing, so that the Merchant was forced to deliver the Wines according to agreement, and was thoroughly convinced from that time that Women, as well as Men, understand the Pleasure of the Bottle.'

Ned Ward found a further target for his satire in the Lord Mayor's Banquet which in the *City Feast* he depicts as a gathering of gluttons engaged in a race to see who could eat and drink the most. With sleeves rolled up and napkins tied round their necks, they all went to work 'with such a rending and tearing, like a kennel of hounds'. Ward continues:

> When done with the flesh, then they clawed off the fish,
> With one hand at mouth, and the other on dish.
> When their stomachs were closed, what those bellies
>   denied,
> Each clapt in his pocket to give to his bride,
> With a cheesecake and custard for my little Johnny,
> And a handful of sweetmeats for poor daughter Nancy.

Others, too, made fun of the excesses then widespread. In 1707 there was sold in London a pamphlet by an anonymous author about 'The Barbecue Feast or the Three Pigs of Peckham Broil'd under an Apple-Tree where the Cooks were Numberless, the Company Masterless, the Meat Carved with Hatchets, and Punch drunk by Pail-fulls'.

VI

GLUTTONY AND GIN

For centuries it had been held in Northern Europe that obesity was essential for good health and strength. It gave you a dignified appearance and plenty of food and drink enlarged the brain. Celebrities like Gustavus Adolphus of Sweden, Martin Luther, Frundsberg, Hans Sachs, Handel, and J. S. Bach were proud of their pot-bellies. Leanness was regarded with contempt. All this originated through excessive consumption of the most popular drink, beer. In Germany, by the beginning of the eighteenth century, it was drunk with every meal. At mid-day, there would be beer soup; for supper, egg-flip made with it. Folk boiled fish and sausages in beer, and added it to all kinds of dishes just like the French did with wine. During the Thirty Years' War drunkenness spread alarmingly as the harassed populace tried to drown their misery.

Alexander Pope in his *Second Satire of the Second Book of Horace* (1717) pours scorn on a well-known glutton of his day named Oldfield, who dissipated a fortune in one year on pandering to the greed of his stomach:

Oldfield with more than harpy throat endued,
Cries, 'Send me, Gods! a whole hog barbecued!'
Oh, blast it, south winds! till a stench exhale

Rank as the ripeness of a rabbit's tail.
By what criterion do ye eat, d'ye think,
If this is prized for sweetness, that for stink?
When the tired glutton labours through a treat,
He finds no relish in the sweetest meat;
He calls for something bitter, something sour,
And the rich feast concludes extremely poor.

The poet goes on to advocate avoiding excess of any kind when we eat and drink:

He knows to live, who keeps the middle state,
And neither leans on this side nor on that;
Nor stops, for one bad cork, his butler's pay . . .
Now hear what blessings temperance can bring . . .
First health: the stomach (cramm'd from every dish,
A tomb of boil'd and roast, and flesh and fish,
Where bile, and wind, and phlegm, and acid jar,
And all the man is one intestine war),
Remembers oft the school-boy's simple fare,
The temperate sleeps, and spirits light as air,
How pale each worshipful and reverend guest
Rise from a clergy, or a city feast!

Later, Pope suggests a self-inflicted punishment for the glutton:

When luxury has licked up all thy pelf,
Cursed by thy neighbours, thy trustees, thyself,
To friends, to fortune, to mankind a shame,
Think how posterity will treat thy name;
And buy a rope, that future times may tell
Thou hast at last bestowed one penny well.

If Parson Woodforde ever read Pope's verses, he like many others in the Church paid little heed to their strictures. Woodforde's meticulously detailed diaries refer time after time to the huge amounts of food ate by his family and friends. In 1774 at 'a very elegant dinner' in Oxford, they had part of a large cod, a chine of mutton, a chicken pie, pigeons and asparagus, a fillet of veal with mushrooms, roasted sweetbreads, hot lobster, apricot tart, syllabubs and jellies, a dessert of fruit, and to drink, Madeira, white and red port. He managed all this on a stipend of £300 per annum plus tithes and what he obtained from his glebe farm in East Anglia, where he was a good employer giving the men at harvest-time, when they had ended a day's work, beef and plum pudding to eat and as much liquor as they would drink.

Once there were unexpected participants in the drinking. Woodforde's journal entry of 15 April 1778, goes: 'Brewed a vessell of strong Beer today. My two large Piggs by drinking some Beer grounds leaking out of one of my Barrels today got so amazingly drunk by it that they were not able to stand and appeared like dead things almost, and so remained all night from dinner time today. I never saw Piggs so drunk in my life.' By next morning, they were still hardly able to stand and tumbled about the yard, but in the afternoon they were 'tolerably sober'.

The ill-effects of excess began to be felt in England in the last decade of the seventeenth century, and as a result, people flocked to Bath for treatment hoping for restoration to good health — and so that they could start indulging in their vices all over again. Ned Ward in *A Step to the Bath* describes with a caustic pen the scene in the fashionable King's Bath when he went there in 1700. In it were

> at least fifty of both sexes, with a score or two of guides, who by their scorbutick carcasses and lacker'd hides made you think they had lain pickling a century in a Stygian lake. . . . In one corner was an old fornicator hanging by the rings, loaded with a rotten humidity; hard by him was a buxom dame cleansing her *nunquam satis* from mercurial dregs and the remains of Roman vitriol. Another, half covered with sear-cloth, had

more sores than Lazarus, doing penance for the sins of
her youth; at her elbow was a young hero, supported
by a couple of guides, racked with aches and intoler-
able pains, cursing Beveridge's dancing school. . . .

Ward exaggerated for the sake of effect and his description of those disporting themselves in the Cross Bath is
equally lurid.

Here is performed all the wanton dalliances imagin-
able; celebrated beauties, panting breasts and curious
shapes, almost exposed to the public view; languishing
eyes, darting killing glances, tempting amorous postures, attended by soft music, enough to provoke a
vestal to forbidden pleasures, captivate a saint and
charm a Jove.

There was a vigorous spark showing off before the ladies
'with several artistic postures, as sailing on their backs,
then embracing the element, sinking in a rapture and by
accidental design, thrusting a stretched arm, but where the
water concealed, so ought my pen'.

The galleries, says Ward, were crowded with men
feasting their eyes on the heavy breasts and other charms
of the women they fancied. He noticed a roaming
nymphomaniac in a crimson gown 'with Monsieur at her
elbow, two devils behind her and Aetna in her face, all the
water in the Severn not able to quench her desires; she
hath already quartered a troop of French dragoons, a
regiment of Dutchmen and is come to exercise a battalion
of Britons'.

The following year, 1701, *The Bath, or the Western Lass*, a
comedy by Thomas Durfey, was presented at the Theatre
Royal, Drury Lane, and in it there is a character,
Hairbrain, who 'will souse into the Bath stark naked as
ever he was alone, and if there be a plump Londoner
there, a fat shouldered lass or so, as we have a great many
crummy dames come here to waste an't please ye, he's on

the back of her in a trice, and tabering her buttocks round the bath as if he were beating a drum'.

Queen Anne herself, who came to the throne in 1702, became so fat through over-eating that she hunted the stag in a special chaise strengthened to support her weight without risk of collapsing. A year prior to her death, she had put on so much weight that it was an ordeal for her to climb stairs, so she was lifted in her chair to the next floor by ropes round pulleys. In the next century, incidentally, another heavyweight, Parson Pike of Kirkby Mallory in Leicestershire, had to be winched by pulley in and out of his pulpit. Queen Anne was also a wine-bibber and the story goes that her statue was erected in London with its back on St Paul's so that her royal smile could be fixed on the street corner opposite where her vintner's premises were situated.

George I, who succeeded Anne in 1714, liked women to be well-upholstered. Lord Chesterfield wrote:

No women came amiss to him if they were very willing and very fat. . . . The standard of His Majesty's taste made all those ladies who aspired to his favour and who were near the statuable size strain and swell themselves like the frogs in the fable to rival the bulk and dignity of the ox. Some succeeded and others burst.

Chesterfield himself found there was a certain advantage in having sex with a fat woman as he revealed in a letter from Venice to another lady friend. It is typical of the frankness about promiscuity in eighteenth-century aristocratic circles.

I beg you, whether there would not be a way on my return for us to pass a night together, or even a day in bed. For example, could you not find some pretext for staying a night in town, and as you value few people in the house, have me let in by your maid through the back door, or if that is not possible, come early in the morning and have me enter the same way. If the thing is feasible, think constantly of the means if possible and let me know. Thus far, my happiness has been imperfect and I begrudge your clothes the part which they have had in our embraces.

Later, in the same letter, Chesterfield tells his inamorata that as he has promised to conceal nothing from her, he confesses that he has had intimate relations with a married lady, but their commerce was 'purely corporal' and the heart had no part in it, so there is no need for his correspondent to alarm herself.

She is an abandoned lady, who welcomes all comers, but who happily nevertheless behaves very well. She is bizarre and uncertain to a supreme degree, now of a marvellous tranquillity, now wild as the devil. Our rendez-vous are every morning at seven o'clock; I throw myself completely nude into her arms, even without a shirt, and as she is of appalling size, I have not the least difficulty in getting at her. With all that, she is of a temperament very cold. But what is singular in our relation is that I emerge from her arms with more vigour and energy than when I went into them, which is good fortune rarely encountered. Finally, you can conclude that I do not love her, and proof of that is that I shall tell you who she is: She is the Sea, the wife of Monsieur the Doge of Venice, and I hope that he and you will pardon me this affair.

Gluttony was prevalent, too, amongst academics, and sometimes with unfortunate effects. Thomas Gray, the poet, wrote from Pembroke Hall, Cambridge, on 12 August 1760:

Our friend Dr Chapman (one of its nuisances) is not expected here again in a hurry. He is gone to his grave with five fine mackerel (large and full of roe) in his belly. He ate them all at one dinner; but his fate was turbot on Trinity Sunday, of which he left little for the company besides bones. He had not been hearty all the week; but after this sixth fish he never held up his head more, and a violent looseness carried him off. They say he made a very good end.

Fastidious Horace Walpole was repelled by the corpulence and gluttony of the country gentry of those days:

I shudder to see them brandish their knives in act to carve, and look on them as savages that devour one another. I should not stare at all more than I do, if yonder Alderman at the lower end of the table was to stick his fork into his neighbour's jolly cheek and cut a brave slice of brown and fat. Why, I'll swear I see no difference between a country gentleman and a sirloin; whenever the first laughs, or the latter is cut, there runs out just the same streams of gravy!

In the last decade of the eighteenth century, John Knyveton in his journals refers to the great anatomist, Dr George Fordyce, who maintained that people were harming their health by over-eating. However, what the advocate of dieting considered permissible might nowadays be regarded as excessive. On 4 October 1791, as Knyveton and a friend were walking down Paternoster Row, a portly, red-faced man almost knocked them into the gutter as, making a great play with his long cane, he entered Dolly's Chophouse as if he owned it. This was the celebrated doctor from Edinburgh who, following the example of the lion, allowed himself only one meal daily and that always at four in the afternoon.

As the clock strikes, he seats himself at a table reserved for him, on which in readiness for his arrival are placed a bottle of port wine, a quarter of brandy, and a silver tankard of strong ale. The moment his loud step and loud voice are heard at the door, a solemn and orderly ritual is set in motion. As one drawer hastens to pull out his chair, the cook puts a pound and a half of rump steak on the gridiron and dishes up a trifle of broiled fowl or a dish of fish, which a second drawer lays before the doctor. Of this he disposes whilst the steak is grilling, and caps it with a drink of brandy. He then sets to work on the steak, washing it down with the strong ale, and finally finishes off the brandy and drinks his bottle of port. . . . And this he has been doing for upwards of twenty years.

Dr Fordyce ate rapidly, spending precisely one hour-and-a-half on the meal, then he would return to his house in Essex Street, pausing at three hostelries on the way to drink a glass of brandy and water at each. In 1802 he died, a martyr to gout and having been afflicted for some years with 'acute rambling pains in his stomach and bowels'.

To show that they were superior and more cultured than those grosser mortals who cared only for the smell and taste of what they shovelled inside them, it became the mode in elegant society during the latter half of the eighteenth century to have the dishes served at dinner exotically decorated. This was soon carried to excess. Horace Walpole in his *Journals* commented:

The last branch of our fashion into which the close observation of nature has been introduced is our desserts. Jellies, biscuits, sugar-plums, and creams, have long since given way to harlequins, gondoliers, Turks, Chinese, and shepherdesses of Saxon china. But these, unconnected, and only seeming to wander among groves of curled paper and silk flowers, were soon discovered to be too insipid and unmeaning. By degrees, meadows of cattle, of the same brittle materials, spread themselves over the table; cottages rose in sugar, and temples in barley-sugar, pigmy Neptunes in cars of cockle-shells triumphed over oceans of looking-glass or seas of silver-tissue. Women of the first quality came home from Chenevix's laden with dolls and babies, not for their children, but their house-keeper. At last, even these puerile puppet-shows are sinking into disuse, and more manly ways of conclud-ing our repasts are established. Gigantic figures suc-ceed to pigmies; and it is known that a celebrated confectioner (Lord Albemarle's) complained that, after having prepared a middle dish of gods and goddesses eighteen feet high, his lord would not cause the ceiling of his parlour to be demolished to facilitate their entrée. '*Imaginez-vous*,' said he, '*que milord n'a pas voulu faire ôter le plafond!*'

French chefs were even more fanciful and Walpole says that the Intendant of Gascony to celebrate the birth of the Duke of Burgundy treated 'the noblesse of the province with a dinner and a dessert, the latter of which concluded with a representation, by wax figures moved by clockwork, of the whole labour of the Dauphiness and the happy birth of an heir to the monarchy'.

Walpole adds that the French Ambassador, the Duc de Mirapoix, gave a dinner with a dessert representing the story of Perseus and Andromeda, where the sea was silver tissue covered with barley sugar; whilst in Germany a Duke in Wurtemberg startled his guests with a dessert representing Mount Etna in which real fireworks were used.

Thomas Jefferson was so interested in the pleasures of the table that, when American President, he sent one of his aides to Italy to learn how to prepare spaghetti dishes, and, writing at the end of the eighteenth century, he observed: 'No nation is drunken where wine is cheap, and none sober where the dearness of wine substitutes ardent spirits as the common beverage.' English social history following the Revolution of 1688 certainly bears this out. Until then, beer and claret had been the most popular beverages, and, ever since the Norman Conquest, the law had forbidden the conversion of malt into spirits except a little for medicinal purposes. In 1689, motivated mainly by anti-French feelings, an Act was passed allowing any one to start up a distillery, and then, in 1695, the duties on wines were sharply raised. By the end of the century, owing to the war, French claret and cognac ceased being imported and stocks dwindled. All this proved a disastrous change. By 1710, the annual quantity of British spirits distilled amounted to two million gallons, by 1735 to 3,601,000 gallons, and by only eight years later it had soared to 5,394,000 gallons.

Tobias Smollett, who lived in the first half of the eighteenth century, wrote of the havoc cheap gin caused:

> The retailers of this poisonous compound set up painted boards in public, inviting people to be drunk for the small expense of one penny, assuring them they might be dead drunk for two pence, and have straw for nothing. They accordingly provided cellars and places strewn with straw, to which they conveyed those wretches who were overwhelmed with intoxication.

Hogarth's 'Gin Lane' was no exaggeration. The spirit turned them into savages. Drunks covered the pavements every Saturday night, and the grand jury of Middlesex declared that the greater part of the rampant poverty, murders, and robberies was caused by it.

But gin was not the only liquor that made the eighteenth century the most intemperate in English history. Even children had a dram of rum several times a day, and mothers' favourite medicine for squalling babies was a few spoonfuls of rum strengthened with opium. Employers paid their workers partly in rum, and allowed them at least a day off every month to get drunk. Farm-hands would quit unless they were kept happy with frequent tots.

Daniel Defoe, after travelling between Honiton and Exeter in 1725, wrote: 'They told us they send 50,000 hogsheads of cyder hence every year to London, and which is still worse that it is most of it bought there by the merchants to mix with their wine.'

In 1725, a report of the Middlesex Justices stated that in the metropolis, exclusive of the City of London and Southwark, there were 6,187 houses and shops wherein 'geneva or other strong waters' were sold by retail catering for a population of about 700,000. There were districts where every seventh house was engaged in selling intoxicants. Belatedly, in 1736, the Gin Act became law which imposed a duty of 20*s.* a gallon on all spirituous liquors and prohibited any one from selling them in smaller quantities than two gallons without paying a tax of £50 a year. This would have resulted in almost prohibition, and mobs rioted to battle cries of 'No gin, no King!' There were mock funeral processions mourning the death of 'Madam Gin'. Shops were ransacked for spirits and there were drunken orgies. The distillers soon found a way of evading the terms of the new law by taking out wine licences and selling gin, spiced and slightly flavoured with wine, under new names, such as 'Cuckold's Comfort', 'Ladies' Delight', 'Cholic-and-Gripe Waters', 'The Last Shift', 'Knock-me-down', etc.

The authorities relied on informers to try and enforce the hated restrictions and some twelve thousand convictions resulted within two years, but, far from consumption falling, by 1742 it was estimated that every Londoner bought on average 14 gallons a year. Urgent action was imperative, so the following year a bill was passed reducing the duties drastically, but even this had little effect and in 1749 over four thousand persons were convicted of selling spirituous liquors without a licence and the number of private gin-shops was reckoned to be in excess of seventeen thousand. London physicians in their report of 1750 revealed that there were under their care some fourteen thousand seriously ill patients, most of them incurable due to their addiction to gin.

Henry Fielding in his pamphlet, *On the late Increase of Robbers*, published in 1751, blamed it on 'a new kind of drunkenness, unknown to our ancestors'. Gin was 'the principal sustenance (if it may be so called), of more than a hundred thousand people in the metropolis. . . . Should the drinking of this poison be continued at its present height during the next twenty years, there will, by that time, be very few of the common people left to drink it.' The annual consumption of spirits had leapt from under six million gallons ten years previously to over eleven whilst for the first time in centuries the population was no longer increasing.

The watchmen or constables were mostly inept and instead of patrolling the streets haunted the taverns. Often they were a menace to the public they were supposed to protect. Horace Walpole in a letter to his friend, Sir Horace Mann, in Italy, dated July 1742, gives us a horrifying example of this:

> A parcel of drunken constables took it into their heads to put the laws in execution against disorderly persons, and so took up every woman they met, till they had collected five or six and twenty, all of whom they thrust into St Martin's roundhouse, where they kept them all night, with doors and windows closed. The poor creatures, who could not stir or breathe, screamed as long as they had any breath left, begging at least for water . . . but in vain. In the morning, four were found stifled to death, two died soon after, and a dozen more are in a shocking way. . . . Several of them were beggars, who, from having no lodgings, were necessarily found in the streets, and others honest labouring women. One of the dead was a poor washerwoman, big with child, who was returning home late from washing. One of the constables is taken, and others absconded; but I question if any of them will suffer death, though the greatest criminals in this town, are the officers of justice. There is no tyranny they do not exercise, no villainy of which they do not partake.

Ten years later, on 22 March 1751, Horace Walpole wrote to Mann: 'One is forced to travel even at noon as if one were going to battle.' That year, however, as far as the problem of preventing the country from sinking in a sea of spirits was concerned, another and more successful bill became law. Distillers were forbidden from either selling spirits themselves or selling them to unlicensed retailers. Licences were granted only to £10 householders or to traders subject to certain parochial rates, and the penalties for unlicensed trading were sharply raised.

VII

PORT AND PASSION

Due to the wars with France very little cognac and claret were imported into England and stocks dwindled. This opened the market to the red wine of Portugal, and the excessive consumption of port that followed affected those in power. It made them gouty and ill-tempered, ready to pick a quarrel. In Queen Anne's reign two leading politicians, Carteret and Pulteney, were alcoholics, and the latter shortened his life through drink. Harley, Earl of Oxford, was dismissed from the post of Lord Treasurer by the Queen on the grounds that he was regularly in various stages of intoxication, causing him to neglect all business, that he was seldom to be understood because his speech was slurred, and that when he did explain himself, she could not depend upon the truth of what he said.

Throughout the eighteenth century many government ministers went to bed drunk. Port altered the appearance of the typical English gentleman; his complexion soon matched the colour of the wine that flowed at the end of his dinner and his swag-belly became the target for the cartoonist. The Irish politician, Sir Hercules Langrishe, when asked if he had finished three bottles of port, without assistance, said: 'No — not quite that. I had the assistance of a bottle of Madeira.' And Theodore Hook, tipsy in his chair three hours after dinner, excused himself, saying: 'When one is alone, the bottle does come round so often.'

A Swiss visitor, De Saussure, wrote in *A Foreign View of England* that he had found water in abundance there, but 'would you believe it, absolutely none is drunk'. The philosopher De la Rochefoucauld's son, writing in 1784, stated how astonished he was by English drinking habits, but described dinner as the most wearisome experience as it lasted for four or five hours. The first two were spent in eating and he had been compelled to exercise his stomach to the full in order to please his host. 'He asks you the whole time whether you like the food and presses you to eat more, with the result that, out of pure politeness, I do nothing but eat from the time I sit down until the time I get up from the table.' All the dishes consisted of various meats either boiled or roasted and of joints weighing about twenty or thirty pounds. After the sweets, the cloth was removed and the table covered with all kinds of wine and in the middle was placed fruit, biscuits and butter 'for many people take it at dessert'.

At this juncture, all the servants left and so did the ladies after drinking a glass or two of wine.

> It is then that real enjoyment begins — there is not an Englishman who is not supremely happy at this particular moment. One proceeds to drink — sometimes in an alarming measure. Everyone has to drink in his turn for the bottles make a continuous circuit of the table and the host takes note that everyone is drinking in his turn.
>
> After this has gone on for some time and, when thirst has become an inadequate reason for drinking, a fresh stimulus is supplied by the drinking of 'toasts' — that is to say, the host begins by giving the name of a lady to whose health he drinks and everyone is obliged to do the same. After the host, someone else gives a toast and everyone drinks to the health of everyone

else's lady. Then each member of the party names some man and the whole ceremony begins again. If more drinking is required, fresh toasts are always ready to hand. Politics can supply plenty. The sideboard, too, is furnished with a number of chamber pots and it is a common practice to relieve oneself while the rest are drinking. One has no kind of concealment and the practice strikes me as most indecent.

At the end of two or three hours, a servant announces that tea is ready and conducts the gentlemen from their drinking to join the ladies in the drawing-room, where they are usually employed in making tea and coffee. After tea, one generally plays whist, and at midnight there is cold meat for those who are hungry. While the game is going on, there is punch on a table for those who want it. I have entered into these details of my experiences at Euston, where I stayed with the Duke of Grafton, because the manner of life is the same throughout England.

Though the French nobleman found such eating and drinking excessive, it was nothing compared with the feats of some English aristocrats. There were two who locked themselves in a room with a hogshead of claret and succeeded in drinking it all as well as several bottles of cherry brandy within a week. Sir Philip Francis mentions as though it were quite normal that two of his cronies finished ten bottles of champagne and burgundy between them over a meal. Lord Torrington corresponding with a friend from Biggleswade in 1793 revealed with pride that he drank three pints of port every day in addition to half-a-pint of brandy without any ill-effects. It was also his practice should he get wet in a downpour of rain to strip and rub himself all over with brandy or gin, which, as an additional precaution against catching a cold, he would sprinkle on his bedclothes if he feared they might be damp. Despite such care, in the summer of 1792 he became ill with bronchitis and tried for a change a non-alcoholic remedy. He wrote on June 2: 'I drank snail tea for breakfast for my chest is very sore.' Four years earlier, Colonel John Byng mentioned in his journal how he had been lavish with the brandy to guard against infection when staying in an inn at Rugby: 'I took off the sheets and employed all the brandy, near a pint, in purifying the room and sprinkling the quilt and blankets.'

Gronow says in his memoirs that he knew several four- and even five-bottle men and the only thing that saved them was drinking very slowly out of small glasses. 'The learned head of the law, Lord Eldon, and his brother, Lord Stowell, used to say that they had drunk more bad port than any two men in England. . . . The late Lords Panmure, Dufferin, and Blayney wonderful to relate were six-bottle men at this time.' Lord Eldon left on his own would eat an entire dish of pig's liver and bacon. His eyes and mouth never failed to water from delight when his nostrils caught the smell of their being fried.

In *The True Drunkard's Delight* William Juniper tells of a Scottish laird who, when his seventh son was born, had a dozen bottles of the oldest Château Margaux brought up from the cellar and christened the child himself with a glass of the claret, gave a glass of it to his wife, then went into the library with the doctor where they finished the remainder between them by breakfast time. The boy when he grew up became both a poet and an innkeeper who wrote *Poet's Pub*.

There was secret drinking by MPs during the proceedings in the House of Commons. Cornwall, its Speaker, later in the eighteenth century, kept a mug of beer by him which was replenished immediately it was empty and he held up debates by falling asleep as a result.

In Ireland the gentry had either laid in huge stocks of claret or had little trouble obtaining it through smugglers. In the early eighteenth century, Beauchamp Bagenal of Dunleckey House, County Cork, after a day in the field, would gather his horsey friends about his table laden with food. Once they were seated, in he came carrying a brace of pistols, which he laid beside his plate. When he and his cronies were replete, footmen brought in a cask of claret and set it at the other end of the dining-room. This was the signal for Bagenal to perform his most appreciated act of hospitality — raising one of the pistols, he shot out the bung. Other bullets, it was said, he reserved for those who fell short of doing justice to his claret.

Jonathan Swift, Dean of St Patrick's, gives a lively picture of the aristocracy dining in Dublin. Lord Smart received the guests at 3 p.m. Eight sat down, including a county baronet, who had no appetite having already eaten a beef-steak and drunk 'two mugs of ale, besides a tankard of March beer when he got up in the morning'. The company drank claret, which their host said should always be drunk after fish. This was followed by puddings, and then a goose during which course 'beer and wine were freely imbibed'. After this, the meal ended and some of the gentlemen took a dram of brandy. Then, Lord Smart bade the butler bring up the great tankard full of October to Sir John, and this was passed from hand to hand and mouth to mouth. The cloth removed, a bottle of Burgundy appeared, of which the ladies were invited to partake before they went to tea. When they left, fresh bottles were brought, the dead man removed. Lord Smart told the butler to bring clean glasses, but a Colonel said: 'I'll keep my glass, for wine is the best liquor to wash glasses in.' At lustier dinners in Ireland that century in houses of the gentry, a giant goblet termed a 'Constable' was set on the table and filled with claret, and any one who neglected his own glass was forced to drink it.

When the first Prime Minister, Sir Robert Walpole, was young, his father would pour into his glass a double portion of wine, declaring: 'Come, Robert, you shall drink twice while I drink once, for I will not permit a son of mine in his sober senses to witness his father's intoxication.' This upbringing turned Robert into a heavy drinker who boasted that at his own table he 'always talked bawdy, because in that all could join'. At the height of his power, for six weeks and longer in the autumn, he would fill his magnificent mansion at Houghton with his dissolute friends in both Houses of Parliament and their friends. Their riotous behaviour was the scandal of the county, often driving Lord Townshend from his neighbouring seat of Raynham denouncing what he called 'Bacchanalian orgies'. Lady Mary Wortley Montagu was shocked to hear that Sir Robert had laughed and joked with his fourteen-year-old daughter about Lord Stair's attempt to seduce her.

Another lecherous eighteenth-century politican was the fourth Earl of Sandwich, twice First Lord of the Admiralty, whose rolling gait caused a wit to jest that 'it was his wont to walk down both sides of the street at once', whilst the poet, Charles Churchill, described his face as that of a man who had been half hanged and cut down by mistake. 'Jemmy Twitcher' was so randy that he kept his mistress during the day in a room near his office at the Admiralty, so that, whenever the urge to copulate came over him, he need take only a few steps to gratify it. As this occurred very frequently, his official duties did not suffer as much as they might had his love nest been further away. As sex and the Royal Navy took up so much of his time, he could not spare any to be absent for a meal, so he would send out for slices of beef laid between thick slices of bread which he could eat at his desk. Others followed his example and the busy man's snack came to be called after him.

When Sandwich left the Admiralty, he would either visit the brothels round St James Street or relax at Medmenham with Sir Francis Dashwood and his fellow-members of the infamous Hell Fire Club, which also included the Chancellor of the Exchequer. There, after drinking whatever aphrodisiac he fancied, a 'Strip Me Naked' or a 'Lay Me Down Softly', he would enjoy a luxurious dinner; after which they would dress up as monks and take part in a Black Mass before indulging in orgies with prostitutes in the Roman Room. As most of these rakehells suffered from VD, they would mockingly greet one another as *Monsieur de Croix de Venus* and *Signor Gonorrhoea*.

Daniel Defoe has been called the first of the great English novelists. He was essentially a journalist who obtained his raw material from life, embellishing where detail was lacking with such consummate artistry that his characters lived and the events in which he involved them seemed real. *The Fortunes and Misfortunes of the Famous Moll Flanders*, first published in 1722, can be regarded therefore as no less faithful an account of the excesses of the period than the journals of Boswell, Horace Walpole, and others. Moll, we are told, was born in Newgate, and was twelve years a whore, five times a wife (once to her own brother by whom she had three children), twelve years a thief, eight years a transport felon in Virginia, at last grew rich, liv'd honest, and died a penitent'. She was a big, strong, buxom woman, who regarded sexual intercourse as mere physical jerks that kept her from starving. The wealthy lechers were the villains.

Defoe makes Moll denounce such men:

There is nothing so absurd, so surfeiting, so ridiculous as a man heated by wine in his head, and a wicked gust in his inclination, together he is in the possession of two devils at once, and can no more govern himself by his reason than a mill can grind without water; his vice tramples upon all that was in him that had any good in it, if any such thing there was; nay, his very sense is blinded by its own rage, and he acts absurdities even in his view; such as drinking more, when he is drunk already, picking up a common woman without regard to what she is or who she is, whether sound or rotten, clean or unclean, whether ugly or handsome, whether old or young, and so blinded as not really to distinguish. Such a man is worse than lunatic; prompted by his vicious, corrupted head, he no more knows what he is doing than this wretch of mine knew when I picked his pocket of his watch and his purse of gold.

These are the men of whom Solomon says, 'They go like an ox to the slaughter, till a dart strikes through their liver', an admirable description, by the way, of the foul disease, which is a poisonous deadly contagion mingling with the blood, whose centre or fountain is in the liver. . . .

Two years later Defoe published another novel in the first person, *The Fortunate Mistress or a History of the Life And Vast Variety of Fortunes of . . . the Lady Roxana in the Time of King Charles II*, in which he makes her admit:

I may venture to say that no woman ever lived a life like me, of six and twenty years of wickedness, without the least signals of remorse, without any signs of repentance, or without so much as a wish to put an end to it. I had so long habituated myself to a life of vice, that really it appeared to be no vice to me. I went on smooth and pleasant. I wallowed in wealth. . . .

She obtains the riches she craves through impersonating a Countess, a Quaker, a Turkish woman, a French aristocrat, and so on.

Samuel Richardson's *Clarissa Harlowe* (1748) is regarded as the finest novel of the eighteenth century. Its villain, Lovelace, seeks power through sexual conquest. He is a sadist with animalistic urges and also a voyeur and a necrophiliac who rapes the drugged Clarissa. She says of him that his 'abominable eyes' have 'at times, such a leering, mischief-boding cast', and, later, Mr Mowbray announces that he had taken 'a pailful of black bull's blood' from Lovelace.

A broad-minded *grande dame* of Victorian times was to say that such goings on might be tolerated as long as they were not allowed out in the streets where they might frighten the horses. But such sentiments would be derided by the populace in eighteenth-century London. With the intention of keeping vice out of St James's Park, its gates were locked at ten o'clock every night, but some 6,500 persons managed to persuade those in charge to allow them keys, and duplicates found their way into the hands of prostitutes who operated there from dusk to dawn. According to a foreign visitor, Schutz, in many of the streets of London themselves, one was accosted at every ten paces.

A young man visiting St James's Park after dark in 1763 was to have had before the age of thirty on his own admission eleven mistresses as well as intercourse with sixty prostitutes in six countries other than England. This was James Boswell, who in his journal for the 25th of March that year confessed: 'As I was coming home this night, I felt carnal inclinations raging through my frame. I determined to gratify them. I went to St James's Park and picked up a whore.' Five days later, he strolls into the Park again and takes the first whore he meets 'whom I without many words copulated with, free from danger being safely sheathed'. On 13 April, he writes:

I should have mentioned last night that I met with a monstrous big whore in the Strand, who I had a great curiosity to lubricate, as the saying is. I went into a tavern with her, where she displayed to me all the parts of her enormous carcass; but I found that her avarice was as large as her a ——, for she would by no means take what I offered her. I therefore with all coolness pulled the bell and discharged the reckoning, to her no small surprise and mortification. . . . I was so much in the lewd humour that I felt restless and took a little girl into a court; but wanted vigour. So I went home, resolved against low street debauchery.

Boswell's good intentions did not last long. On 10 May he admits:

At the bottom of Haymarket I picked up a strong, jolly young damsel, and taking her under the arm I conducted her to Westminster bridge and there in armour complete did I engage her upon this noble edifice. The whim of doing so there with the Thames rolling below us amused me much. Yet after the brutish appetite was sated, I could not but despise myself for being so closely united with such a low wretch.

Then, a week later:

I picked up a fresh, agreeable young girl called Alice Gibbs. We went down a lane to a snug place, and I took out my armour, but she begged that I might not put it on, as the sport was much pleasanter without it, and as she was quite safe. I was so rash as to trust her and had a very agreeable congress.

The following month, on 4 June, we read:

I went to the Park, picked up a low brimstone virago, went to the bottom of the Park, arm-in-arm, and dipped my machine in the Canal and performed most manfully. I then went as far as St Paul's Churchyard, roaring along, and then came to Ashley's Punch-house and drank three threepenny bowls. In the Strand, I picked up a little profligate wretch and gave her sixpence. She allowed me entrance. But the miscreant refused me performance. I was much stronger than her, and . . . pushed her up against the wall. She, however, gave a sudden spring from me; and screaming out, a parcel of more whores and soldiers came to her relief. 'Brother soldiers,' said I, 'should not a half-pay officer roger, for sixpence? And here has she used me so and so.' I got them on my side, and I abused in blackguard style, and then left them. At Whitehall I picked up another girl to whom I called myself a highwayman and told her I had no money and begged she would trust me. But she would not.

On the 18th of the same month, at night, Boswell took 'a streetwalker into Privy Garden and indulged sensuality. The wretch picked my pocket of my handkerchief, and then swore she had not. When I got home I was shocked to think that I had been intimately united with a low, abandoned, perjured, pilfering creature. I determined to do so no more, but if the Cyprian fancy should seize me, to participate my amorous flame with a genteel girl.'

'This afternoon I had some low debauchery with girls who patrol the courts in the Temple,' Boswell records on 13 July, and three days later his conscience troubles him again but without much effect.

> Since my being honoured with the friendship of Mr Johnson I have more seriously considered the duties of morality . . . I have considered that promiscuous concubinage is certainly wrong. . . . Sure that it is that if all the men and women in Britain were merely to consult an animal gratification, society would be a most shocking scene. Nay, it would cease altogether. Notwithstanding of these reflections, I have stooped to mean profligacy even yesterday. Heavens, I am resolved to guard against it.

But, on 3 August, making a lame excuse for his lapse, he unburdens his conscience:

> I should have mentioned that on Monday night, coming up the Strand, I was tapped on the shoulder by a fine fresh lass. I went home with her. She was an officer's daughter and born at Gibraltar. I could not resist indulging myself with the enjoyment of her. Surely, in such a situation, when the woman is already abandoned, the crime must be alleviated, though in strict morality, illicit love is always wrong.

As time went on Boswell started to drink more and more, no doubt as a compensation in his struggle against concupiscence. In *A Journal of a Tour to the Hebrides*, his entry for Sunday, 26 September 1773, reads:

> I drank too much the night before with the innkeeper while Dr Johnson was abed. I then thought that my last night's riot was no more than such a social excess as may happen without much moral blame; and recollected that some physicians maintained that a fever produced by it was upon the whole, good for health. . .

A year later, on 18 September 1774, Boswell wrote:

> It gave me much concern to be informed by my dear wife that I had been quite outrageous in my drunkenness the night before; that I had cursed her in a shocking manner and even thrown a candlestick with a lighted candle at her. It made me shudder to hear such an account of my behaviour to one whom I have so much reason to love and regard. . . . I therefore am most resolved to be sober.

Five years earlier, he had married his cousin.

According to Boswell's own account, he was in a state of inebriation on twenty-six occasions between 27 July 1776 and 25 March 1777. His tendency, when deprived of alcohol, was to gormandize. In 1776, he appeared to be under a compulsion to bring every conversation with Dr Johnson round to the subjects of concubinage and fornication. The following year his conversational obsession was drinking. He needed the strain of abstinence to be relieved by commendation and encouragement.

On 19 March 1777 Boswell lamented that he was having to sell his house through too much drinking of brandy punch. Then, on 28 June, he is ashamed to have come home after excessive hard drinking 'sadly intoxicated even insane'.

A happier side of Boswell's life was, of course, his

biography of Dr Johnson, whom he met for the first time in 1763. Boswell soon learnt that food and drink were of considerable interest to the great lexicographer, who at supper on Friday 5 August, that year, told him:

> Some people have a foolish way of not minding or pretending not to mind what they eat. For my part, I mind my belly very studiously, and very carefully; for I look upon it, that he who does not mind his belly will hardly mind anything else.

Boswell comments that Johnson was not only serious but vehement:

> Yet I have heard him, upon other occasions, talk with great contempt of people who were anxious to gratify their palates; and the 206th number of his 'Rambler' is a masterly essay against gulosity. His practice, indeed, I must acknowledge, may be considered as casting the balance of his different opinions upon the subject; for I never knew any man who relished good eating more than he did. When at table, he was totally absorbed in the business of the moment; his looks seemed riveted to his plate: nor would he, unless in very high company, say one word, or even pay the least attention to what was said by others, till he had satisfied his appetite; which was so fierce, and indulged with such intenseness, that while in the act of eating, the veins of his forehead swelled, and generally a strong perspiration was visible. To those whose sensations were delicate, this could not but be disgusting; and it was doubtless not very suitable to the character of a philosopher, who should be distinguished by self-command. But it must be owned, that Johnson, though he could be rigidly *abstemious*, was not a *temperate* man either in eating or drinking. He could refrain, but he could not use moderately. He told me, that he had fasted two days without interference, and that he had

never been hungry but once. They who beheld with wonder how much he ate upon all occasions when his dinner was to his taste, could not easily conceive what he must have meant by hunger; and not only was he remarkable for the extraordinary quantity which he did eat, but he was, or affected to be, a man of very nice discernment in the science of cookery. He used to descant critically on the dishes which had been at table where he had dined or supped, and to recollect very minutely what he had liked. . . .

When invited to dine even with an intimate friend, he was not pleased if something better than a plain dinner was not prepared for him. I have heard him say on such an occasion, 'This was a good dinner enough, to be sure; but it was not a dinner to *ask* a man to.' On the other hand, he was wont to express, with great glee, his satisfaction when he had been entertained quite to his mind. One day when he had dined with his neighbour and landlord in Bolt Court, Mr Allen, the printer, whose old housekeeper had studied his taste in everything, he pronounced this eulogy: 'Sir, we could not have had a better dinner had there been a *Synod of Cooks*.'

In the essay against gluttony that Boswell mentioned, Dr Johnson preached what he did not practise. Calling the character satirized 'Gulosulus', he says that his sole 'topic of talk or subject of meditation' is feasting.

His calendar is a bill of fare; he measures the year by successive dainties. The only common places of his memory are his meals; and if you ask him at what time an event happened, he considers whether he heard it after a dinner of turbot or venison. He knows, indeed, that those who value themselves upon sense, learning, or piety, speak of him with contempt; but he considers them as wretches, envious or ignorant, who do not know his happiness, or wish to supplant him; and declares to his friends, that he is fully satisfied with his own conduct, since he has fed every day on twenty dishes, and yet doubled his estate.

Johnson believed it unwise for a man to associate with a woman who ate too much, and in a letter dated 26 July 1783, he warned Boswell: 'If once you find a woman gluttonous, expect from her very little virtue.'

As regards Johnson's drinking habits, Mrs Piozzi in her *Anecdotes* of him wrote that 'his liking was for the strongest, as it was not the flavour but the effect he sought for' and that though for most of the last twelve years of his life he gave up wine after having often disposed of three bottles of port after dinner, he made himself some amends by drinking 'his chocolate liberally, pouring in large quantities of cream or even melted butter'. When asked by Boswell why he had stopped taking wine, he replied: 'Because it is so much better for a man to be sure that he is never to be intoxicated, never to lose the power over himself. I shall not drink again till I grow old and want it.' On another occasion, Johnson confided to Boswell:

I used to slink home, when I had drunk too much. A man accustomed to self-examination will be conscious when he is drunk, though a habitual drunkard will not be conscious of it. I know a physician who for twenty years was not sober; yet in a pamphlet, which he wrote upon fevers, he appealed to Garrick and me for his vindication from a charge of drunkenness. A bookseller was so habitually drunk that his most intimate friends never perceived he was more sober at one time than another.

In March 1781, Mr Thrale, a close friend of Johnson's, told Boswell that he had started drinking wine again. Soon after this, when Thrale entertained the two men to dinner, Boswell recorded in his journal:

I observed he poured a quantity of wine into a large glass and swallowed it greedily. Everything about his character and manners was forcible and violent; there never was any moderation. Many a day did he fast, many a year did he refrain from wine; but when he did eat, it was voraciously; when he did drink wine, it was copiously.

On 27 June 1784, when Johnson was seventy-five, Boswell was the guest with him of General Paoli, where the old man loved to dine.

There was a variety of dishes much to his taste, of all of which he seemed to me to eat so much, that I was afraid he might be hurt by it; and I whispered to the General my fear and begged he might not press him. 'Alas!' said the General. 'See how very ill he looks; he can live but a very short time. Would you refuse my slight gratification to a man under sentence of death? There is a humane custom in Italy by which persons in that melancholy situation are indulged with having whatever they like best to eat and drink, even with expensive delicacies.'

On 20 July that year Johnson wrote to his doctor from Ashbourne: 'My appetite still continues keen enough and what I consider as a symptom of radical health, I have voracious delight in raw summer fruit, of which I was less eager a few years ago.' Not long after this, he died.

Other diarists of the period apart from Boswell tell of their meetings with Johnson, and surgeon John Knyveton, when a medical student, was present by chance at a dinner given by the great literary lion in the Devil's Tavern on 11 December 1751.

We found ourselves chairs at the end of the table, my seat being near the door and thereby intolerably draughty but of satisfaction since it afforded me a good view of the Doctor. The waiters did bring in the supper, such a profusion of dishes as I have never seen before, the company being a large one, some twenty souls or more and the occasion an important one. Amongst those dishes that I remember were: a dish of rabbits all smothered with onions; a leg of mutton boiled with capers and served with walnuts and melted butter; a side of beef with frizzled potatoes; a roasted goose with some chickens and other game; a roasted lobster, served very cunning with all the claws arranged as though alive; a dish of fish with their bellies stuffed with pudding; and a currant pudding and a Vast Apple Pie, this last especially ordered by the Doctor.

We did drink Wine and Ale according to our taste with the Meat, but the Doctor kept to Lemonade. . . . About eleven of the clock the remnants of the food were cleared away and nuts and fruit set out and coffee served; some of the gentlemen being overcome with the Heat of the room and the potency of the Wines.

Knyveton says that he did not feel too well himself and noticed that his companion, a Mr Pope, had vanished.

The Doctor, our host, had eaten I do believe more than any one else in the room; I did marvel at the way he crammed all manner of meats into his mouth until his face became purple . . . but he seemed to suffer no inconvenience from it, his face now shining with sweat and merriment until it resembled a Full Moon. Moreover, he never ceased talking. . . . His voice did lull me to sleep . . . and falling beneath the table did there find Mr Pope sleeping as calm as in his bed at home, in company with sundry other gentlemen.

At about one o'clock Dr Johnson began discussing 'the Value of Health as an Aid to Morals' and Knyveton felt so 'infernally sleepy and fuddled' that he left. 'I heard from Mr Pope that the supper party lasted until the dawn, when the Doctor was still in Full Cry but the company much diminished and those present with difficulty keeping their feet and their wits. . . . It was eight in the morning when the last guest left. . . .'

The pseudonym of 'William Hickey' was adopted by a Fleet Street columnist after the waster whose journals like Boswell's bring back to life so well eighteenth-century England. Having embezzled his father's money, he started frequenting the taverns and brothels of Covent Garden before he had reached the age of fourteen. One evening in 1768, together with other wild roisterers of his own age, he went from one den of vice to another round Bow Street, Covent Garden, getting more and more intoxicated and ending up at Wetherby's in Little Russell Street.

> The first impression on my mind upon entering these diabolical regions will never be effaced from my mind. . . . My companions conducted me into a room where such a scene was exhibiting that I involuntarily shrunk back with disgust and dismay. . . . Two she-devils, for they scarce had a human appearance, were engaged in a scratching and boxing match, their faces entirely covered with blood, bosoms bare, and the clothes nearly torn from their bodies. . . .

One might have expected more sedate behaviour at the Lord Mayor's Annual Banquet in the Guildhall, but this was not so when Hickey attended the junketing given by Sir Watkin Lewis on 9 November 1780.

> Five minutes after the guests took their stations at the table the dishes were entirely cleared of their contents, twenty hands seizing the same joint or bird and literally tearing it to pieces. A more determined scramble could not be, the roaring and noise were deafening and hideous, which increased as the liquor operated, bottles and glasses flying across from side to side without intermission. This abominable and disgusting

scene continued till near ten o'clock when . . . the dancing commenced.

Things were not to improve by Victorian times as we shall see later.

William Hickey mentions three bawdy houses in Bow Street alone. When George III became King, there were about 2,000 such places in London, one for every fifty adult males. Mrs Cornelys's Carlisle House in Soho, opened ten years previously for the holding of balls and masquerades, had become a rendezvous for harlots and roués. *The Whisperer*, a mordant weekly, claimed: 'Adultery, debauchery and divorces are now more frequent than in the days of Charles II.' The opening of a rival 'emporium of sophistication', the Pantheon, ruined Mrs Cornelys, who spent her last days selling asses' milk in Knightsbridge. Novelty was essential for success and this was achieved by Mrs Goadby of Berwick Square, Soho, who opened the first bordello this side of the Channel to be staffed by a truly international assembly of strumpets from almost every part of the globe. Charges ranged from 5 to 50 guineas and virgins were available for 20 guineas.

Mrs Goadby's chief rival was Charlotte Haynes of King's Place who made capital out of popular interest in reports of sexual practices which Captain Cook had come across when exploring the South Seas. So she sent out invitations to potential clients in the aristocracy to reenactments of these orgies, such as the Feast of Venus with herself impersonating Queen Oberea of Tahiti and twelve 'spotless virgins' as nymphs who would perform with twelve lusty youths while the guests were served with 'a sumptuous banquet' and could join in the fun if they felt like it.

Mary Wilson made a small fortune catering for a so far neglected section of society, rich ladies who were plain, ugly, or ageing, and who longed for occasional sex with some experienced Adonis. There were those, too, whose husbands were impotent or homosexual. In the *Voluptarian Cabinet* Mrs Wilson describes how her lady clients would lie on couches in darkened alcoves that served as bedrooms whilst the men on offer, elegant, muscular, dark or blonde, filed past displaying all their other attractions. Bells would be rung when minds were made up and the chosen lovers brought in.

Foreigners in their published accounts of visits to London in the latter half of the eighteenth century invariably concluded that it was the most licentious city in the world. Even the Pantheon intended to maintain high standards of decorous behaviour soon degenerated. A report of a masquerade in the *Westminster Magazine* for May 1774 complained about the 'wanton love . . . most base and dishonourable' prevalent there:

> The room was crowded with courtezans: there was not a duenna in town who had not brought her Circassian to market; and towards the conclusion of the debauch, I beheld scenes in the rooms upstairs too gross for repetition. I saw ladies and gentlemen together in attitudes and positions that would have disgraced the court of Comus; ladies with their hair dishevelled and their robes almost torn off.

With the growth of trade the merchant class became more affluent and by the middle of the eighteenth century, instead of picking up prostitutes in public places, they could afford to patronize the ladies of pleasure operating from discreet establishments like Mrs Brown's, described in John Cleland's *Fanny Hill*, or in their own lodgings. Most of these advertized in *The New Atlantis*, published annually. Payment was according to time spent with each customer, and some of these women set up incredible records in the annals of vice. La Croix in his *History of Prostitution* mentions a Mme Dubois of the *Comédie Française* who on the 12th September 1775, boasted that she had had 16,527 lovers.

Aphrodisiacs were greatly in demand, such as the

'Balsamic Corroborant' or 'Restorant of Nature' with its snob appeal claim that a member of the Royal Family and 'several Noble personages' used it regularly. Others tried to find satisfaction for sexual cravings by reading erotica. Some old men clasped young women simply to inhale their breath, believing that this would have a rejuvenating effect. T. E. White in *The Age of Scandal* quotes a Mr Phillip Thicknesse of Bath, who stated in 1779:

> I am myself turned sixty and though I have lived in various climates, and suffered severely both in mind and body, yet having always partaken of the breath of young women, wherever they lay in my way, I feel none of the infirmities which so often strike the eyes and ears in this great city of sickness by men many years my younger.

The medical profession became interested and we read of a physician who carried out experiments whilst lodging in a boarding-school for the daughters of gentlemen.

In the latter part of the eighteenth century and throughout the next century flagellomania became wide-spread in London. The notorious Mrs Theresa Berkeley of 28 Charlotte Street boasted that none of her competitors were so well furnished with such an assortment of appliances for flagellation. We are told in her *Memoirs* that she kept her birches in water so that they remained green and pliant. She had 'shafts with a dozen whip thongs in them; a dozen different sizes of cat-o'-nine tails, some with needle-points worked into them; various kinds of thin bending canes; leather straps like coach traces; battledores, made of thick sole-leather with inch nails run through, and curry-combs.' For scourging 'with which she often restored the dead to life' she employed 'holly brushes, furze brushes; a prickly evergreen called butcher's bush' and during the summer, green nettles.

If a customer wanted to flog instead of being flogged,

then, Ebony Beth or One-eyed Peg or some other strong young lady, would oblige; or, for at least 200 guineas, Theresa herself.

Not everyone considered England to be the worst country for habitual lewdness. Francis Willoughby, describing a visit to Andalusia in 1737, declared:

> For fornication and impurity, they are the worst of all nations, at least in Europe; almost all the inns in Andalusia, Castile, Granada, etc., having whores who dress the meat and do all the business. They are to be hired at a very cheap rate. It were a shame to mention their impudence, lewdness and immodest behaviour and practices.

Daniel Defoe, originally intended for the Nonconformist ministry, believed that the debauchery prevalent in his times was caused by luxurious living and he considered the Italians by far the worst in this respect. He thundered in his *Use and Abuse of the Marriage Bed*:

> All the heats and fires raised with us by the acrimony of the blood, by the inflammation of the spirits and animal salts, are kindled from hell, set on fire by the devil and made to rage and boil up in the veins by the inflaming vitiated thoughts and imagination. Hence the Italians, a nation who revel in all the varieties of luxury, such as rich wines, luscious fruits, high sauces, pickles, preserves, sweetmeats to an excess, how the hellish fires rage in them . . . the more moderate feeding nations round them are in proportion less outrageous in this vice.

But this was written in 1727. Had Defoe been still alive by the end of the century, he might have thought that the English were now worse than the Italians — and, like the then Bishop of Durham, have blamed the Revolutionaries in France for it. 'The Directorate of that country, finding that they cannot subdue us by their arms, appear as if they are determined to gain their ends by destroying our morals,' he accused. They were achieving this in an insidious way through suborning foreign dancers to give 'indecent exhibitions in the theatres'.

It should be borne in mind that what is excessive to one person may not be so to another. That great gastronome, of our times, André Simon, has claimed that excess as regards wine cannot be gauged in terms of quantity. 'It depends entirely on the nature of individual wines and the disposition of individual drinkers. There are people who can drink a bottle of claret with pleasure and profit and yet may be seriously indisposed if they drink a second glass of port.' The converse, he points out is true. 'Neither could be counted among the average drinkers. The average wine drinker would be likely to consider anything over and above a bottle a day as excess in the matter of wine.'

A century earlier the king of gastronomes, Brillat-Savarin, vigorously championed gourmandism. It was the enemy of excess — an impassioned, reasoned, habitual preference for that which gratifies the organ of taste. He had consulted all the dictionaries upon the word and found an endless confusion between it and gluttony, or voracity. Lexicographers had forgotten 'social gourmandism, wherein the elegance of Athens, the luxury of Rome, and the delicacy of France come together and are made one, which to profound design brings skilled performance, and tempers gustaline zeal with wise discrimination: a precious quality, which might well be termed a virtue, being certainly the source of all our purest joys.'

For a brilliantly graphic description of such social gourmandism in the eighteenth century, let us turn to the *Travel Diaries* of that eccentric sensualist, William Beckford, where he dines with the Abbot of Alcobaça in Portugal.

> In came the Grand Priors hand in hand, all three together. 'To the kitchen,' said they in perfect unison, 'to the kitchen, and that immediately. You will then

judge whether we have been wanting in zeal to regale ·you.' Such a summons, so conveyed, was irresistible; the three prelates led the way to, I verily believe, the most distinguished temple of gluttony in all Europe. What Glastonbury may have been in its palmy state, I cannot answer; but my eyes never beheld in any modern convent of France, Italy, or Germany, such an enormous space dedicated to culinary purposes. Through the centre of the immense and nobly groined hall, not less than sixty feet in diameter, ran a brisk rivulet of the clearest water, flowing through pierced wooden reservoirs, containing every sort and size of the finest river fish. On one side, loads of game and venison were heaped up, on the other, vegetables and fruit in endless variety. Beyond a line of stoves extended a row of ovens, and close to them hillocks of wheaten flour whiter than snow, rocks of sugar, jars of the finest oil, and pastry in vast abundance, which a numerous tribe of lay brothers and their attendants were rolling out and puffing up into a hundred different shapes, singing all the while as blithely as larks in a cornfield.

The banquet itself fully lived up to Beckford's expectations. It consisted of not only the most excellent usual fare but also of rareties and delicacies of past seasons and distant countries.

There were exquisite sausages, potted lampreys, strange messes from the Brazils, and others still stranger from China (edible birds' nests and sharks' fins) dressed after the latest mode of Macao by a Chinese lay brother. . . . Confectionery and fruits were out of the question here, they awaited us in an adjoining, still more spacious apartment, to which we retired from the effluvia of viands and sauces. . . . The table being removed, four good-looking novices, lads of fifteen or sixteen, demure even to primness, came in, bearing cassolettes of Goa filigree, steaming with a fragrant vapour of Calambac, the finest quality of wood of aloes.

One might also regard as social gourmands the cook to the Prince de Soubise and the Marquis de Béchamel. The Prince told the cook he intended to give a dinner in celebration of a friend's birthday and asked for a menu to be prepared. The chef presented one with an estimate of what was needed. 'Fifty hams!' exclaimed his master. 'Why, Bertrand you must have taken leave of your senses!'

'No, *mon seigneur*, only one ham will appear on the table. The rest are none the less essential for the *espagnoles*, my *blonds*, my *garniture*, my —'

'Bertrand, you are plundering me!'

'No, *mon seigneur*, respectfully I am not. You do not appreciate my art. Agree and these fifty hams which astonish you I shall put them all into a glass bottle no bigger than my thumb.'

The Prince did not know what to reply, so he merely nodded, silenced by the explanation of his genius of a chef.

The Marquis de Béchamel married Valentine de Rochemont because, like himself, she was a first-rate cook. It proved a perfect partnership and they cooked and ate together, always happy and never ill, and apart from sleeping they were rarely to be found anywhere else than in the kitchen or at the table. A grand feast was prepared to celebrate their golden wedding for which the Marquis had saved a bottle of Constantin, a glorious vintage wine, but just as the bottle was brought to the table the Marquise collapsed and died.

The widower was heart-broken. He put the bottle away unopened and soon he fell desperately ill, and, believing that his own end was near, asked for the Constantin, saying: 'When I meet my beloved Valentine again, she will ask, "What is that perfume, my dear, which I detect upon your lips?" And I shall reply, "It is the Constantin, darling, we had kept for our golden wedding." ' The Marquis drank some of the wine, and then he sank back on to the pillows. Those at the bedside thought he had died, but he was only asleep. Later, he summoned his nephew, and, handing him a key, asked him to fetch a box from a locked drawer in an escritoire. On taking it to his uncle, the youth was astonished when the Marquis took out — not a lock of Valentine's hair or some other relic of hers — but a Périgord pie, dressed with truffles. The old man ate it with relish, then his head fell back once more.

'Listen!' the doctor exclaimed. 'I hear the death rattle in his throat!' But the Marquis was only snoring, and he went on living for another fifteen years, dying at the age of ninety, and having invented many more dishes the fame of which outlasted him.

VIII

LOUIS XV AND HIS SERAGLIO

Following the death of Louis XIV in 1715 and the transfer of power to the dissolute Regent, Philippe II, Duc d'Orléans, during the minority of Louis XV, excess of the worst kind became fashionable among the aristocracy, some 25,000 of whom led the lives of sybarites in the environs of Versailles. Both men and women vied with one another trying to collect the most lovers and enticing desirable ones away from competitors. The Marquis d'Argenson wrote in his memoirs:

> I prophesy that lack of affection and incapacity to feel will lead the country to perdition. We have no more friends, we do not love our mistresses. People do not have passions any more. Debauchery and false love are rife.

Cuckolding was often treated as a joke. It was said that the Duchesse de Montbazon was in bed one night with a lover when her old husband, who used to sleep on the floor below, came upstairs and opened her door. 'I heard a noise,' he called. 'Is it a rat?' And the Duchesse replied: 'Don't worry — go back to bed — I'm holding it!'

When Regent, Orléans, married to Henrietta, sister of

Charles II, treated her disgracefully and gossip alleged that he belonged to the 'Sacred Fraternity of Glorious Pederasts' who had taken an oath to have no sexual intercourse with women except to obtain heirs, and who all wore a medallion showing a man standing on a woman. They performed fellatio when they met.

Under the Regency other court libertines formed exclusive groups for sex that met in private locations. The Aphrodite was housed in a magnificent mansion near Montmorency in extensive grounds concealed from curious eyes by high walls and it cost a great deal to become a member. The main building, the Hospice, contained a huge rotunda in the middle of which was an altar encircled by statues of the deities of love. There were a number of elegantly equipped private boxes for couples to disport themselves in, and these had cunningly camouflaged peep-holes for voyeurs.

M. du Borsage, the architect who designed the whole place, had devised an apparatus he named *une avantageuse* which removed all discomfort from long periods of lovemaking. Jean Hervé in his *Les sociétés d'amour au 18ème siècle* gives this description of it:

> After having gripped two supports in the form of vigorous phalluses on the right and left of her, a lady lets herself fall back upon a thick and firm, satin-covered cushion supporting her from head to buttocks. With legs stretched out like open scissors at a right angle, she rests her feet in softly padded stirrups, whilst her gentleman positions himself above her with knees resting on cross bars. With his hands grasping two cylindrical supports fixed on the outside of the piece of furniture, he is able to reach with ease his objective.

No more than two hundred adepts were allowed membership, all aristocrats and top clergy, and they had to pass a practical examination in sexual ability and technique that went on for three hours and was supervised by experienced judges who crowned the most proficient candidates with laurels. Rarely were those winning less than seven crowns admitted to the secret society. The acceptance ritual was an elaborate one accompanied by feasting and expertly managed bacchanalia.

Jean Hervé quotes from the journal of a noble lady giving detailed records of her amorous achievements whilst a member of the Aphrodite. She claimed to have had a total of 4,959 assignations over twenty years of which 272 were princes and bishops, 439 monks, 93 rabbis, 929 army officers, 342 bankers, 119 musicians, 117 valets, as well as two uncles and twelve cousins and 1,614 Englishmen and other foreigners whilst in exile in London during the French Revolution.

The promiscuity of the aristocracy was copied by many in the lower ranks of society. An extreme example was Restif de la Bretonne, a sheep farmer's son, who also kept comprehensive records. He spent ten years walking the banks of the Seine, picking up prostitutes and inscribing dates and other details on the parapets and in his diaries. He published no fewer than 203 books on the subject.

The Aphrodite was still in existence at the time of the Revolution when it was closed; then, in 1793, the Assembly decided to clean up Paris. All prostitutes were arrested and either imprisoned or installed in state-run brothels where they had to sit in drawing-rooms for an eight-hour day either reading approved literature or doing needlework whilst awaiting clients.

The attitude of those who condoned liaisons and marital infidelity is explained by Montesquieu, who lived during the first half of the eighteenth century. He wrote in his *Lettres Persanes*:

> A husband who wishes to be the only one to possess his wife would be regarded as a public kill-joy. The French do not take a pride in constancy. They believe that it is just as ridiculous for a man to tell a woman that he will

love her for ever, as it would be for him to affirm that he will always enjoy good health, or that he will always be happy.

Louis XV himself when he assumed power led an utterly frivolous life. It was said of him that eating was the only serious occupation of his life and that he drank each year enough champagne to fill a lake. He has been credited with the invention of the disappearing table that ascends through the floor fully set and descends once the meal is finished. His wife found his ardour exhausting and complained that she was always either in bed, or pregnant, or being brought to bed. Eventually, her doctor forbade her after a miscarriage to have any more sex, so for the rest of her life she locked Louis out of her bedroom.

The King, whose amours up till then had never lasted, now took a Countess as mistress, who had four sisters, three of whom had reached puberty. It was not long before this trio also achieved their ambition of becoming his concubines. When, on attaining the age of sixteen, the youngest refused to join the seraglio, Louis was affronted. Soon after this he was taken ill and, fearing death and hell-fire, dismissed them when his confessor refused absolution unless he did so. However, he recovered and they were succeeded by the favourite he loved most, whom he created Marquise de Pompadour. When she died, Mme du Barry from the stews of Paris replaced her together with the harem he kept in the Parc aux Cerfs, which was stocked with young girls of average age fifteen, either kidnapped or bought from their parents by the King's agents, specially employed to comb the country to find the types that would appeal to him. Sometimes, when parents were uncooperative, the police were called in to apply the necessary pressure. Each recruit was installed in her own apartment in the commodious, beautifully furnished building at Versailles. Over one hundred million francs were thus spent by Louis.

Louis liked to give his seducing a veneer of respect for

religious duties, therefore before getting into bed with a girl he would make her kneel with him and say their prayers. Terrified of contracting syphilis, he had to be certain that those recruited for his pleasure were virginal. Nuns, in particular, attracted him and four that he admired on a visit to the Convent of Bon Secours found themselves transferred next day to the Parc aux Cerfs.

So loose were the morals of the times that even the nobility offered their daughters to the King. One letter to his chief procurer preserved in the Paris archives reads:

> I should be exceedingly obliged if you could be kind enough to try and gain a place for my third daughter, aged fifteen, in that happy little house where are kept those intended for the ardent love of our worthy King. She is completely innocent, ignorant of the difference between the sexes. . . . I await, Monseigneur, your reply with impatience. . . .

Raoul Vèze, in his *La Galanterie Parisienne au XVIIIme Siècle*, gives the names of many who were Louis's sexual toys in the Parc au Cerfs. There was a quick turnover for he liked variety, and, on leaving, they would be handsomely pensioned. So it is not surprising that the Duchess of Devonshire went to the trouble of bringing to Paris from London a protégée of hers, a Miss Witist. She was given 'a pretty little house' in the Parc, a housekeeper, a *femme de chambre* and two lackeys like the others.

IX

ROISTERING IN RUSSIA
— AND PHALLIC GODS

Excess was widespread in seventeenth-century Russia. Those from the West, who visited what was then known as Muscovy, were unanimous in their judgement that drunkenness and immorality were rife. Tsar Alexei's English physician wrote that his employer enjoyed watching the antics of his courtiers after imbibing beakers of vodka 'that would take away the breath of anyone not used to it'. According to Dr Collins, to be drunk was regarded as a daily routine and as proving that one was hospitable. In his book, published in 1671, he wrote that women were 'often the first to become raving mad with immoderate draughts of brandy and are to be seen, half naked and shameless, in almost all the streets'. The worst debauchery occurred during religious festivals. Muscovites were convinced that the saints would wish their devotees to have a good time on such occasions. In the last week of the carnival before Lent, they drank 'as if they were never to drink any more'.

Another traveller, Olearius, in his *Voyages*, published nine years earlier, observed the Muscovites 'doing all things according to their unbridled passions and appetites'. They were 'wholly given up to licentiousness, even to sins against nature, not only with men but also with beasts. . . . The postures of their dancing and the insolence of their women are infallible marks of their bad inclinations. We have seen at Moscow both men and women come out of the public brothel houses stark naked and incite some young people of our retinue to naughtiness by filthy and lascivious expressions.' The women had 'lewd tongues, are given to wine, and will not let slip the opportunity to pleasure a friend'.

Peter the Great (1672-1725) made it his ambition to civilize his country. Although he himself spent many a night in roistering, drinking to excess and insisting that his companions should do the same, his mental and physical strength enabled him to rise at dawn whilst they were still lying unconscious. In the society of women what he enjoyed most was to see them drunk. His second wife, Catherine, contemporaries described as 'a first-rate toper'.

Peter shocked the religious by the burlesque of the Orthodox Church's ritual perpetrated by the Most Holy and Most Drunken Synod. Proselytes were asked 'Dost thou drink?' instead of 'Dost thou believe?' Those who dared to give up drink would be excommunicated with terrifying rites. In 1698 he took part in a procession in which the mock Patriarch, Zotof, wearing a mitre decorated with a figure of Bacchus, led a troop of disorderly bacchants, their heads adorned with bundles of lighted tobacco instead of vine leaves. Twenty-six years later, the same thing was still going on. During the pre-Lent Carnival of 1724 some seventy courtiers, army officers, priests (including the Tsar's confessor, Nadajinski) rampaged with Peter through the streets. These people, chosen from among the worst drunkards and debauchees in the country, formed a regular brotherhood, called 'the Council which knows no sadness'. They met on fixed days and indulged in orgies occasionally lasting for twenty-four hours.

Peter, after he had chosen a mock Pontiff, proceeded to appoint cardinals and a conclave taken from the most dissolute of the brotherhood. Their first duty was to present themselves at the house of the *Knes-papa*, known as the *Vaticanum*, and offer him their homage. Four stutterers acted as spokesmen during the visit when the new arrivals were invested with the red robes which became their future official costume. Thus attired, they entered the Hall of the Consistory, the only furniture of which consisted of casks ranged round the walls. At the end of the hall, on a pile of barrels, bottles and glasses, was the throne of the *Knes-papa*, who sat astride on a wine-butt drawn by four oxen and was attended by mock monks. The sham cardinals were taken up to a gallery lined with narrow beds on which they laid, with casks sawn in half and filled with food on either side of them. Certain conclavists, attached to the person of each cardinal, were charged with the duty of inciting them to drink and eat. The Tsar was always present, listening and making notes. The conclave lasted three days and nights.

At another conclave held on 10 September 1723 to elect a new Patriarch the mock prelates had to drink wine and brandy for twenty-four hours without going to sleep after which they elected him.

In 1714 Peter decided to vary the monotony of the proceedings by celebrating the wedding of the then *Knes-papa* Zotof, aged eighty-four, to sixty-year-old Anna Pashkof. He ordered immense preparations to be made, four months in advance. The whole court had to take part and send detailed descriptions of their chosen disguises to the Chancellor, so that there might not be more than three of any character.

On the appointed day, at a signal given by a cannon, the male and female masqueraders gathered and, crossing the frozen Neva, made their way to the Church of St Peter and St Paul, on the opposite bank, where a priest over ninety years old, specially brought from Moscow for the purpose, awaited the bride and the bridegroom who was dressed in pontifical robes as the mock Patriarch. They arrived on a high sledge, surrounded by Cupids and with a goat seated behind them.

All the top people in the capital — ministers, aristocrats,

and the diplomatic corps — followed, some of them more than a little constrained and uncomfortable, but none dared offend the Tsar by staying away. Prince Menshikof, Admiral Apraxin, General Bruce, and Count Vitzthum, garbed as Hamburg burgomasters, played on hurdy-gurdies, and the Russian Chancellor and four Princes dressed as Chinamen played on flutes. The Austrian and Dutch Residents and the Hanoverian Minister, as German shepherds, blew bagpipes. Three noblemen had been excused from performing on musical instruments on account of their age, but they had to put in an appearance. The Tsarina and her ladies played flutes, whilst Peter in his favourite costume of a Dutch sailor rattled on a drum. He was surrounded by a motley crew of Venetians blowing shrill whistles, Poles scraping violins, Kalmuks strumming balalaikas, Honduras savages brandishing lances, Norwegian peasants, Lutheran pastors, monks, mock bishops with stags' horns on their heads, and others. The noise of the instruments, the clang of the bells ringing out from every church tower, and the shouts of the thousands of spectators was deafening.

The marriage ceremony ended with a banquet which soon turned into an orgy, during which some trembling octogenarians acted as cupbearers. The festivities went on for nearly a week.

When Zotof died in 1717 Peter drew up fresh and grotesque regulations for the election of his successor which included public verification of all candidates' sex. Chosen after scenes of debauchery, with the Tsar acting as Subdeacon to the conclave, was Peter Ivanovitch Boutourlin, mock Archbishop of St Petersburg 'in the diocese of drunkards, gluttons, and madmen' and a member of one of the most distinguished families in Russia. Three years later, Peter decided to marry Boutourlin to Zotof's widow. A bed was set up within a stone pyramid built in 1714 to commemorate a victory over the Swedes. The newly weds were put to bed dead drunk and subjected to all manner of coarse indignities by those of the carousing public still on their feet.

In 1723 Boutourlin, too, passed away and on the 10th of September, Campredon, the French Resident, wrote in a despatch to his Foreign Office:

> The ceremony of the installation of the new Patriarch will take place at Moscow. The conclave will be held in a small island near Préobrajenski, on which there is a peasants' cottage. The mock cardinals will assemble there on the appointed day. They will have to drink wine and brandy for four-and-twenty hours, without going to sleep, and after that fine preparation, they will choose their Patriarch.

The following year the Saxon Minister described in a despatch to his monarch how the Tsar had 'baptised a church with 3,000 bottles of wine'. Waliszewski in his life of Peter in explanation of such behaviour makes the point that it was typical of a society 'in which nothing stable, nothing consecrated, and, therefore, nothing sacred existed'. He goes on: 'From the days of Ivan the Terrible, all the remarkable men in this society had been *eccentrics* — "*Samodoury*," according to the expressive national term. Peter was the same. . . . He was full of elementary forces and instincts.'

When Peter went out hunting he would usually be attended by about five hundred persons, and every visitor, of whatever rank, who entered his presence, was forced to drink a huge glass of his favourite drink, coarse brandy, seasoned with pepper, served by a tame bear which growled threateningly. If the brandy were refused, the animal dropped the tray forthwith and hugged the man.

Peter had a passion for robust cheeses and in particular Limburger. Before it was removed from the table, he would carefully measure what was left with a compass as a warning to his servants not to steal any. In 1698, when returning to London from a visit to Portsmouth, he and his party numbering twenty-one stopped at an inn in Goldalming. On arrival, they rested in their bedrooms and ordered seven dozen eggs with salad to be sent up to them. Then for breakfast, they ate half a sheep, nineteen pounds of lamb, ten pullets, a dozen chickens, and drank three quarts of brandy. Later, for supper, they had five ribs of beef weighing three stone, one sheep weighing four, three-quarters of a lamb, a shoulder roasted, a loyn of veal trussed with bacon, eight pullets, four couple rabbits, two dozen of sack, one dozen of claret, and bread and beer proportionately, also before going to bed six quarts of mulled sack. The total bill came to £1 and is preserved in the Bodleian.

Peter's appetite for sex was enormous. He slept indiscriminately with women of all classes and any age. When he died, probably from venereal disease, the crown was seized by his second wife, Catherine, a gluttonous virago, illegitimate daughter of a Livonian peasant, who had had a soldier husband still alive when she married Peter, as well as having been the slave or mistress of a score of generals. A veritable Empress of Excess she died of drink within a couple of years. But her sensuality was matched by Elizabeth Petrovna who ruled for twenty-one years from 1741. Since puberty she had slept with all in the regiment protecting her. On accession, she promoted her chief lover, Sergeant Grunstein, to the rank of major-general and made all the soldiers officers, as well as distributing twenty thousand roubles among them. The majority of the latter were unprincipled sots and, when their demands became too outrageous, they would be transferred to posts in distant parts of Russia. Occasionally, Elizabeth went off to some secret love nest and could not be found, thus holding up the business of the country. She was also drunk for weeks at times, and had an affair with the hermaphrodite Chevalier d'Eon. There were persistent rumours that she had married him.

Catherine the Great, who ascended the throne in 1762, easily outstripped her predecessors in the extent and variety of her sexual activities. She admitted having had intercourse with at least a dozen men in her lifetime, but some biographers claim that the numbers are more likely to have approached four hundred — and one alleges that she died after a virile young courtier mounted her. She made no secret of her hunger for sex and advocated having it six times daily. She admitted that what appealed to her most in a man was not his face or his brain but his genitals.

Between 1762 and 1796 ten official favourites served Catherine. Most were of Herculean build and in the prime of life — though as she grew older she selected younger and younger men. They cost the country some ninety million roubles. A possible favourite had to submit to a thorough medical examination by her trusted personal physician. Then those he passed as fit had their virility assessed by a lady-in-waiting employed for that work, Mlle. Protasoff. If she approved of an aspirant's performance, he would move into a fine apartment on the floor just underneath Catherine's and communicating with it by a secret staircase. Here he would find awaiting him 100,000 roubles for linen. If his first night in her bed proved a success, a further sum would follow, and more after every repeat performance. When his reign as emperor of the night ended, his golden handshake might be in the form of money or of a large estate complete with several thousands of peasants to toil for him.

Catherine's third favourite, Potemkin, was astute enough to realize that she would eventually cool off, so, when this happened, he helped her to find a successor and, for the rest of his own life, devoted a great deal of time searching for and selecting suitable lovers for her. He always made sure that they were of such character that they would remain grateful and loyal to him. An up-to-date file on young officers was kept, and, on sensing that the Empress felt in need of a change, he would send one of these men to her with a picture. The candidate had to say that he had brought it from Prince Potemkin for her to examine and decide whether or not she would like to add it to her collection. If she rejected the painting, it meant that the visitor did not attract her and Potemkin would go on trying out others on his list until she signalled her satisfaction.

When Catherine was in her sixties, an obsessive appetite for sensual gratification led to her starting a secret society of libertines and lechers of both sexes who perpetrated Roman-style orgies in the Hermitage. After feasting, they would sometimes draw lots and pair off for intercourse. As a result of these excesses, so many society ladies were stricken with venereal disease that Catherine founded a hospital where fifty of them were treated in secret. She herself had grown so corpulent that she could hardly move and eventually died from an apoplectic fit.

Catherine and Martha Wheeler in their *Russian Journals* described their gastronomic experiences in Moscow in 1804. One mid-day they went to a Count Ostrowman's residence. Immediately on arrival, they were led to a table where what was called a breakfast was displayed.

> That is little odds and ends of dried fish or caviar, of cheese, bread, etc. and *eau de vie* were presented to us to give us an appetite for dinner which was announced almost immediately. We assembled in the Hall . . . surrounded by a sort of gallery which was filled with men, women, dwarfs, children, fools, and enraged musicians who sang and played with such powerful effect as to deafen those whom Heaven had spared. . . .

There came such a terrific blast on a trumpet that everybody became silent.

> A crystal vase filled with champagne was presented to the Master of the Castle. He stood up and quaffed the sparkling draught to the health of the Lady of the feast. A trumpet sounded a second time, and the goblet

was presented to Princess Dashkow, who went thro' the same ceremony. A third time, the trumpet sounded, and a third person quaffed from the same crystal vase to the same toast. In short, the ceremony was repeated for every individual, and as there were a party of forty-six you may judge the time which all the pomp and parade took up.

Martha Wheeler added:

Many a bad dinner I made from the mere fatigue of being offered fifty and sixty different dishes by servants who come one after the other and flourish ready carved fish, flesh, fowl, vegetables, fruits, soups of fish, etc., before your eyes, wines, liqueurs, etc., in their turn. Seriously, the profusion is beyond anything I ever saw.

At that time the Tsar reigning over Russia was Alexander I, who had a great interest in cooking. Later, at the Congress of Vienna in 1815, Talleyrand, representing Louis XVIII, spotted the Austrian statesman, Prince Metternich, conversing in a low voice with Alexander in a corner. Hoping to overhear some secret deal, the wily diplomat tiptoed behind a pillar and learnt instead a recipe for plum pudding.

South of Russia, as the English infiltrated India in the eighteenth century, the more prudish were taken aback by the extent to which phallicism played a part in Hindu rites and in the decoration of temples. In *A New Account of the East Indies*, Captain Hamilton, in 1727, wrote that he found those of the phallic god, Gopalsami, were decorated 'with obscene effigies of men and women in indescribably indecent postures, and of demons whose genitals were of prodigious size in proportion to their bodies'. In Ganjam, he visited a pagoda containing a huge image of the same god.

This deity is sometimes carried in procession through the streets, and in the coach in which he sits, there are pictures of gods and goddesses in copulation, similar to those in his temple. One of his attendants on the coach has a stick about two feet in length, one end of which is carved in the shape of a phallus. The stick is placed between the idol's legs with the end projecting before him. Virgins and childless married women come and worship the stick, and the priests bestow blessings on them to make them fruitful.

Krishna, one of Vishnu's incarnations, was reputed to have 16,000 wives, and another writer complained that the temples where Siva and Vishnu were worshipped had their interior walls 'covered with shocking representations of sexual passion' whilst the adoration of Siva's wife, Dirga-Kali, degenerated into 'orgies of drunkenness and sexual immorality'. It was in the sacrificial rites performed in the chief temple dedicated to Juggernaut at Orissa that the excesses took their worst form. Once a year his grotesque image standing on a vehicle would be dragged by devotees through the streets where others in their frenzy would hurl themselves beneath the wheels. Similar commemorations took place elsewhere in Bengal.

According to Francis Bernier in his *Travels in the Mogul Empire*, once the procession had returned to the temple, the Brahmins would chose the most beautiful maiden available to be Juggernaut's bride, and, locked inside for the night, she had to await his commands. He would lie with her and say whether the year ahead would be a fruitful one and what offerings he required the people to give the priests in return for his favours. During the hours of darkness, one of the Brahmins would enter by means of a secret entrance, deflower the girl on behalf of Juggernaut, and instruct her as to what she must tell the populace next day.

Rájendralála Mitra in *The Antiquities of Orissa* says he saw depicted in its temples 'human couples in the most disgusting of sexual positions' and again that in the Great Temple of Puri 'a few of the human figures are disgustingly obscene'.

Christian missionary Dr Alexander Duff, in a book published in 1839 about India, alleged that 'there are not merely hundreds of thousands, but literally millions, simultaneously engaged in the celebration of orgies, so stained with licentiousness and blood, that, in the comparison, we might almost pronounce the Bacchanalia of Greece and Rome innocent and pure'. The British did take steps to suppress the worst excesses not in accordance with the ritual stated in the *Puranas*.

W. E. Griffs in *The Religions of Japan*, published in 1895, described the Shinto temples of Japan as the scenes of bacchanalian sexual orgies. He wrote: 'The reason for the temples being devoted to unashamed phallicism is indicated by a study of the *Kotiki* and the *Nihongi*, the sacred books of Japan the contents of which because of their obscene nature cannot be translated into English.' Horace Grant Underwood is more explicit in *The Religions of Eastern Asia* (1910).

X

COFFEE, CHOCOLATE, TEA —AND COCKTAILS

There were three seductive stimulants, all non-alcoholic, introduced into England in the middle of the seventeenth century which were eventually to be drunk to excess.

In 1598 the inveterate traveller Sir Anthony Shirley, on reaching Aleppo, was served with a drink made by roasting and grinding the seeds of a tree and which he found wholesome though 'nothing toothsome' and which would 'soon intoxicate the brain'. In due course quantities of this were imported into England, and, in 1650, a Mr Jacobs opened the first coffee-shop at the Angel in Oxford and it attracted an increasing number of addicts in a very short time. In London, one Daniel Edwards, a merchant trading with Turkey, brought with him from Smyrna a youth, Pasqua Rosee, who prepared the beverage for him every morning. Friends and business acquaintances, invited to partake of it, were so smitten with this novel nectar that they kept returning for more and bringing others with them. As a result, Edwards allowed Rosee, in partnership with another man, to sell it to the public in a coffee-house in Cornhill.

Rosee proved himself an adroit publicist. A handbill of his headed *The Verture of the Coffee Drink* went:

The quality of this drink is cold and dry; and though it be a drier, yet it neither heats nor inflames more than hot posset. It so encloseth the orifice of the stomach and fortifies the heat within, that it is very good to help digestion; and therefore of great use to be taken about three or four o'clock in the afternoon, as well as in the morning. It much quickens the spirits, and makes the heart lightsome; it is good against sore eyes, and the better if you hold your head over it and take in the steam that way. It suppresseth fumes exceedingly, and therefore is good against the headache, and will very much stop any defluxion of rheums that distil from the head upon the stomach, and so prevent and help consumptions and the cough of the lungs. . . . It is observed that in Turkey, where this is generally drunk, that they are not troubled with the stone, gout, dropsy, or scurvy, and that their skins are exceeding clear and white. It is neither laxative nor restringent.

Rosee's success led to coffee-house after coffee-house opening up and in the reign of Charles II it became fashionable to patronize them. But even three years before the Restoration, during the Commonwealth, there was excessive trade in it, and James Farr, who kept the Rainbow in Fleet Street, was prosecuted for 'making and selling a sort of liquor called Coffee, whereby in making the same, he annoyeth his neighbours by evill smells, and for keeping of fire the most part night and day, whereby his chimney and chamber has been set on fire, to the great danger and affreightness of his neighbours.'

Alexander Pope in *The Rape of the Lock*, however, found merit in the liquor, declaring:

Coffee, which makes the politician wise,
And see through all things with his half-shut eyes.

In France Charles II's sister, the Duchess of Orleans, approved on religious grounds: 'Coffee is not necessary to ministers of the reformed faith as to Catholic priests. The latter are not allowed to marry, and coffee is said to induce chastity.'

The owners of ale-houses, angry because coffee-drinking diminished their trade, denounced the stuff as 'syrup and soot', and in 1674 some women in London petitioned King Charles II to have all coffee-houses closed accusing the 'base, black, thick, nasty, bitter, stinking, nauseous puddle water' of making their husbands stay away from home and neglect domestic duties, and worse still too much rendered them sterile and even impotent — 'as unfruitful as the sandy deserts from whence that unhappy berry is said to be brought'.

The coffee-houses had also become meeting-places for those opposed to the King, so he took advantage of the women's petition to issue a Royal Proclamation on 29 December 1675, ordering that all such establishments must be closed down within two weeks. However, there was such an outcry from the public that the measure had to be rescinded, and more and more were opened until by 1739 there were over 500 in the city alone.

Others were to attack coffee, such as Brillat-Savarin who in *La Physiologie du goût*, published in 1826, wrote:

> A man of good constitution can drink two bottles of wine a day throughout a long lifetime; but he would not stand the same quantity of coffee so long. He would become an idiot or die of consumption. In Leicester Square, London, I have seen a man whom the immoderate use of coffee had reduced to the state of a helpless cripple.

In the 1890s *Hints and Advice for the Healthy* was published by Sebastian Kneipp, a Bavarian parish priest, and it went into twenty-two editions. Six years previously, he claimed, there came to see him the daughter of 'an honourable family', who had been completely given up by the doctors and was wasting away. She told him that she drank coffee three times a day and no longer relished solid food. He persuaded her to take nothing but a spoonful of milk every hour and thrice daily a small portion of bread soup. Thanks to this diet and the avoidance of all coffee, she recovered her health. Kneipp commented: 'I am fully convinced that coffee is the chief cause of anaemia among women. What will it lead to, if the evil is not checked in time? Many young mothers told me in tears how infirm and miserable they were owing to addiction to coffee and how, in consequence of their inability to perform their domestic duties, they were forsaken and despised by their husbands.'

It may well have been that much of the coffee used by these women was adulterated. John Mitchell, in his *Treatise on the Falsification of Food*, published in 1848, revealed that it was then almost impossible to buy pure coffee, as so much of what was sold contained large proportions of chicory, roasted corn, the roots of various vegetables, and colouring matter such as red ochre.

Brillat-Savarin, in *Gastronomy as an Art*, gives a cure for excess:

> Let, then, every man who has drunk too deeply from the cup of pleasure, every man who has devoted to work a considerable part of the time due to sleep . . . every man tormented with some fixed idea which deprives him of the liberty of thinking — let all such people, we say, prescribe to themselves a good pint of chocolate mixed with amber in the proportion of from sixty to seventy grain to the pound and they will see wonders.

The Spaniards were the first Europeans to taste chocolate when they conquered Mexico. One of Cortez's companions describing a banquet given by Montezuma wrote: 'They brought in above fifty great jars filled with frothy Cacao and drank it, similar jars being served to the guards and attendants to the number of 2,000 at least.'

The earliest reference to the use of chocolate in England is an announcement appearing in the *Public Advertiser* for 16 June 1657 that informed the public: 'In Bishopsgate Street in Queen's Head Alley at a Frenchman's house is an excellent West Indian drink called Chocolate to be sold.' In France, about the same time, chocolate started being drunk in fashionable milieux in Paris thanks to the faculty of medicine recommending it. After a time, however, strange rumours spread, and we find Mme de Sévigné writing to a friend: 'The Marquise de Coetlogen took so much chocolate, being pregnant last year, that she was brought to bed of a little boy who was as black as the devil.'

Tea was first introduced into England in the 1650s. An advertisement in the *Mercurius Politicus* ran:

> That Excellent and by all Physitians approved China Drink called by the Chineans Tcha, by other nations Tay, alias Tee, is sold at the Sultaness-head, a cophee house in Sweetings Rent by the Royal Exchange, London.

Thomas Garway, the owner, brewed the tea in an urn and customers either sat and drank cups of it in his parlour or sent an employee to collect some in a jug and heat it up again on their premises. This was hardly the best way of serving tea, so it is not surprising that people did not think much of it at first. It was the marriage of Charles II with Catherine of Braganza, who preferred tea to any other beverage, that gave the drink a boost despite its high cost. In 1664, shopkeepers charged 95*s*. for 2 lb. 2 oz. Only the rich could afford it and those largely in towns. When a Londoner sent a gift of some to a country friend, the recipient did not know what to do, so she experimented by boiling it, straining off the leaves to which she added melted butter and salt before serving it in a dish to her expectant friends, who spat it out in disgust.

As tea became more popular, an increasing amount was smuggled into England to evade the high Customs duty and it has been estimated that half the tea sold was contraband during the eighteenth century at the commencement of which duty-paid importations totalled annually 20,000 lb. These in the next hundred years were to increase a thousand-fold. The poor dried the leaves after a brew and used them again and again, and also bought spent ones from the kitchen staff at the houses of the better-off.

Even clergymen bought contraband tea. On 29 March 1777 Parson Woodforde put down in his diary:

> Andrews the smuggler brought me this night about 11 o'clock a bagg of Hyson Tea 6 pound weight. He frightened us a little by whistling under the parlour window just as we were going to bed. I gave him some Geneva and paid him for the tea at 10/6 per pound.

As the eighteenth century progressed an increasing number of people started drinking tea with all meals. The great physician, Boerhaave, imbibed on average a 100 cups of it a day. Such excesses were soon attacked. Baron von Pollnitz in his *Amusements de Spa*, published in 1727, wrote that he was present when another physician demonstrated to the abbess accompanying him the dangers of tea-drinking. He stirred a spoonful of tea into a glass of crystal-clear water from a fountain at Spa and it turned purple and then black. He asked the abbess if it were wise to fill one's stomach with such a vile concoction. 'Clearly,' he went on, 'tea must sour the ferment of the aliments and disturb their trituration, irritating the fibres of the stomach.'

The author of a later book about Spa in 1784 found that all the tea-drinking there was 'fatal to morals'. Whores walked in the Gardens of the Capucins, making assignations with male addicts to the stuff 'which kept the apothecaries busy'.

In England, John Wesley was convinced of tea's wickedness and made a searing attack on it, and so did Jonas

Hanway in his *Essay on Tea* of 1757, claiming that tea which should not be exposed to the air was being sold out of wheelbarrows or brought over as packing for oriental porcelain, in place of sawdust.

> Can any reasonable person doubt that this flatulent liquor shortens the lives of great numbers of people? . . . It is an epidemical disease. If any seeds of it remain it will engender an universal infection. To what a height of folly must a nation be arrived when the common people are not satisfied with wholesome food at home, but must go to the remotest regions to please a vicious palate?

Hanway claimed he had been told that in some places where no one family could afford to buy a kettle, a tea-pot, or anything else needed for tea-making, they carried what they had to each other's house 'to the distance of a mile or two and club material for this fantastic amusement! What a wild infatuation is this!'

Tea's popularity, however, intensified despite such onslaughts. Rogues were already adulterating it with blackberry leaves and dust, and colouring it with ferrous sulphate, a substance used in tanning and dyeing and hardly suitable for a human stomach. A century later, in the London of the 1840s, there were at least eight factories busily engaged drying used tea-leaves and reselling them to fraudulent dealers. According to George Phillips, then head of the Chemical Department of the Inland Revenue, the practice was to buy up the exhausted leaves from hotels, restaurants and other places at $2\frac{1}{2}d.$ and $3d.$ per lb. These were taken to the factories , mixed with a solution of gum and redried. After this, the leaves, if for black tea were mixed with rose-pink and black lead to 'face' them as the trade term was. No wonder that, as Thackeray complained, the tea on channel steamers tasted like 'boiled old boots'.

At the top end of the social scale there were gourmets

like Alfred de Rothschild who would have his guests served only with exquisite, carefully-chosen teas. The footman wheeling in the breakfast would ask: 'Shall it be China, Indian, or Ceylon, sir? . . . Lemon, milk, or cream? . . . Jersey, Hereford, or Shorthorn?'

In the summer of 1985, visitors to Britain's zoos were dismayed to hear that chimpanzee tea parties were having to be phased out. The official reason was that the chimpanzees taking part in them had begun to prefer tea to sex.

People have always experimented with drink and fortunes have been made by those successfully catering for the human race's longing for novelty with such concoctions as cocktails and coke. It was also in the seventeenth century that someone invented 'Cock Ale', probably the cocktail's ancestor. According to Smith's *Compleat Housewife* to make it:

> Take ten gallons of ale and a large cock, the larger the better. Parboil the cock, flea him and stamp him in a stone mortar until his bones are broken. You must craw and gut him when you flea him. Put him into two quarts of sack and add to it three pounds of raisins of the sun stoned, some blades of mace and a few cloves. Put all of these into a canvas bag and a little while before you find the ale has done working, put the ale and bag together into a vessel. In a week or nine days, bottle it up, fill the bottles but just above the necks and leave the same to ripen as other ale.

Since the last century cocktails have become increasingly popular although many gourmets have spurned them as excesses of vulgarians with no palates. Paul Claudel wrote: 'A cocktail is to a glass of wine as rape is to love.' And in his *Diet and Pleasure*, published in 1932, Paul Reboux scoffed at books of cocktail recipes, describing the mixtures prescribed as enough 'to make a shark retch or a crocodile vomit'. It horrified him to find champagne shaken up with gin, orange juice, and kirsch, and curaçoa with green peppermint and anisette. He agreed with Curmonsky, 'prince of epicures', who had decried cocktails as like drinking medicaments, dentifrices and explosives beaten together.

According to Reboux, the modern cocktail was first prepared by an American publican, who used to keep the dregs of bottles of spirits in a flask and clean brass with them. Somebody passed out after a brawl and in the consequent confusion the contents of the flask were poured down his throat. He high-jumped at once.

For a long time in Paris the cocktail was confined to bars frequented by those with Anglomania. There they served the 'Earthquake', consisting of equal measures out of every bottle on the shelves. Alphonse Allais created the 'Stars and Stripes', the latter being formed by letting spirits of different densities and colours flow slowly into a glass. As to the stars, one sip was enough to make one see a dazzling galaxy. 'The ultimate degradation is "Black Velvet", a blend of stout and champagne,' accused Oscar Mendelssohn in his *Dictionary of Drink and Drinking*. 'Both are honest beverages in their own right, but to mix them — one might as well spread onions on ice cream.'

Among the exhibits at the 1985 International Salon of Inventors in Geneva was an armchair-cocktail cabinet devised by a Frenchman and fitted with mirrors so that lazy addicts might see the ranks of bottles stored in the side of the chair without moving. The new concoctions include the garish, sickly 'Pina Colada', the 'Depth Bomb', the 'Glad Eye', the 'Between the Sheets', and the 'Good Night, Ladies' cocktails.

The *Sunday Mirror* for 15 December 1985 was concerned over 'the craze for trendy cocktails' among teenagers. It commented: 'The sweet-tasting drinks with glamorous names seem harmless enough, but pack a lethal punch. At up to £3.50 a time, they often contain the equivalent of a triple scotch. Teenagers up to seventeen years old are now spending £220 million a year on booze.'

XI

GEORGE IV
AND FRENCH CUISINE

G. W. M. Reynolds, in *The Mysteries of the Court*, published in instalments from 1850 onwards a highly coloured account of the Prince Regent's private life at Carlton House during the early nineteenth century. Aimed at the sensation-hungry public, it depicts him as looking like a walking feather-bed when he rises late in the morning after a night of debauchery. Paintings hang on the bedroom walls, showing Antony using Cleopatra's naked bosom as a pillow, Lucretia being ravished by Tarquin, Mars and Venus entangled, Andromeda roped provocatively to a rock; then the voluptuous Lady Letitia enters via the back stairs disguised as a man. She is soon sporting with him in his orientally splendid bathroom with its mirrored walls.

On another morning the Prince is in a perfumed room with 'six beauteous votaries of the Terpsichorean art'. The dancing had degenerated into licence when his father, King George III, bursts in and berates him: 'Hey-day! Am I in Carlton House or in luxurious brothel? 'Pon my word, George, your taste is very vicious — very vicious indeed.' He then reveals that in order to reform him he has sent an emissary to Germany to select a wife, but the marriage is a disaster and the Prince finds solace watching three girls pirouetting on a tight rope across his bedroom 'with the most exquisite refinement of sensual provocation' for an hour, except for intervals when he pours them out champagne. The dancers, Reynolds writes, had 'strong heads, even if their morals are weak'. His penny-dreadful also introduces the reader to Mrs General Hamilton, the procuress, and says: 'Hundreds of blooming victims were annually sacrificed on unhallowed altars by this high priestess of debauchery.' Scholarly footnotes assisted in lending apparent authenticity to all this farrago which judging by the sales of the book was regarded by the populace as a fairly correct account of George IV's private life.

To get an accurate picture, one must consult the letters and journals of the more reliable of the King's contemporaries. As regards his eating habits, he had a passion for fine food with dire effects on his figure. For a time he wore a corset, then gourmandise won the battle, and he threw it away. Lord Folkestone wrote on 23 February 1818: 'Prinny has let loose his belly, which now reaches his knees.' Then, when George was ill, the Duke of Wellington wrote on 10 April 1830:

> What do you think of His breakfast yesterday morning for an Invalid? A Pidgeon and Beef Steak Pye of which he ate two Pidgeons and three Beef Steaks, Three parts of a Bottle of Mozelle, a Glass of Dry Champagne, two Glasses of Port, and a Glass of Brandy! He had taken Laudanum the night before, again before breakfast, again last night, and again this Morning.

It is not surprising to learn that the Regent by this time had to be lifted into his mount's saddle after being wheeled up inclined boards to a platform which was then raised sufficiently to allow the horse to pass under it.

George believed that truffles if eaten regularly improved sexual performance. Davenport wrote:

That Coryphaeus of voluptuaries, George IV, so highly appreciated this quality in truffles, that his Ministers at the Courts of Turin, Naples, Florence, etc., were specially instructed to forward by a State messenger to the Royal Kitchen any of these fungi that might be found superior in size, delicacy, or flavour.

The King's contemporary, the poet Thomas Moore, once his guest at Carlton House, later to his distress attacked him, describing his daily life as 'a sick epicure's dream, incoherent and gross' and his favourite luncheon as mutton cutlets and strong curaçoa. He was also addicted to laudanum in large doses, and in an age of extravagant drinking scored off all competitors with the recipe for Regent's Punch, prepared from three bottles of champagne, two of Madeira, one of hock, one of curaçoa, one quart of brandy, one pint of rum, and two bottles of seltzer water, flavoured with four pounds of bloom raisins, Seville oranges, lemons, white sugar candy, and diluted with iced green tea.

After a night of guzzling alcoholic mixtures such as this, prostrate Regency bucks would be carried out by their valets, put in their coaches and taken home. Occasionally, the valets were not themselves too sober, causing substitutes to take their places. As a result, masters would sometimes be put in the wrong coaches and conveyed to strange houses much to the astonishment of the wives. John Knyveton in his diaries records being stopped in the Mall one morning by the Hon. Mr Rowley who asked his opinion of the best cure for a hangover. He replied: 'There is of course but one sovereign remedy for all gentlemen of dissipation, rhubarb — it makes them brave next morning.'

Regular companions of George IV as Prince of Wales were Fox and Sheridan, and, most dissipated of all, the eleventh Duke of Norfolk, known as the 'Jockey', whose boast it was that he could drink all his fellow-peers as well as any MP under the table. Once he had achieved this at a dinner party, he would go on to another. The pattern was repeated until at last he himself would lie drunk on a bench or tumble into the gutter from where he would be retrieved by his servants. He so disliked washing that it was the only time they could scrub him with soap and water. He was also a glutton, and in recognition of his prowess as a trencherman he sat in a Chair of State raised up above the other members when he attended dinners of the Beefsteak Club. He had no difficulty in eating more steaks than everyone else and yet maintain a reputation as a witty and knowledgeable conversationalist. He often engaged in drinking contests with the Prince Regent and his brother, the Duke of Clarence, and was the only guest George's knock-out brandy 'Diabolino' never floored.

Antoine Carême's fame as a chef of genius had spread from Paris to England, and the Prince Regent's passion for *haute cuisine* led to Carême's engagement in 1818 to take charge at the Royal Pavilion in Brighton where for seven months he remained constantly on duty. He claimed later that during this while the Regent never once suffered from gout, whereas previously owing to dishes being overspiced he had been tortured by it, day and night.

To give some idea of Carême's menus, here are the entrées alone for a luncheon of forty covers served to the Prince: *sauté de volaille à la Lyonnaise, côtelettes de mouton à la Soubise, timbales de nouilles à la Reine, ailes de poulardes à la Chevalier, matelotte de foies gras au Madère, petits canetons de poulets à la Nivernaise, escalopes de faisans au truffes de France, noix de veau au beurre de Montpélier, émincé de levrauts à la Clermont, turbans de filets mignon à l'Ecarlate.*

The first important banquet staged by Carême at the Pavilion was in January 1817, when the future Tzar Nicholas I came to stay and when there were nine courses with 100 dishes. Exaggerated accounts of this and the Regent's style of living led to stones being thrown at his coach by a mob when he opened Parliament on the 28th of that month, and a Whig MP damned his ménage as more like 'the pomp and magnificence of a Persian satrap in all the splendour of Oriental state than the sober dignity of a British Prince'.

After two years in the Prince Regent's employ, Carême left. The English weather did not agree with him, and he had received a tempting offer to work for the Russian court. But, once in St Petersburg, the close watch that was kept over expenditure in the kitchens irritated him — especially after the Prince Regent's open-handedness — so he returned to Paris. Later, the Prince when King tried unsuccessfully to lure the culinary prodigy back, offering to double his previous salary.

On 19 July 1821 George IV was crowned King and the banquet held afterwards in Westminster Hall was a gargantuan affair. The food assembled in the kitchens for the meal consisted of: beef, 7,442 lb; veal, 7,133 lb; mutton, 2,474 lb; lamb, 5 saddles; house lamb, 20 quarters and 20 legs; grass lamb, 55 quarters; sweetbreads, 160; calves feet, 400; cow heels, 389; geese, 160; capons and pullets, 720; chickens, 1,610; fowls for stock, 520; bacon, 1,730 lb; lard, 550 lb; suet, 250 lb; butter, 912 lb; eggs, 8,400.

To wash all this down the throats of those assembled nearly a thousand dozen bottles were provided of champagne, burgundy, claret, hock, moselle, Madeira, sherry and port, as well as a hundred gallons of iced punch. The total cost, including the Coronation, came to £238,000. Such extravagance was much criticized with the result that care was taken when William IV succeeded George in 1830 for him to be crowned for only a fifth of this amount.

By the peace treaty of 1815 France was committed to pay the victorious allies 50 million francs within three years, besides claims for compensation from private citizens. National bankruptcy was predicted, but to the astonishment of all financial experts the payments were made with ease, and, during the whole time this punishment lasted, the balance of exchange was in France's favour, which meant that more money came into the country than went out of it. This was due to the gourmandise of British and other foreign visitors, who, says Brillat-Savarin, brought with them 'a rare voracity and stomachs of extraordinary capacity' and spent their money lavishly on French food and drink.

Louis XVIII celebrated his restoration to the throne in February 1815 with gastronomic splendour. Some 1,200 guests were entertained at a banquet in the great gallery of the Louvre prepared by 100 cooks with Carême in charge of the *entrées froides* and the *entremets de sucre*. This was followed by what must have been the largest military dinner in French history. It was held under the trees in the Champs Elysées and attended by 10,000 men. The list of supplies reads: 6 cows, 75 calves, 250 sheep, 10,000 turkeys, 1,000 chickens, 1,000 partridges, 500 hams, 500 tongues, 1,000 carp, 1,000 pike, 1,000 pies, 1,000 cakes. Liquid refreshment provided consisted of 18,000 bottles of Macon and 145 casks of wine.

The following February, Carême was responsible for the planning, cooking and presentation of the meal served to 3,000 at the *Grand Bal de l'Odéon*. Aristocratic gourmets who had escaped the guillotine all agreed that never even in the extravagant times before the Revolution had dishes of such quality and in such abundance been provided at any function. Carême describes the scene in his memoirs:

> In the foyer I directed the helpers to construct a huge buffet nine tiers high, and when it was laid out with the *grosses pièces*, the fish, the entrées, the centre pieces of pastry, the dishes of roasts, the entremets and the desserts, it presented a sumptuous sight. . . . I can still see the room of the Odéon, shining, glittering with beauty, the lights of a thousand candles. . . . The Bourbon family was there, radiant and laughing. . . . The evening was of an elegance and manner that no country on earth could rival.

Dancing has sometimes caused the excessive consumption of alcohol. In the late 1820s, galops became fashionable and at a party given by Alexandre Dumas, *père*, which lasted until 9 a.m., 300 bottles of champagne, the same of Bordeaux, and the same again of white wine were drunk. The novelist was an indefatigable satyr who proudly used to claim that he had sired five hundred bastards. His son once complained: 'Really, father, it's not fair, you're always giving me your old mistresses to sleep with and your new boots to break in.' To which the reply came: 'What are you grousing about? You ought to regard it as a compliment. It proves you have a thick prick and a narrow foot.' He boasted that, if left alone with five women and a play to write, at the end of an hour he would have finished five acts and had sex with all the women.

The elder Dumas was also an excellent cook and among his writings on the subject are a Dictionary of Cuisine in which, after mentioning that Montaigne called gluttony 'the science of the gullet', he continues: 'The greatest example of this from classical antiquity is that of Saturn, who devoured his children for fear they would dethrone him, and did not even notice that it was a paving stone he swallowed instead when it came to Jupiter's turn. This sort of gluttony requires a strong stomach.'

Dumas tells a tale about a French minister who was sent as a present two huge sturgeons, weighing 324 lb and 374 lb respectively. He discussed the matter with his chef. To serve both for dinner would look excessive and in bad taste, and to have the larger one that evening and the smaller one next day or vice versa would be monotonous as well as excessive. A clever solution to the problem was decided upon. Musicians playing flutes and violins led a number of footmen carrying torches into the dining-hall. They were followed by the chef bearing high the smaller sturgeon resting on a bed of roses and his assistant brandishing knives. Up and down, they paraded before the guests. Then, just as the fish was about to be set on the table, the chef pretended to stumble and dropped the dish on the floor. The company groaned in disappointment. After waiting to make his announcement more impressive, their host commanded to general relief and delight: 'Serve the other!'

Dumas's boast that he had fathered 500 children out of wedlock would not have surprised his contemporary, Balzac, who, in his *Physiologie du mariage*, quoted statistics to support his claim that there existed a floating mass of approximately 150,000 illegitimate persons per year. In view of this, he advised his readers against admitting eligible bachelors into their homes.

> Get rid of such furniture as divans, sofas, etc. They can lead to disaster. I have never been able to look at these without fear, for it has always seemed to me that the devil was installed there with his horns and cloven hoof. Cupboards of every description must be securely nailed up, so that no one can hide inside them. Beware of hangings round the bed. The *Marriage of Figaro* will have warned you not to let your wife have her bedroom on the ground floor. . . . Fireplaces must have grilles to cover up all possible exits and hiding-places, even if this obliges you to have them unsealed every time the chimney is swept. As for the bed, this is an object to which you must give careful thought. On no account have heavy curtains draped round it — choose only light, diaphanous ones. . . .

Balzac was probably speaking from personal experience for he had many mistresses during his life. 'A woman is a well-served table that one sees with different eyes before and after the meal,' he observed. Like Dumas, he loved food and ate enormous amounts in restaurants often disposing of a hundred oysters just as starters. In fact, gourmandise became so widespread that those addicted to it challenged each other to contests to see who could eat the largest number of steaks or chickens, etc., at one sitting. In one instance, an entire calf had to be consumed.

Whilst Gustave Flaubert usually lit and smoked a cigar when screwing a whore, he disapproved of people who over-indulged themselves and wrote: 'The whole trend now in Paris is towards the colossal. Everything is becoming wild and out of proportion. If we are not careful, we shall end up like ancient Rome.' (Incidentally, Théophile Gautier prided himself on being able to solve a complicated mathematical problem as he copulated.)

The new interest in gastronomy led to an increase in gifted chefs to cope with the demand. King Louis XVIII himself was not only a gourmand but an excellent chef. His main interest was devising new dishes. He found that by grilling chops between two other chops, the flavour was enhanced and this formed a perfect trap for their juices. His masterpiece was *truffes à la purée d'ortolans*, the recipe for which he kept secret from all in the royal kitchens and prepared himself assisted only by a trustworthy Duke. On one occasion, Louis's passion for his *plat* led to his cooking enough for half-a-dozen diners, but the two men greedily ate it all.

In the early hours of the morning the Duke was taken ill with the most excruciating indigestion, and a physician rushed to his bedside feared fatal consequences. Loyal to the last, the Duke sent an attendant to the palace with urgent instructions to have Louis woken up and treated by every available antidote lest he, too, perished.

'Dying? Dying from eating my *truffes à la purée d'ortolans!*' cried Louis. 'Why, I never felt better. I was right then — I always said I had a stomach far superior to his.'

Whilst other monarchs did not attempt to emulate Louis, they did engage French chefs. François Tany went to Russia, Marie-Antoine Carême to England and Austria, and Urbain-Dubois to Germany — and their example was followed everywhere by the aristocracy and those in the middle classes sufficiently wealthy. Everything concerning cooking from recipes to restaurants became excessively French.

Thackeray in *Fitzboodle's Confessions* suggested that any-one who set up in business as a gastronomic agent in London might make a great deal of money through exploiting the craze for banquets. He goes on to describe in amusing fashion how such an agency might operate. Customers would be received in a library furnished with massive bookcases containing, according to the titles on the spines of the volumes, all the works on cookery and wines in every known language in the world.

> Any books, of course, will do, as you will have them handsomely bound, and keep them under plate glass. On a side-table will be little sample-bottles of wine, a few truffles on a white porcelain saucer, a prodigious strawberry or two, perhaps, at the time when such fruit costs much money. In the library will be busts marked UDE, CARÊME, BECHAMEL, in marble (never mind what heads, of course); and, perhaps, on the clock should be a figure of the Prince of Condé's cook killing himself because the fish had not arrived in time; there may be a wreath of *immortels* on the figure to give it a more decidedly Frenchified air. The walls will be of a dark rich paper, hung round with neat gilt frames containing plans of menus of various great dinners, those of Cambacérès, Napoleon, Louis XIV, Louis XVIII, Heliogabalus, if you like, each signed by the respective cook.

After the prospective customer has gaped about him at this array, 'which he does not understand in the least, especially the truffles which look like dirty potatoes', you, as agent, enter dressed in dark clothes 'with one handsome enormous gold chain, and one large diamond ring; a gold snuff-box, of course, which you will thrust into the visitor's paw before saying a word'. When he has done sneezing, you ask him to sit down and explain your system which will vary according to circumstances. First, you must impress the inquirer with your qualifications. Belonging to one of the best families in England, you have either yourself, or through your ancestors, been accustomed to good living for centuries. In the reign of Henry V, your maternal great-great-grandfather, Roger de Gotylton — 'the name may be varied, of course, or the King's reign, or the dish invented' — was the first who discovered the method of roasting a peacock whole, with its tail-feathers displayed; and the dish was served to both the French and the English Kings at Rouen. Throughout your life, you have dedicated yourself solely to the study of the table and have to that end visited the courts of all the monarchs of Europe, obtaining recipes from their cooks with whom you are on terms of intimate friendship and often obtaining these at enormous expense to yourself.

You are similarly acquainted with all the vintages of the continent 'having passed the autumn of 1811 (the comet year) on the great Weinberg of Johannesberg; being employed similarly at Bordeaux in 1836; at Oporto, in 1822; and at Xeres de la Frontera . . . the year before. You travelled to India and back in company with fourteen pipes of Madeira on board of the *Samuel Snob*, East Indiaman, Captain Scuttles, and spent the vintage season in the island, with unlimited powers of observation granted to you by the great houses there.'

You are able at a glance to recognize the age of mutton, the primeness of beef, the firmness and freshness of fish of all kinds, thanks to having attended Mr Graves of Charing Cross and Mr Giblett of Bond Street in a course of purchases of the same. You have 'visited the Parks, the grouse-manors, and the principal gardens of England in a similar professional point of view.'

Should the inquirer be sufficiently impressed by all this to employ you as his dinner-master, you agree to engage, through subordinates, cooks 'worthy of the strictest confidence', prepare a menu according to price, purchase what is required 'sending to Paris, if need be', and provide 'dextrous table-waiters'.

The agent's fee for these services, wrote Thackeray, might be five guineas (which should be multiplied by a hundred at least, to reach today's values). He also gives a specimen letter that 'George Gormand Guttleton' might send to all tradesmen and which reads:

> Every Monday evening during the season, the Agent proposes to give a series of trial-dinners, to which the principal gourmands of the metropolis and a few of the Agent's most respectable clients, will be invited. Covers will be laid for *ten* at nine o'clock precisely. And as the Agent does not propose to exact a single shilling of profit from their bills, and as his recommendation will be of infinite value to them, the tradesmen he employs will furnish the weekly dinner *gratis*. Cooks will attend (who have acknowledged characters) upon the same terms. To save trouble, a book will be kept, where butchers, poulterers, etc., may inscribe their names in order, taking it by turns to supply the trial-table. Wine merchants will naturally compete every week promiscuously, sending what they consider their best samples . . . and let all remember that the Agent is a very keen judge, and woe betide those who serve him or his clients ill!

Thackeray ends his satire by claiming that if the gastronomic agency is not a profession — 'a new one — a feasible one — a lucrative one — I don't know what is'. If a man attended but fifteen dinners daily at five guineas a time, he could earn fourteen thousand three hundred pounds for a season of six months. 'It will not be necessary that he should have done all that is stated in the prospectus; but, at any rate, let him *say* he has; there can't be much harm in an innocent fib of that sort, for the gastronomic agent must be a sort of dinner-pope, whose opinions cannot be supposed to err.'

XII

VICTORIAN VICE AND THE 'DEMON DRINK'

Two years before Queen Victoria came to the throne, the London Society for the Prevention of Juvenile Prostitution was founded and in his first report, Mr Talbot, its Secretary wrote: 'There is no country, city or town where the evil is so systematically, so extensively and so openly carried on as in England and her capital.' Dr Ryan in *Prostitution in London* (1839) revealed that, according to the police, there were getting on for 100,000 prostitutes in London, at least half of whom were less than twenty years old. The position had not improved much by 1857 when the *Lancet* stated that there were no fewer than 80,000 prostitutes in the capital out of a population of 2,235,344, that one in sixty houses was a brothel and that one in every sixteen women was a harlot.

Flora Tristan, the French social reformer and Gauguin's brilliant grandmother, visited England in the late 1830s and in her book, *Promenades dans Londres*, gave a pungent account of the vice that she had observed there. In order to gain first-hand knowledge, Flora, accompanied by two men friends armed with canes, went to Waterloo Road, which was entirely peopled by prostitutes and their protectors. It was a hot summer's evening and the girls were either stationed at the windows or seated outside the front doors sporting with the pimps. Some were half-clothed, others were naked down to their waists. Later, the trio sat on the Bridge, watching the girls setting out in bands for the West End. They would be back between eight and nine next morning.

Everywhere that was crowded, there the girls flocked. Performances in the theatres began between six and seven, and at 9.30 p.m. all empty seats were reduced to half price. Then the prostitutes would invade the theatres and take over the foyers and the crush rooms to use as their saloons. After the play, they rushed off to 'finishes', which Flora described as places of refreshment where people went to finish the night. They were as popular with the English as beer cellars were with the Germans and cafés with the French. In the more wretched ones, solicitors' clerks and shop assistants drank ale, smoked vile tobacco and became tipsy in the company of tawdrily dressed whores. In the better-class establishments, men of fashion drank punch or cognac, French or Rhine wine, sherry and port, smoked fine cigars, laughed and tumbled about with beautiful young girls, richly dressed. But, in both settings, it always ended in debauchery.

In order to obtain copy for her book, Flora Tristan visited one of these 'finishes', escorted by her two men friends. The huge room 'lit by a thousand gas jets' was divided into two, half-way across its length. In one section was a row of tables, separated by wooden partitions, with sofas on either side. Opposite, in the other section, was a stage where the girls displayed themselves, provoking the men with their looks and remarks. When a man responded, they would lead him to one of the tables, all of which were laden with food and alcoholic beverages of every kind.

Towards midnight, the regular customers began to arrive. This particular 'finish' was frequented by the aristocracy. Flora watched the young sprigs lie down on the sofas, light up their cigars, and start fooling with their pick-ups. She wrote:

Then, after many drinks, the liquor began to excite their passions, and the milords, including some very honourable Members of Parliament, whipped off their coats, untied their cravats, threw off waistcoats and braces. . . . The orgy reached its peak between four and five o'clock in the morning. It needed a certain amount of courage for me to remain there a silent witness of all that went on.

According to Flora, one of the most popular amusements in the 'finishes' was to make a prostitute intoxicated. When unconscious, she would be forced to swallow vinegar in which mustard and pepper had been added; this nearly always caused her to go into convulsions which the men found uproariously diverting. A prank also much appreciated in these fashionable gatherings was to throw glasses of anything over girls laying in stupors on the floor. In another place, Flora noticed an exceptionally attractive Irish girl who created a sensation when she arrived at 2 a.m. elegantly dressed in spotless white satin and rose-coloured shoes. Three hours later Flora saw her sprawling on the ground. Her gown was now filthy with a confused medley of stains, and her shoulders and breasts were thickly streaked with red wine, brandy, beer, coffee, etc. The waiters stepped across her as though she were a heap of rubbish.

The revellers left between six and seven in the morning. As for those still lying dead drunk, the waiters dressed them as best they could with the clothes nearest at hand, and carried them out to cabs for the drivers to deliver at their homes. When addresses were not known, these human packages would be dragged down into the basements and deposited on straw until they regained consciousness.

The working life of a London prostitute, Flora was informed, lasted between three and four years. In rare exceptions some kept it up for seven or eight. Many died from venereal disease or consumption in hospitals, or, if they could not gain admittance, expired in frightful slums. While she was in London, a city merchant, finding that he had caught syphilis, attributed its origin to a certain prostitute and induced her to meet him. Then, he pulled up her skirts above her head, tied them together with cord so that she was enclosed as if in a sack, whipped her and, when he had exhausted himself, threw her into the middle of the street. The shrieking, stifling woman rolled about in the mud, vainly trying to extricate herself, but nobody went to her assistance until at last a policmen cut her free and dragged her to a hospital. When the merchant was charged with committing an outrage on a public highway, the magistrate fined him only six shillings.

Mr Talbot of the Society for the Prevention of Juvenile Prostitution informed Flora Tristan that he estimated there were at least 5,000 brothels in London, as many as there were shops selling gin, while about the same number of men and women were employed as procurers, the best prices being obtained for girls between the ages of ten and twelve. He also estimated that some 400,000 persons were interested either directly or indirectly in the vice, and that £8 million was spent annually on it. To satisfy the requirements of an expanding market, girls were also being procured by agents in Holland, Belgium, France and Italy. Once an agent reached a town, he would set about finding the names and addresses of families with daughters who might like to go to England in the employment of some respectable family. He would visit the parents, ingratiate himself with them, make all sorts of promises and persuade them to allow him to take their daughter to London to be employed as a nursemaid, milliner, embroideress, florist, and so on. A sum of money would be left with the parents as a guarantee for the carrying out of the engagement.

Sometimes it was even agreed that a fixed percentage of the girl's wages would be sent home every quarter and, as long as she remained in the establishment whose agent had brought her to England, the exact sum promised was sent regularly to the parents, who without realizing it thus received benefits from the prostitution of their child. If the girl moved from the house where she was employed, a letter would be sent to her parents stating that she had left her position and that the remittances would cease. A girl imported into England in this way cost between £20 and a £100. When she was known by all the regulars and no longer appealed to them, she would be transferred to a second-class brothel.

Talbot also told Flora that out of five thousand such venues for sex approximately two thousand provided young boys for their patrons. Agents were paid £10 for each boy, who would be usually picked up when looking into the window of a sweet shop. Nearly all boys between 12 and 15 sent to prison had slept with prostitutes and were regularly visited by their mistresses, who pretended to be their sisters. There were in London about 14,000 prostitutes aged between 10 and 15. In the space of eight years some 2,700 patients of that age range had been admitted to Guy's Hospital with venereal disease, and an even larger number had been refused treatment for lack of beds. He had seen up to thirty of them turned away though they could hardly walk.

Flora was outraged to learn from Talbot that English law appeared to favour the activities of the agents of vice. Thus the keeper of a brothel who had corrupted children in this way would be sentenced to a maximum of ten days' imprisonment, while a working class woman arrested for selling fruit or vegetables in the street would be shut up for thirty days.

Whilst in England Flora Tristan went to the Ascot Races, but she was not impressed. She claimed that the main pleasure of all classes came from eating and drinking. She saw grand ladies balancing on their knees plates piled with enormous slices of ham, beef, pâté, etc., which they forced down with port, sherry and champagne. The races lasted for three hours, and she noticed that in some barouches the occupants never stopped eating for the whole of that time. 'I waited in vain for the moment when some gaiety would enliven the scene. There were ladies being sick over the sides of their carriages, others sleeping, tipsy men making coarse advances to women, men so drunk they reeled about; but of true gaiety, there was none among the rich.' At last, towards six o'clock, the vehicles started on the way home. The police made sure that the horses were harnessed first to the carriages of the aristocracy. Coach-men whom they regarded as too drunk to drive were replaced by sober substitutes. The extremely inebriated were put inside, whilst those who were only half intoxicated were settled on top between two steady companions to prevent them from falling off. 'Such an outing', Flora wrote, 'is known in England as a pleasure jaunt.'

Flora Tristan's picture of the English is almost unre-lievedly black, which appealed to French readers still smarting from defeat in the war that had ended less than twenty years previously. It is interesting to compare the figures she quotes for London with those given in the rolls of the Paris police which number the prostitutes in that city for 1814 at about 1,900 and for 1832 at 3,558 with 220 tolerated brothels. By 1897, the prostitutes had increased to about 4,500.

A side of the English moral scene that Flora Tristan does not cover is the erotica, described as memoirs but clearly fiction and mostly written to a set pattern, that was increasingly being published in the late Georgian and early Victorian periods. Repetitious in style and floridly worded, it would describe in detail sexual intercourse. Anyone picking up *The Modern Rake; or, The Life and Adventures of Sir Edward Walford* would learn from the first page that it contained 'a curious and voluptuous history of his luscious intrigues, with numerous women of fashion, his laughable *faux pas*, feats of gallantry, debauchery, dissipation, and concubinism; his numerous rapes, seductions, and amatory scrapes; memoirs of the beautiful courtezans with whom he lived, with some ticklish songs, anecdotes, poetry, etc.' It was 'enriched with many curious plates'.

Another typical example of this sort of book was the *Memoirs of Rosa Belle-fille; or A delicious bouquet of Amorous Delights. Dedicated to the Goddess of Voluptuous Pleasure, and her soul-enamoured votaries.* When the heroine recollects how disguised as a man she eloped with her lover, we read:

> Velocitous as our speed was, we had not proceeded half a mile before — propulsive pruriency stimulating the energy of procreant zeal — the members of innoculative union stood erect in impatient condition for active duty! My inamorato, with one hand thrust into my swelling bosom (in celestial ramble over my bubbies) and with the other removing the leculottin-empêchement (the close breeches obstruction) inserting his finger up the temple porch prepared the venerous agent within for immediate sacrificial offering! Placing himself procumbent with his shoulders against the back, and his toes stretched against the front of the chaise, and I putting myself, Buttock over him, in an incubative attitude. . . .

The advertisements promoting this squalid sustenance for the sex-starved were full of similar hyperbole. *La Rose D'Amour; or, The Adventures of a Gentleman in search of Pleasure,* its publisher claimed was:

> One of the most remarkable works of the present day. Possessed of unbounded wealth, and of frame and of stamina of body apparently inexhaustible, he pursues pleasures with an appetite that grows by what it feeds on, and is never tired or wearied in the pursuit; this hero ravishes, seduces, and ruins all the females that come within his reach — rich and poor, gentle and simple, rough and refined, all fall down before his sceptre of flesh, his noble truncheon, his weapon of war. His great passion is for maidens, for young and unfledged virgins, for those in whom the secret instinct of propagation has hardly had time to develop itself.

> He travels the seas for new victims of his raging lust: he buys maidens by the score, he initiates them into all the mysteries of Venus, and finally, retires to his château with a seraglio of beauties such as Solomon might envy and David long for in vain. Every page is a picture of sensual delight.

The considerable profits to be made from the large sales of such books made their publishers strive to make their wares more and more sensational. In 1811, the medical profession was incensed by the publication of *The Amatory Experiences of a Surgeon* in which the anonymous author was portrayed as a never satisfied bed-hopper. This sold so well that a rival publisher brought out *The Amours of a Medical Student.* Opera lovers were shattered when the alleged autobiography of the famous singer, Wilhelmina Schroeder-Devrient was published posthumously, supposed to be based on her letters to a doctor discovered after his decease by his nephew, and in which her obsession with sex was luridly depicted.

The medical profession were attacked for setting patients a bad example by the German writer, Iwan Bloch, in his much discussed sociological study of *Sexual Life in England*, first published in his own country in the late nineteenth century. He also maintained that the excessive consumption of meat and of alcoholic beverages by the English had unnaturally stimulated their sexuality and led them into devious paths. Gabriele d'Annunzio in *Lust* and Tolstoi in the *Kreutzer Sonata* had vividly portrayed how luxurious feeding could incite lasciviousness. Indulging in gourmet suppers and midnight dinners paved the way to sexual excess. Alcohol diminished a man's restraint and made him an easy prey to seduction, but, whilst increasing desire, it almost always hindered erection and delayed the orgasm. Requiring a longer time for the completion of the sexual act increased the danger of venereal infection.

In the case of women, Bloch quoted various authorities, who, as a result of their researches, had established that chronic alcoholism was an important cause of late prostitution above the age of twenty-five. All engaged in this profession were aware of 'the peculiar influence of alcohol upon the libido sexualis and upon the psyche' and it was precisely 'this discriminative duplex influence' which was utilized by them. Not only in drinking saloons with women attendants and in the brothels did alcohol play this part; street-walkers, too, found drunken men easy prey. This was common elsewhere in Europe, too.

At a great public dinner which in 1890 the city of Berlin had given in the Rathaus to the members of the International Medical Congress, some 4,000 persons had consumed 15,382 bottles of wine, 484 gallons of beer, and 300 bottles of brandy, causing 'the most disgusting scenes of drunkenness'. Outside the Rathaus 'swarmed prostitutes who found a rich booty among the drunken, staggering guests'.

The crusading zeal of the Victorians against lax morals found in the Demon Drink one of their main targets and in order to scare heavy imbibers into signing the pledge they were subjected to such propaganda as that alcohol if taken in large quantities rendered them liable to spontaneous combustion. In 1810, reports circulated that an old Frenchwoman addicted to spirits had one day begun to smoulder in her chair and that an Italian nobleman who took a daily bath in brandy had also gone up in smoke. A medical witness told the Buckingham Committee in 1834 that such cases were 'quite possible', and Charles Dickens in *Bleak House*, published in 1853, made Krook drink so much that he eventually exploded from internal combustion. When challenged as to whether this was possible in real life, the novelist quoted thirty other cases mostly from the past, but contemporary examples came from Canada, where a heavy drinker was said to have glowed with 'a widely extended silver-coloured flame' and from Boston where a man caught fire after belching near a lighted candle.

The publicity gained by this controversy encouraged the temperance supporters to bring out a pamphlet later giving other instances of gruesome deaths suffered by other drunkards. In San Francisco, in 1877, one after lighting his pipe at a gas jet had fallen on the floor, his head and neck veiled in smoke while blue jets of flame issued from his ears, mouth and nostrils.

The most insidious and effective weapons employed by the white man in his subjugation of black Africa were rum and gin. The Revd William Taylor served for thirty-three years there and was Missionary Bishop for Africa in the Methodist Episcopal Church between 1884 and 1896. In his reminiscences he describes how, on his first voyage down the west coast lasting three months, the Kroo boys handling the cargo were paid their wages in gin of wretched quality given them when they left. It was so poisonous that it made them 'temporarily insane'. At Malange in Angola he found that the following method of commerce was used: caravans arriving from the interior with ivory and rubber were instructed to deposit their loads in the trader's compound. The natives were then debauched with rum for several days, when they were told how much their goods were considered to be worth. If they expostulated that it was far too little, the trader's bullies would inform them that as he had already taken possession of the stuff, the blacks must accept his terms. When forced to do so, they were paid in kind — with rum. There were at that time, Bishop Taylor wrote, some 200 steamships engaged in the rum trade of Africa.

Another cleric, the Revd Charles Morris, wrote that he travelled up and down the west coast of the dark continent on boats that were 'simply wholesale liquor houses — rum in hogsheads, in casks, barrels, kegs, demijohns and stone jugs'. He added that 'Gin, gin!' was the cry all along the coast.

Most of the rum came from the United States, the quantities and values for exports from Boston for the year ended 30 June 1899, were to: England, 26,210 gallons

@ $34,162; British Africa, 790,556 gallons @ $1,099,743.

John O. Gough, arguably the greatest temperance speaker of the nineteenth century, would end his onslaught on intoxicating liquor with a panegyric on water which enraptured his packed audiences. He became known as 'the American high priest of the pump', and holding up a glass, he would begin:

> Here is our beautiful beverage, water, pure water. . . . There is no necessity to drink, except to quench one's thirst. . . . Our beverage is beautiful and pure, for God brewed it not in the distillery, but out of the earth. . . . Beautiful water! How it weaves a golden gauze for the setting sun and a silvery tissue for the midnight moon! Watch it descending in the feathery snow-flake, or painting with fairy pencil flowers and leaves upon the window pane. . . . Look at it as it trickles down the mountain side, like silver ribands, mixing with the heather bloom. . . . Beautiful water! It never broke a mother's heart. . . . Never did pale-faced wife or starving child . . . weep into it a bitter tear. Never did drunkard howl back from his death-bed a fearful curse upon it.

A common failing is to take things to extremes, and those who drank too much water found themselves suffering from water intoxication. At an inquest held in Great Yarmouth in March 1985, a verdict to this effect through misadventure was returned on 31-year-old Richard Cox who drank gallons every day. He was once seen to gulp thirteen half-pint glasses of it in succession, insisting it was good for the kidneys.

Pathologist Dr John Ball stated that a post-mortem showed severe excess fluid in the brain tissues, fluid in the lungs, and the stomach greatly dilated and filled with fluid. Death was due to water intoxication. A hundred such cases had been recorded world-wide. When water entered the brain tissues, the effect was similar to drunkenness. 'The person becomes disorientated, incapable of speaking properly,' Dr Ball said.

In order to reassure the public, a medical specialist affirmed that anyone drinking up to eight pints a day was not at risk.

In an article headed 'Do drinkers have water on the brain?', in the *Sunday Express*'s 'Science and Medicine' feature for 17 November 1985, Emma Bryer reported that researchers at the University of Edinburgh and the Royal Edinburgh Hospital had employed a sophisticated technique called magnetic resonance to look at the brains of drinkers during and after drinking. They found that the brains of heavy drinkers of alcohol became waterlogged when supplies of it were cut off, but if the addict could keep off intoxicants for three weeks, the water level would fall back to normal.

The research team's account in the *Lancet* stated that if the water could be reduced by drugs during the week after stopping, it might make giving up less traumatic, and ease the way to fighting alcoholism. More research was required to see whether an alcoholic thirst can be cured in this way.

The eminent gastronome, André L. Simon, once gave his reason for never drinking water was that he did not want to become rusty inside. Another gourmet, an elderly Frenchman, told an American: 'Wine is the only safe and sanitary beverage. Look at me. At the age of eighty-seven I am in perfect health. And why? Because water has never passed my lips.'

'Do you mean that literally?' asked the other.
'*Absolument, monsieur.*'
'What about brushing your teeth?'
'For that, I use a very light, dry wine.'

XIII
THE REIGN OF THE COURTESANS

The second half of the nineteenth century in Paris saw immorality rife in high places and courtesans making fortunes. There was Cora Pearl, born in Devon. Seduced in her teens by a merchant, she ran away to London and joined a bagnio. Having learnt the tricks of the trade, she started up on her own in Paris and soon proved adept at attracting rich and influential admirers such as the third Duc de Rivoli, Prince Achille Murat, and a Serbian Prince over whom she and Marthe de Vere fought a duel armed with whips. Their faces were so wounded that they had to wear thick veils for weeks by which time the object of their dispute had left the country. William, Prince of Orange, next fell in love with Cora, but his habits irritated her, especially as he was mean about money. Then, one January, when skating on the ice, she became friendly with Napoleon III's half-brother, the Duc de Morny. He introduced her to the Emperor's cousin, Prince 'Plon-Plon', who in his turn became so enamoured of Cora that he set her up in a fine establishment with a generous allowance.

Despite her new position, Cora made no attempt to curb her wantonness. At a party, the only woman present among a crowd of men, she hinted suggestively: 'There is only one of you with whom I am still a virgin.' Once she won a bet that she could serve for dinner meat nobody could cut by having herself carried in naked on a silver platter. La Belle Otero was to be similarly dished up to her admirers in St Petersburg. Cora was greedy for costly presents and when Alexandre Duval gave her a book she hurled it contemptuously into the fire and then learnt to her dismay that the pages were interleaved with one thousand franc notes.

La Paiva, originally a child beggar, made the most money out of selling her favours. After serving her apprenticeship in a Turkish pasha's harem, Thérèse charmed the Portuguese Marques, George de Paiva, who married her. Installed in a magnificent mansion on the Champs-Elysées with its onyx staircase, she asked playwright, Emile Augier, to suggest a suitable inscription to embellish the first step and he wisecracked — 'Like Virtue, Vice has its degrees'.

The German Count Guido Heinkel became so besotted with La Paiva that he spent a 100 million francs on buying her a resplendent residence at Pontchartrain, where, to gratify one of her whims, he had a replica of the grand canal at Versailles dug in the grounds.

There was a cruel streak in Thérèse's character. She let Lasalle, one of the *jeunesse dorée*, dissipate his inheritance in a vain attempt to become her lover. The day came when he told her that he had only 10,000 francs left. 'Very well,' she relented. 'Bring them to me tomorrow. We'll set fire to them, and I'll be yours till the flames die out.'

Lasalle could not sleep that night, and, when at last he was ushered into Thérèse's salon, she smiled up at him from the couch on which she lay, her voluptuous nakedness teasing him from a gap in her négligé. He held out the notes to her with trembling hands. She took them nonchalantly, dropped them into a silver bowl on the table beside her, and applied a match. Then she threw the négligé wide open. The young man's attention was so riveted on the burning money that he completely ignored her charms. La Paiva leapt up laughing. He had reacted exactly as she had expected.

Of all nineteenth-century courtesans, Caroline Otero had the most astonishing life. She was the daughter of a Spanish prostitute and never traced her father. A savage rape at the age of eleven by a village shoemaker who broke her pelvis left her incapable of having children. Three years later she started living with a Catalan dancer, Paco Coli, and as a result learnt to sing and dance. He had no money and he made her sleep with men to support them both. They went to the French Riviera where she obtained an engagement in a music-hall and was soon rising to stardom as *La Belle Otero*. Her association with Coli ended when he attempted to marry her.

It seems that the effect of her terrible childhood experience was to turn her into a nymphomaniac. Some have suggested that she wanted to punish men for it. According to Monte Carlo gossip, one night she had intercourse with eleven men in a close-at-hand hotel spending less than a half-hour with each so that she could return to her real love, gambling at the tables, where she lost a fortune during her life. 'If I had saved it instead,' she said later, 'I could have endowed a university for prostitutes. What a variety of courses one could have provided!'

Otero must have been the only courtesan to have had sex in a balloon. This was with Baron Lépic as it floated for more than an hour high above the French river Aude. 'It was an amorous adventure every woman should experience,' commented Caroline in her memoirs, where she claimed to have had more crowned heads as her lovers than any other *femme fatale*. There was Tsar Nicholas II who always had armed guards at their bedroom door, 'some at every window, and if there were a back entrance, he would have a regiment stationed there'. She almost felt as if she were undressing in 'an army barracks or a bull-fighting arena'. Should she suddenly move a chair or drop a perfume bottle, Nicholas would leap out of bed 'screaming with fright'. Nevertheless, she became very fond of him although he had 'the oddest views about sex'. Her affair with the Shah of Persia lasted five years and he, too, was 'very strange in his desires'. His visits lasted from two to five in the afternoon and shortly after his departure one of his aides would call and hand her maid a gold, inlaid casket, containing a superb jewel which Otero would remove and send back the empty container.

King Leopold II of Belgium patronized Caroline first in 1894, when over sixty, and she found him 'not very generous at the start', but she taught him 'how to give' and he became an apt student and rewarded her with 'several residences' during an intermittent association lasting four years. Also in the Nineties, Prince Albert of Monaco went to bed with her. She had the knack of making the near impotent perform which proved necessary in his case. To be told by her that he was 'formidable' made him strut round the room, accommodate her in a splendid apartment and shower her with jewels. When the affair cooled off, the future King of Montenegro, Prince Nicholas, went to live with her there and paid for his lodging with a 'gorgeous diamond brooch and at least five exquisite watches'. He coaxed her into visiting his country, but she saw next to nothing of it for all he wanted to do was 'to make love to me so I complied'.

In Cairo, la Belle Otero danced and sang before the Khedive, and, as a result spent three nights of intense sex with him in his palace and left with yet another ring bearing 'a ten carat diamond surrounded by a dozen pearls and of the first water'. In St Petersburg, later, a newspaper reported:

'Señora Otero is burning everybody's head. One evening, Colonel X of the *Chevaliers-Gardes* had the brilliant idea, in the course of a supper at Cula's, to present her to the company, served *au naturel* upon a silver dish. One may imagine that the Señora, fashioned like a Velasquez or a Murillo Virgin was a *succès fou*.' In Berlin, according to Caroline, Kaiser

William II, spoke of her as 'the little savage', whilst in Paris Albert, Prince of Wales, soon to become King Edward VII, 'often sent for me to dance after supper at Voisin's, Durand's, or the Café Anglais'.

She adds: 'He was surprisingly virile and generous, but he had to disappoint me one night in London when Lily Langtry arrived unexpectedly.'

Caroline's youngest and last royal lover was King Alfonso XIII of Spain who, in 1905, in her flat at Monte Carlo was given his first lessons in making love by her. Aged nineteen, he was young enough to be her son. Remaining fond of his Belle Otero, in 1913, he arranged for her to have an apartment in Madrid so that he could visit her when he felt like it. Thrones were to topple following the First World War, and Caroline now found herself a leading statesman instead as her special friend. This was Aristide Briand whom she described as fat, hideously ugly, badly dressed, and who, when she first met him in 1909, was too poor to be able to give her more than an occasional cheap jewel or flowers. Nevertheless, she found him more fascinating than any other man. 'Once he made love to me eight times before morning, and he was fifty at the time.' They parted after ten years when his eminent position forced him to become more discreet.

In her heyday, la Belle Otero charged two thousand pounds on average for a night with her — either in cash or in the form of jewels. When she died at the age of ninety-seven her fortune had been gambled away at the casino tables. She told a journalist, who called on her just before the end in Nice: 'I have been a slave to my passions, but never to a man.' She was the sexiest woman of her day whose breasts it was said preceded her 'by a quarter of an hour' and which reminded Colette of 'elongated lemons, firm and upturned at the tips'. When the Hotel Carlton in Cannes was built, its architect, who admired her, used them as models for its twin cupolas, which ever since have been called locally *les boîtes de la Belle Otero*.

Of all the painters who practised their art in late nineteenth-century Paris, Henri de Toulouse-Lautrec perhaps captured closest on canvas the essential character of its artistes and demi-mondaines. Although only slightly over five foot in height, he had the sexual equipment of two men of his size and once described himself as a coffee pot with an extra large spout. It was in Montmartre at the age of nineteen that he made his home, began studying night life and having affairs with models. Fame came to him in 1891 with his first poster for the *Moulin Rouge*. When his liaison with Berthe La Sourde ended, he started visiting brothels. Such surroundings he found enabled him to pay close attention to the female body in natural and uninhibited attitudes as well as catering for his fierce sexual hunger. Three years later he went to live in a reputable establishment in the Rue des Moulins and spent the rest of his days there and in other residences for prostitutes. 'I found professional models like stuffed owls,' he explained. 'These daughters of joy are alive.'

Toulouse-Lautrec was an aristocrat spurned by women of his own class and his artistic genius would never have attained such full fruition had he not thus in this way found a milieu that suited him so admirably. No man could have been more popular with the prostitutes. He entertained them on their rest days in his studio, took them out to the theatre followed by supper at some fashionable restaurant, remembered their birthdays, bought them presents, and no one among all their clients could compare with him as a lover. He exhausted them and they enjoyed it.

The artist was upset when, in 1894, Mireille, the model of whom he was the most fond, went off to the Argentine, so he moved to a new *maison close* in the Rue des Moulins. He had already taken heavily to drink and was rarely sober. Given commission on liquor sold to their customers, the prostitutes coaxed him into consuming more and more until he was imbibing daily in excess of all the other male patrons put together. To get rid of him during the day, they would drag him out of his bed and bundle him, in an alcoholic daze, into a fiacre which would deposit him at his studio. There, after washing and shaving, he gulped down a few strong cocktails before starting work. Despite all those who feared that his insobriety would damage his brilliance, he painted with greater insight and assurance for his experiences had provided him with fresh subjects for his brush.

In 1897 Toulouse-Lautrec lost his heart to Aline, a girl related to him, and promised to renounce all alcoholic drink except port and submit to treatment in a clinic. But when Aline's father prevented him from seeing her again, he drowned his disappointment in worse dissipation, and this brought on an attack of delirium tremens. Detention in an asylum failed to cure him, for within a short period after being discharged he relapsed into his old ways.

A voluptuary, Lautrec enjoyed feasting his eyes in turn on the various parts of a woman's body. Red-heads he found irresistible. In his book, *Un Henri de Toulouse-Lautrec*, Thadée Natanson, who knew him intimately, wrote how he watched the artist 'purr with pleasure as he plunged his face into a woman's bosom, so that her huge breasts enclosed his neck'. He would snatch up from the floor a pair of women's stockings, roll them into a ball and breath in their scent with his eyes shut. Being so short, the first thing he noticed on looking up at a women was her nose and a beautifully shaped one acted as a magnet for his desire. It was this and something else that attracted him to the actress, Marcelle Lender. Every night at the theatre he sat in the same reserved seat, an end one on the left of the centre gangway in the orchestra stalls where he had a clear view of her dancing the bolero. Asked after his twenty-first visit, why he was doing this, he replied: 'I come simply to study her back. It's magnificent. Just look — you'll never see anything like that anywhere!'

As Laurence and Elisabeth Hanson point out in their life of Lautrec his drinking differed from the normal — the commonplace bored him. 'What greater fun than to mix one's own drinks, force them on hesitant and downright alarmed friends and swallow them oneself without turning a hair.' In his studio stood a table crowded with bottles containing every kind of alcoholic ambrosia likely to appeal to connoisseurs. The moment a visitor appeared, the artist would leave his easel, seize an apron, fasten it round his waist, turn up his sleeves, and set about preparing cocktails for them both. He was constantly experimenting with new combinations and the end product would be of a strength that made even the most inured toper blench. There was no sipping it slowly — just the opposite, followed by another and another. Ultimately, when his addiction peaked, he poured indiscriminately from all the bottles into a jug — brandy, rum, whisky, even absinthe — shook it, drank with abandon and made his guests do so, too.

XIV
GLUTTONY IN
THE GUILDHALL

Thomas Creevey in his memoirs describes the gluttonous behaviour prevalent at a Lord Mayor of London's banquet he attended in 1820. Above his table were three niches where sat 'three men in complete armour from top to toe, with immense plumes upon their helmets' and whose duty it was 'to rise and wave their truncheons when the Lord Mayor rose and gave his toasts; which they did with great effect, till one of them fainted away with the heat and fell out of his hole upon the heads of the people below'. For another such feast held in the Guildhall on 13 November 1828, the fare included 200 tureens of turtle, 60 dishes of fowls, 10 sirloins of beef, 50 roasted turkeys, and over a 1,000 dishes of dessert.

Free food and drink have been used down the ages for political and business purposes. At Horsham during the General Election of 1844, every public-house and place selling intoxicating liquor was taken over by the candidates and flew Blue or Pink flags to denote who was giving the free drinks inside. Labourers usually unable to afford anything dearer than small beer were able to order whatever they fancied. As a result, many of the male population of Horsham were continuously drunk for the whole six weeks before Polling Day.

In *My Life and Loves*, Frank Harris claimed that the striking reduction in drunkenness among the aristocracy in the latter part of the nineteenth century was brought about by Edward, Prince of Wales. Before he and his 'Smart Set' led the fashions, it was still the custom at dinner parties for the ladies to go and gossip in the drawing-room and leave the men to get sozzled on claret and port. But the Prince chose to drink black coffee and smoke a cigarette after the meal. No one, wrote Harris, who smoked could appreciate the bouquet of fine claret, and so the cigarette and coffee ended the habit of drinking heavily after dinner.

The Prince also preferred champagne to claret, and in the course of a single decade it became good form in society to join the ladies after having sipped a glass or two of champagne and a cup of coffee afterwards while smoking. 'Sobriety became the custom,' claimed Harris, 'and a man in society who drank to excess would soon find it impossible to discover where he would be tolerated.'

The old habit of eating and drinking to excess, however, still prevailed in the 1880s at civic dinners. Harris describes how he first experienced this on attending a Lord Mayor of London's banquet in 1883. He never missed one for years after this because of the light such functions cast on English habits. What struck him most was the extraordinary gluttony displayed by seven out of ten of the city aldermen. The one next to him gulped down his soup like an ogre, then whilst waiting for a second plateful, he took a swig from the jeroboam he kept on the floor beside him like his colleagues. Suddenly, he noticed the pieces of green meat remaining on Harris's plate and prodded them. 'Why do you leave that?' he demanded. 'It's the best part.' And before Harris could think of a reply, the 'ogre' was gobbling down the soup the waiter had served him. In barely a minute, the plate was again empty and the alderman was signalling for a third supply. 'I'll remember you, my man,' he whispered to the waiter, 'but see that you get me some green fat — I want some Calapash.'

'Is that what you call Calapash?' Harris inquired, pointing at the green gobbets on his own plate.

'Of course,' the other answered. 'They used to give you Calapash and Calipee with every plateful.' He explained that the former came from the upper shell and the latter from the lower shell of the turtle. 'Now eat that up. It'll go to your ribs and make a man of you. I gained three pounds at my first banquet I did — but then I'm six inches taller than you.'

Harris continues that his neighbour went on to fill his huge frame with 'a bellyful of Southdown mutton, three or four years old, that melted in one's mouth' and ended the evening by being sick before Harris could help him to his brougham. 'No place like this,' he declared nevertheless. 'The best food and the best drink in God's world and nothing to pay for it, nothing.'

It is not surprising that the alderman was so keen on turtle soup, for, according to John Timbs, in Victorian times some forty turtles were needed to make 250 tureens of soup. The poet, Thomas Hood (1799-1845), so concerned with the plight of the poor in *The Song of the Shirt*, in a convivial moment confessed:

> Of all the things I ever swallow
> Good, well dressed turtle beats them hollow.
> It almost makes me wish, I vow,
> To have two stomachs, like a cow.

Frank Harris who innumerates his sexual adventures in *My Life and Loves*, despised gluttons and wrote: 'Self indulgence in eating and drinking is simply loathsome and disgusting to all higher natures.' He gives another example of the excess that revolted him. It was at a dinner party given by Sir William Marriott, MP for Brighton, where Sir Robert Fowler, twice Lord Mayor of London, was also a guest together with half-a-dozen city magnates. Fowler was a large man at least 5 ft. 10 in. in height and 'much more in girth'. Harris was placed on 'washed-out, prim, little, kindly but undistinguished Lady Marriott's left-hand' opposite Sir Robert, who, on first sitting down, talked to them both, but, after the roast beef had been served, ignored them. 'Never have I seen a man stuff with such avidity. First, he had a helping of beef, then Yorkshire pudding and beef again. . . the veins of his forehead stood out like knotted cords and the beads of sweat poured down his red face.'

When they started on the game, Harris found the atmosphere in the small dining-room appalling. The partridges were so high that they fell apart when touched.

> I had never cultivated a taste for rotting meat and so I trifled with my bread and watched the convives. . . . Suddenly there came a loud unmistakable noise and then an overpowering odour. I stared at the big glutton opposite me, but he had already finished a third plateful of the exquisite Scotch beef and was wiping his forehead in serene unconsciousness of having done anything out of the common. I stole a glance at Lady Marriott. She was as white as a ghost and her first helping of meat still lay untouched on her plate. The quiet lady avoided my eyes and had evidently made up her mind to endure to the end. But the atmosphere got worse and worse, the smells stronger and stronger, till I rejoiced every time a servant opened the door, whether to go out or come in.

All the guests were eating as if their lives depended on how much they ate, and the butler and the four men-servants were plainly insufficient to cope with the situation.

> I have never in my life seen men gormandize to be compared with these men. And the curious thing was that as course followed course their appetite seemed to increase. Certainly the smell got worse and worse, and when the savoury of soft herring roes on toast came on the board, the orgy degenerated into a frenzy.

Harris writes that there was another unmistakable explosion and his hostess went deadly pale. 'I'm not very well,' she murmured to him. 'I don't think I can see it through.' Rising, he responded, 'Why should you? Come upstairs — we'll never be missed.'

Lady Marriott drew a long breath as they sat down in the pure air of the drawing-room, and then she confided that it was her first experience of eating in the company of City bigwigs. She added: 'And I hope devoutly it may be my last. How perfectly awful men can be.'

Back home, Harris gave himself what he describes as a 'good wash-out' with his stomach pump, a gadget which he considered essential to health on such occasions.

Frank Harris clearly felt like Joseph Addison, who, in the early eighteenth century, wrote in *The Spectator* for 13 October 1711:

> It is said of Diogenes that meeting a young man who was going to a Feast, he took him from the street and carried him to his Friends, as one who was running into imminent danger, had he not prevented him. What would that Philosopher have said had he been present at the Gluttony of a modern Meal? . . . For my part, when I behold a fashionable Table set out in all its magnificence, I fancy that I see Gouts and Dropsies, Fevers, and Lethargies, with the innumerable Distempers lying in Ambuscade among the Dishes.

And nearer our days E. C. Dodds, discussing diet, exercise and weight in the *Middlesex Hospital Journal* for October 1933, calculated that — 'to work off the calories provided by a single good City banquet it will be necessary to take exercise equivalent to climbing Ben Nevis five times'.

The City banquet surpassing all others in the nineteenth century was undoubtedly that given on the 25th of October 1851, in the Gothic Hall at York, by all the Mayors of England, Wales, and Northern Ireland to Prince Albert and the Lord Mayor of London. The great chef, Alexis

Soyer, prepared the most expensive dish of his career for the royal table, which he called: *L'Extravagance Culinaire à l'Alderman* or *The Hundred Guinea Dish*. In his memoirs, Soyer wrote: 'The opportunity of producing some gastronomic phenomenon for the royal table was irresistible, accordingly the following choice morsels were selected from all the birds mentioned in the general bill of fare, to form a dish worthy of his Royal Highness and the noble guests around him. The extravagance of the dish, valued at 100 guineas, can be realised by supposing that if an epicure were to order one for a small party he would be obliged to provide the undermentioned articles.' Soyer then listed what he used: 5 turtle heads, part of the fins, and green fat, 2 noix only in each case from 24 capons, 18 turkeys, 18 fatted pullets, and 16 fowls; the noix only of 20 pheasants, 45 partridges, 100 snipe, 40 woodcocks, 36 pigeons; the whole of 10 grouse, 6 plovers, 36 quails; 72 stuffed larks; and ortolans from Belgium. The garniture consisted of cocks' combs, truffles, mushrooms, crawfish, olives, American asparagus, croustades, sweetbreads, *quenelles de volailles*, green mangoes, and a new sauce created by him.

The purpose of all this excess was in this case a worthwhile one. The idea of holding the Great Exhibition of 1851 had been Prince Albert's, but the Cabinet had refused to finance the enterprise so he campaigned to raise the money privately and the banquet was organized to gather together under one roof those wealthy enough to contribute the large sums required. The plan succeeded and the Exhibition made a handsome profit justifying the Prince's imaginative project.

Temperance reformers were delighted that no alcoholic drinks were allowed to be served inside the Crystal Palace. The public paid 6*d*. a glass instead for lemonade, soda, or ginger beer — a total of 1,092,336 bottles of this being supplied.

XV

EDWARDIAN VOLUPTUARIES

Even before King Edward VII's accession, in the reign of Queen Victoria, large amounts of food were delivered daily at Buckingham Palace from the royal estates. She often served her guests with quail stuffed with pâté de foie gras, surrounded by oysters, truffles, prawns, mushrooms, tomatoes and croquettes. She regarded Welsh lamb as the most tender and would have only that at her table. There would normally be ten courses at luncheon and twelve at dinner, and half-way through the meal sorbets flavoured with port or brandy refreshed one's palate.

Queen Victoria herself was a light eater, unlike some of her ministers. Denison, the Speaker of the House of Commons, recorded in his diary details of a dinner to which Lord Palmerston invited him in 1865:

> Dined with the Prime Minister who was upwards of eighty years of age. He ate for dinner two plates of turtle soup; he was then served very amply to a plate of cod and oyster sauce; he then took a pâté; afterwards he was helped to two very greasy looking entrées; he then despatched a plate of roast mutton; then there appeared before him the largest and to my mind the hardest slice of ham that ever figured on the table of a

nobleman, yet it disappeared, just in time to answer the inquiry of his butler, 'Snipe, my lord, or pheasant?' He instantly replied 'pheasant', thus completing his ninth dish of meat at that meal.

In the provinces, according to Abraham Hayward, the lord lieutenant of one of the western counties ate a covey of partridges for breakfast during the season, and a popular MP would eat a Solan goose as a whet.

Edward VII rarely missed his elevenses at Buckingham Palace, usually a lobster salad or cold chicken. There were normally fourteen courses at luncheon and the same at dinner. He was particularly fond of a dish that had been popular with his father's family in Germany — a turkey stuffed with a chicken which contained a pheasant and inside which was a woodcock packed with truffles. The whole was covered with pastry and served cold. The richer the dish, the more he enjoyed it, such as grilled oysters, crayfish cooked in Chablis, deer pudding, and quails filled with foie gras in a sherry-flavoured jelly. As he often felt hungry in between meals, side tables in the royal apartment were kept stocked with sandwiches, York cakes, and Parmesan biscuits, as well as a quail or a cutlet. By his bed would be placed a cold truffled chicken which his valet used to find picked to the bones in the morning.

The Coronation banquet was a triumph for the chef, Menager, and the forty-five members of his kitchen staff, the *pièce de résistance* being the *côtelettes de bécassines à la Souvaroff*, the boned snipe full of forcemeat and foie gras, grilled in a pig's caul, and served with Madeira sauce on a bed of truffles. The following year, 1903, Lord Roseberry delighted the King by entertaining him to a marathon dinner of twenty-two courses. Freed from his grumbling appendix, 'Tum Tum', as Edward was nicknamed, went on indulging in five meals a day until he died.

Rudyard Kipling called Edward VII 'a corpulent voluptuary' and news of his many amours spread round the world. In the United States, *Town Topics* told its readers:

'There is nothing between the Prince of Wales and Mrs Langtry.' Then, a week later, it added: 'Not even a sheet'. In Paris, the police regarded him as a satyr, after they had shadowed him visiting a dozen demi-mondaines during one visit alone. They included the self-styled greatest whore in the world, Giulia Barucci. According to William Wiser in *The Crazy Years*, the Prince would disport himself at 12 Rue Chabannais 'in sumptuous private chambers furnished with a copper baignoire filled with champagne, and a throne of his own design that permitted semi-reclining dalliance with more than one favourite at a time'.

Men from the English upper classes were not usually regarded as powerful lovers by the courtesans of Paris, which was perhaps why Napoleon III's mistress, the Contessa di Castiglione, said 'Yes' when the fourth Marquis of Hertford wrote to her: 'Give me one night of love, without excluding any erotic refinements, in exchange for one million francs'. Once in her house overlooking the Café des Anglais, he proved to be a stallion. After he left, she was so exhausted that she could not move for three days.

Other English aristocrats with similar inclinations to Hertford's enjoyed gatecrashing two annual balls that ignored all bourgeois restrictions and gave rein to excesses of all kinds. That of the *Interns* took place in the autumn to celebrate the end of examinations and was restricted to members of the Medical School and their guests. Nudity was obligatory. Soon after midnight vehicles would collect the students from the hospitals and unload them at the *Salle Wagram* near the *Etoile* which had been let to them for a night of ribald revelry. The proceedings began with the choosing by popular vote of a Queen of the Ball, followed by a display of erotic tableaux vivants on floats. Many bore prodigious phalluses encircled by fauns and satyrs who gambolled and ravished shrieking nymphs. Although the ball was supposed to be attended only by those connected with the medical profession, attractive young girls eager to pass the night amorously were smuggled in. Some came from afar, hoping to pass the time until dawn touring the hospital boxes and enjoying sexual fun.

With the spring came the *Bal des Quatz' Arts,* first held by art students at the *Elysée-Montmartre* in 1891. One year everybody was supposed to be dressed as ancient Egyptians, another year as Romans and so on, but not much attention was paid to historical accuracy. The four arts in question were painting, engraving, architecture, and sculpture. Again it was more like a saturnalia than a ball, rising to a climax for its celebrated characteristic, the 'uprising' when the carousing crowds surged across the Seine from the Left to the Right Banks.

A leader of Edwardian voluptuaries was the Duke of Devonshire's heir, Lord Hartington, known as 'Harty Tarty', who before entertaining King Edward VII to dinner bought eighty new liveries of gold cloth for his house footmen, while his father would welcome the King to Chatsworth with torchbearers stationed on either side of the long avenue and fireworks bejewelling the sky. To please his royal guest's passion for ortolans, the Duke imported these costly buntings from France and had them served, three to a plate, at dinner, whilst a brilliant orchestra, specially engaged for the visit, played waltzes for Queen Alexandra's delight.

During such house parties, when they were not eating, ladies spent much of their time changing their clothes, which they did on the average six times a day, bringing with them for that purpose many huge trunks. At breakfast the sideboards would be packed with silver dishes, heated by spirit lamps, and filled with porridge, cream, haddock, poached eggs, bacon, chicken, woodcock, whatever game was in season, savouries, and cold meats. Of course, there was an array of China and Indian teas, coffee, and cold drinks as well as toast, marmalade, honey, all sorts of jams, and heaps of melons, nectarines, peaches, and other fruit. For lunch, one expected at least eight courses. Tea was a meal in itself and dinner with often more than twelve courses did not end the day's stuffing for who could sleep without a snack of sandwiches and devilled chicken moistened with a whisky and soda or brandy?

J. B. Priestley in *The Edwardians* wrote that the English house party of those times gave opportunities for discreet love affairs. A guest's bedroom door held a tiny brass frame into which the hostess would insert a card bearing the name of the occupant which facilitated visits to single or divorced ladies or those unaccompanied by their husbands. 'The lusty males, crammed with all that Edwardian food and inflamed by all its drink, were constantly tempted . . . avidly longing to discover what the women were really like once the frippery and finery and social disguise were removed.' After a little tap, the male in search of sexual sport would open the door and enter the room where 'the delicious creature with bared bosom, and those great marmoreal thighs, was waiting'.

Lord Cardigan, surprised by a husband he had believed miles away suddenly arriving, was quick-witted enough to whisper: 'Hush! Don't wake her — I was passing — thought I smelt smoke, but all's well.' Lord Charles Beresford, however, leapt onto the double bed crying: 'Cockle-a-doodle-doo!' and found himself between a bishop and his wife.

Those not so fortunate as to be visited by lovers found vicarious excitement in the pages of the new genre of romantic novels that shocked the prudish, such as those of Elinor Glyn, who wrote in *Three Weeks*:

> A madness of tender caressing seized her. She purred as a tiger might have done, while she undulated like a snake. She touched him with her finger-tips, she kissed his throat, his wrists, the palms of hands, his eyelids, his hair. Strange subtle kisses, unlike the kisses of women. And often, between her purrings, she murmured love-words in some fierce language of her own, brushing his ears and his eyes with her lips the while. And through it all, Paul slept on, the Eastern perfume in the air drugging his senses.

Two million copies of this were sold by 1916 and five million by 1933. Basically, it is not all that different from the permissive novel of today — just add a few four-letter words and 'pubic' in front of 'hair'.

Not only did high society eat excessively but there was excessive waste in its preparation. Gabriel Tschumi wrote in his memoirs about his experiences as royal chef. After a banquet, he revealed:

> Sometimes dozens of pheasants or soufflés in which four or five dozen eggs had been used found their way to the garbage pails. So did quantities of salmon, sturgeon, trout or foie gras, which had been spoilt at some stage of their preparation. No one can learn cuisine without making a good many mistakes in the process, and it is essential that those learning have the best materials at their disposal. The standard of cuisine was so high in Victorian days at Buckingham Palace simply because there was ample food with which they could demonstrate their skill.

Similar prodigality went on in the kitchens of the aristocracy. For example, Lord Alvanley always had his *suprême de volaille* made of the oyster bits instead of the breast fillets, so that it took twenty fowls to complete a single dish.

One might have thought that a banquet to publicize Apollinaris water would have had fewer and simpler courses than customary. When the English company which had launched it decided to exploit the Johannes source at Zollhaus, they engaged César Ritz to organize the affair. The Prince of Wales, Grand Duke Michael of Russia, Lord and Lady de Grey, and others taking the cure at Bad Homburg to lose weight and regain better health, went to the source for the luncheon and were served with *Caviar Astrakhan, Consommé Viveur, Truite au bleu Zollhaus, Selle de Chevreuil Grand-Duc, Purée de Marrons, Gelée de groseilles, Désirs du Prince de Galles, Salade Argenteuil, Pêches Melba,* and *Corbeille de Fruit.*

175

As Marie Ritz points out in *Host to the World*, it is amusing to note that, although the object of the banquet was to promote a mineral water, not a single bottle of Apollinaris or of any other kind was served. The following wines and liqueurs accompanied the various courses instead: *Marcobrunner, Bernkasteler Doktor, Moët et Chandon Poysère 1884, Musigny 1860, Château Yquem 1865, Grande Fine Champagne de Napoléon 1800, Grande Chartreuse 1812.*

Marie Ritz wrote that 'a repast of the most fantastic order' took place in 1891 at the exclusive Amphitryon in Albemarle Street, London, when King Milan of Serbia gave a dinner party in a private room the walls of which were completely covered with orchids. The King had no table manners, ate the meat with his fingers, and threw the chicken bones on the carpet. One of the most gluttonous celebrities her father had ever watched eat was the French statesman, Gambetta, who devoured three *perdreaux truffés* and four *sorbets au rhum* at one sitting.

Somerset Maugham used to tell a story about a peer much given to an extravagant night life and on whom he called one morning. 'What time does his Lordship usually breakfast?' Maugham asked. He said that the butler's impassive reply was typical of the mood of the Edwardian era. It was: 'His Lordship does not breakfast, sir. His Lordship is usually sick at about eleven.'

In America, the most gluttonous character of those times must have been 'Diamond' Jim Brady who weighed eighteen stone, had three chins and a stomach six times the size of normal, and who would eat a twelve-course dinner, plus three extra helpings of each main dish, finishing with a twelve-egg soufflé. It was said that Jim liked his oysters 'sprinkled with clams' and his steaks 'smothered in veal cutlets'. Strangers often bet on whether or not he would be carried out feet first from Rector's, as they watched the disappearance of four dozen extra-large oysters, followed by the restaurant's famed Lobster American (with two crustaceans instead of the usual one), and a dozen hard-shelled crabs — after which he was ready for his main dish. 'Whenever I sit down to a meal', Brady once disclosed, 'I always make it a point to leave just four inches between my stummick and the edge of the table. And then when I can feel 'em rubbin' together pretty hard, I know I've had enough'.

Whilst some men like Brady were proud of their girth, there were others who made occasional attempts to reduce it, especially if it began to affect their health. In Europe, there were several fashionable spas where one could take the cure for obesity. Some were so gross that they could hardly walk, like the Egyptian merchant Achmed el Gamel who weighed thirty stone. *The Tatler* for 22 July 1903, stated: 'The paramount reason for going abroad after Goodwood is consciousness of embonpoint, especially among women.'

XVI

'YAMA THE PIT'
AND 'DEAD SOULS'

There have been few in Western Europe able to match the capacity of Russians to drink heavily and yet stay sober. King Edward VII's brother, Alfred, Duke of Edinburgh, when in command of a naval squadron in the Mediterranean, managed this and later advised a friend faced with the same problem. 'I can give you a recipe,' the Duke said. 'Whenever I am invited to dine on a Russian ship, I always take the precaution of drinking half a liqueur glass of salad oil, just before I start. I can then drink brandy to their claret and drink them all under the table. The oil prevents any fumes rising to the brain so that I remain perfectly sober. Of course, I take a strong purge directly I get back.'

In Russia itself, the fare provided at great banquets dwarfed that served at similar functions in the West. In his *Memoirs of a British Agent*, R. H. Bruce Lockhart tells how three days of gargantuan feasting ended with a banquet held in an immense palace of a hotel and given by the sugar kings of Moscow.

> I describe it in detail because it gives an amazing picture of the Moscow which existed before the war and which will never come again. To meet the British

delegates, every official, every notable, every millionaire in Moscow had been invited, and when I arrived I found a throng like a theatre queue struggling on the staircases. The whole house was a fairyland of flowers brought all the way from Nice. Orchestras seemed to be playing in every antechamber.

At long narrow tables, vodka and the most delicious *zakuski*, both hot and cold, were being served by scores of waiters to the standing guests. When, at last, they sat down to dinner, Lockhart says that so many courses and so many varieties of wine were served that he lost count of them. 'The meal lasted till eleven o'clock and would have taxed the intestines of a giant.'

Exiled after the Revolution, some Russians still retained an appetite for food, drink and sex that those in the lands where they settled found excessive. For example, the Grand Duchess Anastasia Michaelovna resided in a villa in Eze on the French Riviera from which she would descend regularly in search of lusty young men. When she came across one she fancied, she invited him to her eyrie. He would emerge some days later, exhausted. One of the Grand Duchess's victims encountering another, gasped: 'She is like the measles. Everybody should go through the experience. Once you've had it, you never want to have it again.'

The excesses of prostitution in Russia itself were exposed in Alexandre Kuprin's brilliant novel, *Yama the Pit*, which portrays with uncompromising realism and some satire life in the brothels regarded as a public service under the Tsars. Kuprin begins by taking us to a small southern town far from Moscow where towards the end of the nineteenth century both main streets came to be occupied by over thirty houses of ill fame, except for five or six beer halls and general stores catering to the needs of the prostitutes. The most expensive establishment, Treffel's, provided large German women with ample breasts in low-cut, fur-trimmed ball gowns or dressed as hussars, pages, schoolgirls and so on. An hour cost three roubles, and a whole night ten. The other brothels in Great Yamskaya were two and one roubles houses, while in Little Yamskaya, frequented by soldiers, artisans, petty thieves and the like, squalid dives charged only fifty kopecks or less. Here, the inmates in rags of coloured printed calico or in sailor costumes were for the greater part 'hoarse or snuffling, with noses half fallen through, with faces preserving traces of yesterday's blows and scratches and naïvely made up with the aid of a red cigarette box moistened with spit'.

Kuprin goes on to evoke the ceaseless carnival of lust.

> All the year round, every evening — with the exception of the last three days of Holy Week and the night before the Annunciation . . . till the very morning thousands of men ascend and descend these stairs . . . half-shattered, slavering ancients, seeking artificial excitements — military cadets and high school lads — bearded paterfamilias — honourable pillars of society in golden spectacles — disappointed bridegrooms — renowned professors — murderers and liberal lawyers — strict guardians of morals — pedagogues — authors of impassioned articles on the rights of women . . . the timid and the brazen, those knowing woman for the first time, and old libertines . . . pot-bellied, haemorrhoidal apes. They come as to a restaurant; they sit, smoke, drink, assume a feverish merriment; they cavort, executing lewd antics. . . . And the women with indifferent readiness, with uniform words, with practised professional movements, satisfy their desires, like machines. . . . And so, day after day, for months and years, they live a strange, incredible life in their public harems, outcast by society, victims of the social temperament, cloacas for the excess of the city's sexuality, the guardians of the honour of the family — four hundred foolish, lazy, hysterical, barren women.

But the world is constantly changing. 'For decades,' wrote Kuprin, 'life flows evenly, and suddenly after some altogether insignificant incident or other . . . new elements rush in, and, behold, after two years there is not one of the previous people on the spot.' Something resembling this overtook Yama. It originated with an unusually abundant crop of sugar beets leading to the building in the vicinity of three refineries, the advent of electricity and new main roads, followed by a frenzy for building which seized the whole town.

> Two new steamer lines came into being, and they, together with the ones already in existence, competed with each other. This became so fierce that rates for third class passengers were lowered from seventy-five to five, three, two, and even one kopeck. In the end, one line in desperation offered a free passage to all the third class passengers. Then its competitor at once added to the free passage half-a-loaf of white bread as well. But the biggest enterprise was the extensive development of the river port which attracted thousands of labourers.

Yama, apart from its brothels, had a famous monastery nearby and when this now celebrated its millennial anniversary countless pilgrims flocked there. 'The population of the city increased well-nigh fourfold. Stonemasons, carpenters, painters, engineers, technicians, agriculturists, shady business men, river navigators, thieves . . . all this noisy, foreign band full of easy money . . . insatiable beasts in the image of men, with all their massed will clamoured: "Give us women!" '

For the casual arrivals, servants were demanded, and hundreds of peasant girls moved from the surrounding villages into Yama. It was inevitable that the demand on prostitution should become unusually high. And so from all over Russia, even from abroad, flocked a multitude of cocottes. 'Despite the fact that the madams had increased their staff to more than double and trebled prices, their poor demented girls could not catch up in satisfying the demands of the drunken, crazed public squandering money on sex. The waiting-rooms were packed and there were queues outside.'

It was then that Simon Yakovlevich Horizon arrived in Yama.

Now he was one of the chief speculators in the body of woman in all the south of Russia. He had transactions with Constantinople and with the Argentine; he transported whole parties of girls from the brothels of Odessa into Kiev; those from Kiev he brought over into Kharkov; and those from Kharkov into Odessa. He also shifted from important cities to second rate ones goods which had been rejected or had lost their bloom. He had built up an enormous clientèle among people with prominent social positions as well as with the owners of brothels, madams of houses of assignation, *cocottes solitaires*, go-betweens, *souteneurs*, touring actresses and chorus girls. His amazing memory, which enabled him to prudently dispense with written records, stored thousands of names, addresses, characteristics. . . . Two or three times he had been jailed, but this had in no way dampened his daring and every year he had become more inventive and enterprising.

Fifteen times he had managed to marry and every time had contrived to collect a fine dowry. Having possessed himself of his wife's money, he, one day, would suddenly vanish without a trace, and, if possible, he would sell his wife profitably to a secret house of depravity or to a *chic* public establishment. . . . He had changed his name so many times that he could not remember them all.

Remarkably, he did not find anything criminal or reprehensible about his business activities. He regarded them just as though he were trading in herrings, flour, beef or lumber. . . . He was attracted to the business rather by its tang, risk, and a professional self-conceit. To the women, he was perfectly indifferent, although he understood and could value them, and in this respect resembled a good chef, who knows all about food but suffers from a chronic lack of appetite.

With Horizon's coming, everything changed on Yamskaya Street. From Treffel's, girls were transferred to Anna Markovna's two-rouble establishment, and from hers to a one-rouble establishment, and from the latter to a half-rouble one. There were no promotions — only demotions.

And then, one night, two dragoons, short-changed in a one-rouble brothel, protested angrily and were beaten up and thrown out by Horizon's strong-arm men.

Battered and bruised they staggered back to the barracks. A hundred enraged comrades made for Yamskaya Street and began to wreck house after house. They were joined by an immense drunken mob, which smashed all the window panes. The naked women were driven outside with the ripped-open feather beds, and for some two days the countless bits of down flew and whirled over the town like flakes of snow. The rabble also looted the taverns and drink-shops in the vicinity, and beat three porters to death. . . .

The rioting went on for some seven hours until the military and the fire brigade finally succeeded in repulsing and scattering the multitude. However, next day the tumult again flared up; this time all over the city and its environs. And, a week later, the governor-general ordered every brothel in Yama to be immediately closed down.

Crushed and plundered, ludicrous and pitiful, the aged, faded proprietresses and fat-faced, hoarse housekeepers hastily packed up their remaining possessions and departed. And a month later, only the name Yamskaya

Street reminded one of the sexual excesses that used to thrive there. But even that name was soon replaced by another more respectable one. . . .

And all these women — always naïve and foolish, often touching and amusing, and in the majority of cases deceived and perverted children — were scattered through the big city. From them evolved a new stratum of society, the strolling, solitary street-walkers.

Alexandre Kuprin ends his novel by saying that about their lives 'just as pitiful and incongruous, but tinged by other interests and customs' he would some time tell. But the cataclysmal events of the First World War and the Russian Revolution prevented him from doing so.

An earlier novelist, Nikolai Gogol (1809-52), satirized other excesses of society in the Russia of his time. In *Dead Souls*, gluttony is one of his targets. Chichikov operates an ingenious confidence trick, travelling through the country buying dead serfs from landowners who otherwise would have to pay a tax on each one to the government until the next census, as the law regarded them as alive until then. Having acquired them, his plan is to purchase land, people it on paper with these defunct workers thus increasing enormously its value, raise a large mortgage and decamp abroad with the money. Several of the characters Chichikov encounters make food and drink their main interest in life, such as Pyotr Petrovich Petukh whose entire income is spent on extravagant hospitality and who is heavily in debt as a result. When Chichikov dined with him, six decanters of wine stood upon the table together with every kind of tempting savoury snacks. After these appetizers had been consumed, the meal proper was served.

As soon as Petukh noticed that a guest had only one piece of anything left on his plate, he helped him to another, saying: 'Neither man nor bird or beast can survive without pairing.' If one had two morsels left, he added a third, declaring: 'Two doesn't go far. God favours the Trinity.' Three bits left would make him cry:

'Have you ever seen a cart run on three wheels?' He had an apt phrase for four morsels and also for five.

'Chichikov had eaten almost a dozen slices of meat and was telling himself: "Well, now that's floored him." But he was quite wrong, for without a word his host laid on his plate several grilled veal chops including the kidneys — and what delicious chops they were, too! "I reared that calf for two years on milk," said Petukh. "I looked after him as I would my own son."

' "I really can't manage any more," protested Chichikov.

' "But you must try them first before you say that."

' "I've no room left."

' "There was no room in church, but when the Mayor came in, room was made for him," Petukh retorted. "Yet there was such a crush that an apple couldn't have fallen to the floor. Just try — imagine that morsel is the Mayor!"

'Chichikov tried and the veal did manage to squeeze into a space that he had not thought existed. "How will such a man survive in St Petersburg or Moscow?," he asked himself. "With such a hospitable nature he would ruin himself within three years." . . .'

Petukh was equally generous with the wine. He kept replenishing the glasses of the guests and when they refused to drink any more, he gave what remained to his sons, who finished it in no time. By the end of the feast the diners could hardly drag themselves on to the verandah and sink into armchairs. Their host settled himself in one that could have held four average-sized persons and promptly fell asleep. 'His corpulent person was transformed into a bellows; from his open mouth and his nostrils he began to emit sounds such as not to be found even in the most modern music. All the instruments were represented such as the drum, the flute, and an intermittent dog-like bark. . . .'

They gorged again over supper. When Chichikov retired at last to his bedroom, he felt his stomach as he got into bed. 'No Mayor could squeeze into it now,' he said to himself. It so happened that his host's bedroom was next door. The wall was a thin one and through it could be heard what was being said on the other side. Petukh was instructing his cook to prepare a veritable banquet for next day's lunch.

'And it was enough to revive a corpse. "Make the fish pie a four cornered affair," he was saying as he sucked in his breath. "In one corner put the cheeks of a sturgeon and the jelly from its back — in another some buckwheat, mushrooms, and onions, and some soft roe and some brains — and something else — you know. . . . Yes, and see that the crust is well browned on one side and a trifle less on the other. And as for the underpart, see that it's baked just right and doesn't crumble, but is soaked in juice and melts in the mouth like snow." Petukh smacked his lips as he spoke.

' "Confound him! He won't let me sleep," Chichikov thought and he tucked his head under the quilt. But even through its thickness he could hear his host saying: "And stuff the sturgeon well with beetroot, smelts, mushrooms, turnips, carrots, beans, and anything else you consider appropriate. And see that it's richly garnished. And as for the pig's belly when you fill that with minced meat and buckwheat, add a little ice to make it swell up properly."

'Petukh ordered many other dishes. Chichikov could hear him urging the cook to "bake it thoroughly", to "roast it right", and to "stew it properly" — and he fell asleep listening to the instructions for a turkey.'

After lunch next day the guests ate and drank so much that when they departed, one of them, Platinov, was incapable of mounting his horse which had to be ridden by a stable boy instead. 'At last they were in the carriage. The big-headed dog, having also gorged and gorged, padded unsteadily after it. "It's too much," said Chichikov when they had driven out of the courtyard. Platinov agreed. "And yet he is not bored with it all!" he added. "What a pity!" '

XVII

ABANDON IN AMERICA

Turning to the American scene, we find that McDowell's revelations of how rampant vice was throughout both the city and state of New York caused a sensation in the 1860s. As it gave the names and addresses of so many brothels, the flippant called it the 'Whorehouse Directory'. Puritans were disgusted to read first-hand accounts of American sailors' indiscriminate sex when they went ashore at ports in the Mediterranean, at Hawaii and elsewhere, and of the orgies aboard warships when South Sea virgins were entertained in Tahiti harbour. McDowell made a mistake in holding an exhibition of obscene books, prints, and instruments for unnatural sex, admission to which was supposed to be limited to clergymen. He was attacked on the grounds that he was publicizing wickedness. One social reformer, Robert Dale Owen, only supported him, arguing that if the Magdalen Society's estimate of 20,000 active prostitutes in New York City were correct and if each one had three customers a day that gave an annual turnover of 10 million, which could be interpreted as meaning that half of the males in the city's adult population had illicit intercourse thrice weekly.

The Civil War boosted prostitution and Bishop Simpson of the Methodist Episcopal Church claimed that at the height of hostilities there were in New York just as many prostitutes as members of his persuasion, whilst Dr Edward Bliss Foote estimated that there were then some 100,000 prostitutes in the whole country. An English visitor, William Hepworth Dixon, who edited *The Athenaeum* in London, wrote in *New America* in 1867:

> Men who know New York far more than myself assure me that in depth and darkness of iniquity, neither Paris in its private haunts, nor London in its open streets, can hold a candle to it. . . . For largeness of depravity, for domineering insolence of sin, for rowdy callousness to censure, they tell me Atlantic City finds no rival on earth.

Two years later, a widely-read American writer, George Ellington, in *Women of New York*, referred to the 'grossest immoralities' and 'Bacchanalian orgies' that rendered many of the city's parks unsafe.

The hordes that made for California in search of gold provided a new market for vice of all kinds. Prostitutes flocked there from Europe and South America as well as from the East Coast, and the French Government solved the problem of the glut of demi-mondaines in Paris by shipping over 300 of them.

It was only human that those with excessive wealth should be tempted into spending much of it on mistresses and lavish living. No attractive maid remained long unmolested in Commodore Vanderbilt's household, and Leonard K. Jerome, who had fountains playing eau de cologne and champagne at his balls, would shock the prudish on Sundays by driving up Fifth Avenue in his carriage with his harem of lovely ladies, while his wife stayed at home. Also to be seen taking the air, after a hectic Saturday night, might be lovely Josie Woods, owner of the city's most expensive bordello. And on the corner of Fifth Avenue and 52nd Street stood an obese brownstone palace built with the lucre collected by the millionairess and abortionist, Mme Restall. Those who prided themselves on upholding moral standards flaunted their opulence in other ways. Mrs William Backhouse Astor, Junior, dressed her servants in blue liveries that were faithful copies of those worn by Queen Victoria's. Guests at dinner ate for three hours, course after course, off heavy gold plates. In her ballroom, Mrs Astor sat on a kind of throne, wearing a tiara on her transformation and diamond stars pinned to the uncovered parts of her false hair, whilst round her neck she flaunted a three-tiered diamond necklace. Twelve rows of diamonds fell over her bosom, below which scintillated her diamond stomacher. For effect, when going to sit in her box in the Metropolitan's Diamond Horseshoe, she would kick at the large jewel suspended from a gold chain attached to her waist.

The top people in this moneyed aristocracy, known as the 'Five Hundred', competed with one another in acquiring whatever their insatiable appetites craved — from titled husbands for their daughters to the latest gold-plated plumbing. Victor Herbert's hit song expressed well their attitude — *I Want What I Want When I Want It*. César Ritz prospered because he understood them. 'Always serve the thinnest toast,' he instructed a commis. 'Our clients like to taste the caviar.'

'Smiling' Charlie Schwab of the Bethlehem Steel Corporation wanted food to be constantly and immediately available, so he had his mansion on Riverside Drive, New York, furnished with an outsize refrigerator storing twenty tons of every kind of meat, and Schwab kept three chefs at his beck and call to cook it. What five Texan brothers, oil millionaires, the Dorns, wanted perfectly mixed whenever they wanted them were dry Martinis, so they went to vast expense to have a fridge fitted with gadgetry that supplied them with these every time the door was opened. For several days and nights they held parties drinking with their pals, then they lost all interest.

When heiress, 'Fifi' Widener of the gigantic bust, whose annual income exceeded $1,000,000, rented Blair Castle for seven years from the Duke of Atholl, she never at any time had fewer than thirty-six guests staying with her, and each breakfast tray sent up to a bedroom would be laden with a large jug of cream and a pound of butter — most of which was later thrown into the kitchen fire. In London, American hostess, Laura Corrigan, had a steady stream of strangers ringing her front door bell on the flimsiest pretext because she had given instructions that every caller was to be served with a cocktail. Often, acting on a whim, she would decide to give a party and phone Fortnum and Mason and order everything on sale in their delicatessen department.

Prohibition was intended to destroy the Demon Drink in the United States, but instead, it spawned a legion of more Demons. Within a short while the suppressed 15,000 legal saloons in New York were replaced by 32,000 speakeasies. Shops thrived selling complete kits for making hooch at home together with all the necessary ingredients. Stomach linings were scarified by boot-leg liquor of appalling quality appropriately dubbed coffin varnish, craw rot, rot gut, horse liniment, tarantula juice, strike-me-dead, belch, sheep-dip, etc. The code word for bourbon was hypo and a gin drink, nitric acid. Whisky was aged with an electric needle. All the States were awash with liquor.

The permissive society was the result in many respects of the futile attempt to enforce prohibition. 'The deportment and language of the gangsters and their molls were aped by the swells,' as one writer pointed out, 'and the patois of prison-yard and call-house became the lingua franca of society. It was the saloon and not the salon which set the tone.'

As Polly Adler, owner of New York's most notorious bordello in those times, stressed in her reminiscences some of the saloons and night clubs most frequented by socialites had gangsters as proprietors, such as Jack Diamond, Dutch Schutz, and Larry Fay. At 'The Mansion', Belle Livingstone made her customers pay more than elsewhere for the privilege of doing their boozing on the floor,

Japanese style. 'A man could get hurt,' she quipped, 'falling off a bar stool.' The twenties were a period, says Polly, of 'senseless cavortings, determined squandering, guzzling and wenching of the newly rich monsters outrageously at play.' She admits frankly: 'If I had all history to choose from, I could hardly have picked a better time in which to be a madam.'

In 1926, there were banner headlines in the New York papers above vivid descriptions of Earl Carroll's bath-tub party during which a Miss Joyce Howley was immersed nude in champagne and several hundred guests queued to help her wash. The party was actually given to welcome to the States the Countess of Cathcart, following her detention at Ellis Island on charges of moral turpitude, alleging that she had lived in sin in Africa with an English peer. Later, Carroll was tried for perjury because, when prosecuted for having champagne in his house, he had sworn that it was only water.

During the winter of 1935 Polly Adler's girls were working at Colette's in Florida where they had to masquerade as the film stars they most resembled. A blonde might call herself Lana Turner, a brunette Hedy Lamarr, and so on. This caught on, and men congregated at Colette's in order to be able to brag next day: 'I slept with that passion flower, Pola Negri,' or whoever was his favourite movie pin-up. At the time, it was estimated that there were a million prostitutes in the States.

The most talked-about madams in the history of American vice were the Everleigh Sisters who opened their luxurious three-storeyed mansion on South Dearborn Street in Chicago on 1 February, 1900. They had fourteen reception rooms with appropriate names, such as the Rose Room, the Moorish Room, and the Gold Room which was furnished with cuspidors, a grand piano, chairs, and drapes, all of 18 carat gold. The bedrooms had special features, one in Turkish style (like the ballroom) had a mattress on the floor, and another at the touch of a button sprayed perfume upon the love couch. The two sisters,

Minna and Aida, prided themselves on their appreciation of art and their knowledge of literature and they had a gallery of fine paintings and a library full of 'classics' on which they spent a good part of their profits. Minna loved roses and the house was filled with fresh ones at all seasons. Their fame spread so swiftly and even to Europe that, when, in 1902, the Kaiser's brother, Prince Henry of Prussia, came to the States and was asked which of its many wonders he would like to see most, he immediately answered: 'The Everleigh Club.' Many other foreign royalties were to follow his lead. Famous sportsmen, like Gentleman Jim Corbett, and actors, like John Barrymore, passed at least a night there. The members of a Congressional committee conducting an investigation in Chicago concluded that the most convenient way of combining business with *joie de vivre* was to stay at the Everleigh and they did a great deal of their interviewing in the boudoirs upstairs.

As the years went by the Everleigh Sisters improved the facilities of their establishment, installing central heating for smugness in winter and electric fans for coolness in summer. There was valet service available day and night, and three four-piece orchestras — and, of course, thirty hostesses, all more lovely, Minna and Aida believed, than any elsewhere in the country. In 1911 their pride in all this led them into publishing an illustrated brochure giving these particulars. It was a false step. The city fathers were faced with a flood of complaints that such open flaunting of morality was a public menace, and they were obliged to order the Club's closure.

Another well-patronized bordello was run in St Louis by Babe Connors, who had diamond-inlaid teeth, and where Paderewski once accompanied bawdy songs on the piano.

Not far from Reno in Nevada is Sparks where prostitution was permitted like elsewhere in that State, if the townspeople voted in favour of it, and, availing himself of this concession, Joe Confonte started there what became the most thriving cooperative of whores in America. To ensure that the community's annual poll did not ever go against him, Joe arranged for the families and relatives of his women to move to Sparks.

Clients were guided to the Mustang Ranch by arrows painted on rocks in the desert. After ringing a bell by the entrance in the high fence encircling the property, they were admitted and eventually conducted into a room where all the thirty to forty daughters of joy stood in a neat semi-circle allowed only to smile and give their names to avoid any unseemly display of rivalry. All had been certified as wholesome by the physicians after regular check-ups and the fixed rates were fair.

At midnight, Joe would settle in cash with the women deducting half the amount earned for board and lodging. Then all records regarding such transactions would be burnt. In due course, came nemesis in the shape of the taxman and Confonte was convicted for failing to pay $5 million, so he made off to South America.

If the Everleigh Sisters lived today, they certainly would have been amazed at the rooms with mats for communal sex, the disco dancing in the nude, and the public orgies to be found at Plato's Retreat and New York City's other sex clubs where swinging is common even among strangers. Some psychologists now condone orgies on the grounds that, as Burgo Partridge in his book on the subject puts it, they serve not only 'the useful purpose of providing relief from tension caused by abstinence, but also of re-arousing by contrast an appetite for the humdrum temperances which are an inevitable part of everyday life'.

Artie Shaw asked why he had wed seven wives explained: 'Because in my time, you married them.' In the 1980s, even civil marriages have been going out of fashion. Film star Warren Beatty has had affairs with many Hollywood beauties but has made not one of them his bride. The legal fraternity may well soon be faced with a slump in divorce proceedings if the number of marriages plummets.

Regarding the sexual excesses of modern society, Janet

Flanner has written: 'Not since the early Romans when, after they'd eaten, gorged, and debauched all the boys, the girls already having been debauched — and tickled the back of their throats with a scarlet feather in order to start all over again, has one seen such carryings-on.'

Moderation may be a bore to some, like millionairess Barbara Hutton, but in time so, too, becomes excess, as Erica Jong implied when she said: 'My reaction to porn films is as follows — after the first ten minutes, I want to go home and scream. After the first twenty minutes, I never want to screw again as long as I live.'

XVIII

SOME TWENTIETH-CENTURY SYBARITES

Barbara Hutton was aged sixteen when she lost her virginity to an English tennis coach at Cannes. She revealed later: 'It was my first experience with a man who devoured me. I have never felt like this before. It is like being captured and drained. It is not altogether pleasant, and it certainly isn't very graceful.' When she left Miss Porter's School for Girls, Barbara's father engaged a security guard to protect her — and she seduced him within a week and entered in her diary: 'He was as rampant as a bull, literally tearing himself out of his clothes, then driving on top of me. His recuperative powers were admirable. We made love repeatedly and for hours.'

For her coming out Barbara had a tea party for 500 guests, a dinner and dance for the same number in Central Park Casino, then on 21 December 1930, she gave a ball for twice as many in the Ritz-Carlton, costing $60,000, with four orchestras, 200 waiters, 2,000 bottles of pink champagne, a seven-course dinner and breakfast for all. For décor, there were some 10,000 American Beauty roses and 30,000 white violets together with scarlet poinsettias, mountain heather and silver birch trees, whilst the night sky was simulated by dark blue gauze sparkling with electrically-lit stars and a full moon, and everywhere there was glistening artificial snow. Guests on arrival were greeted by Maurice Chevalier in Santa Claus get-up who with laden helpers handed out as gifts gold jewellery cases inside which were unmounted emeralds, rubies, sapphires and diamonds.

In June 1933, when Barbara married the phony Prince, Alexis Mdvani, presents poured in and she was obliged to rent an additional hotel suite in which to put them. She herself followed his first wife's precedent and bought him a second string of Argentinian polo ponies. For her twenty-first party that November there were lavish celebrations with waiters dressed as Cossacks. Then the Mdvanis' reputation received a blow when Alexis's brother Serge was divorced by opera singer, Mary McCormick, who retracted her original description of him as 'the world's greatest lover' and now called him 'the world's worst gigolo'.

When Marie-Louise Ritz published her biography of her famous father, she described Barbara's twenty-second birthday party held at the Ritz in Paris as possibly the greatest triumph in its history. All the restaurants and the huge ballroom were taken over and exotically decorated to resemble the Rue La Koutabia in Casablanca. Three planes were chartered to bring friends and the Jack Harris orchestra from London; 150 dined and 2,200 came to a ball. 'Every possible whim of a rich young modern was indulged in,' commented Mlle Ritz. It all cost £50,000.

The following year, at Rome, Barbara divorced Alexis and, within a day, was remarried to Count Reventlow from whom she later parted on the grounds that he was a sado-masochist. And so it went on. Apart from her marriages, there were several short-lived affairs. Fashion designer Oleg Cassini told David Heymann, one of her biographers, how they met at a party of hers and, later, she said she had fallen in love with him and suggested a deal. She would give his wife a million dollars if the lady gave him his freedom. Then Barbara and Cary Grant, her current husband, would divorce, and she would wed Oleg. Nothing came of it, but Oleg thought he understood her character. Most people when they were in a depressed state of mind or bored found a cure in buying a new dress or a car. 'But this did not work for Barbara, for when you can buy anything, buying is no fun — unless perhaps you can buy the ultimate, another person.' He believed men to be the chief stimulus in Barbara's life. 'She bought and sold them, bartered them or replaced them in much the same way as a stockbroker operates on the Stock Exchange.'

Barbara longed to be loved for herself and not for her fortune. To achieve this, she was convinced that a slim figure was essential. Unfortunately, she enjoyed eating rich foods and sometimes yielding to temptation she would gorge all she craved. To prevent this happening she took appetite depressants and ate hardly anything. Kept awake at night as a result, she resorted to stronger and stronger sleeping pills. She consulted doctor after doctor. Her health deteriorated as drugs of all kinds became increasingly her principal diet.

Lovers and husbands came and went. She rhapsodized over them at first, then went to the other extreme and jettisoned them as though they were garbage. By 1953 she was drinking hard and there were bottles of liquor tucked away under her bed and in the dressing-room of her suite at the Ritz in Paris. It was then that she married 'Always Ready' Porfiro Rubirosa as her No. 7. His mighty organ of generation was so talked about in fashionable restaurants that the sophisticated would ask the waiter for the 'Rubirosa' and be brought a carved 16-inch pepper mill. Such a sure-fire stallion not surprisingly had already filled with bliss film stars like Jayne Mansfield, Marilyn Monroe and Evita Peron. Not that he was in any way a snob, for all was grist to his mill. In Palm Beach he would go round the nightspots hunting for birds to drive back to his apartment. Their social status didn't really matter to him, David

Fields, who then published the *Palm Beach*, has said, 'as long as they were good-looking and good in bed'.

It cost Barbara $2,500,000 before Rubirosa would marry her. She was exhausted on the wedding night, so he slipped out and spent the remaining hours until breakfast with a showgirl. The marriage only lasted fifty-three days and, rid of Rubirosa, Barbara resumed her quest for the perfect lover. She spent the summer of 1954 with a young interior decorator, Daniel Rudd, and a weekend, the following January, with film actor, Michael Rennie, in Palm Springs and wrote in disillusion afterwards:

> There are times when I like sex and times when I don't. When I'm in the mood for it, I like nothing better. But I don't enjoy cruelty. I hate it when somebody I don't know comes out wearing a rubber diving suit, with a battleship in one hand and a jar of vaseline in the other.

James Dean and Barbara met by chance one night in a Hollywood café. They drank a lot and talked. She took him to her hotel. 'It was late, so I asked him to stay. He removed his shirt and pants and climbed into bed and I snuggled in next to him. We made love and we made love again. . . .' Two months later, Barbara married Von Cramn. He failed to overcome his homosexuality and the marriage was never consummated. It hurt her vanity and she found comfort in more and more booze and novel sexual distractions, followed by divorce and a new husband. And so the pattern repeated itself until she died, a pathetic joke.

One of the most colourful gluttons who enlivened the social scene in the 1920s onwards was the Irish peer and journalist, Lord Castlerosse, who never weighed less than seventeen stone as an adult and was about twenty-two stone when he attended the *Bal des Quatz' Arts* wearing nothing but a leopard skin. Four chump chops, an entire ham and six lobsters he regarded as a snack and not a dinner. When a new waiter brought him a slice of game pie at his club, he growled: 'Bring the whole pie, you fool.' Asked what his handicap was when visiting the Walton Heath Golf Club, he replied frankly: 'Drink and debauchery.' His motto ought to have been: 'Excess, always excess' — for he had a wardrobe full of fancy waistcoats and sable-collared, mink-lined top-coats, bought several dozens of shirts at the time and cigars by the thousand. When the piped water failed at the Carlton Hotel in Cannes, he had his bath filled with 800 bottles of Vichy water charging it to his employer, Lord Beaverbrook, as expenses.

Two impresarios, also greatly overweight and with outsize personalities, were Henry Sherek in London and Gilbert Miller in New York. Kitty Black says that dining with Sherek was like watching 'a Magimix at work'. The two men were compulsive eaters and other diners at the Ivy or the *Ecu de France* would watch incredulously as these twentieth-century Falstaffs devoured double helpings of every dish that was the most fattening.

Lord Castlerosse used Vichy water for his bath in an emergency, but pop star Michael Jackson bathes twice a day using 300 bottles of Perrier water a time. According to the *Sunday Mirror*, when he stayed at the Montcalm Hotel, London, in March 1985, he spent £8,000 in three days on keeping clean. He did not drink any, instead he had cranberry juice cocktails specially flown in from the States. It appears that his only excess is eating bags and bags of nuts between meals.

Indian Princes were so fabulously rich that it is not surprising that they should spend their wealth on excessive display and practices. Scandals erupted through their sexual marauding. There was the giant Maharajah of Patiala who spent £30,000 a year on underwear alone and was so active in his 350-strong harem and elsewhere that he was called 'His Exhausted Highness'; the Maharajah

Tukoji Rao of Indore and the shooting affray in Bombay over a fugitive mistress that caused his abdication; the sadistic perversions of the Maharajah Jay Singh of Alwar that forced the British to depose him; the dog and bitch marriage fiestas staged by the canine-crazy ruler of Junagadh, which, with other extravagant excesses, bankrupted his state; and, comparatively normal, the habits of a Maharajah of Mysore's brother who employed a servant to be in attendance, day and night, with silver flasks full of brandy.

The most extraordinary dishes were prepared for banquets such as the one for which the recipe reads:

> Take a whole camel, put a goat inside it and inside the goat a peacock, inside which put a chicken. Inside the chicken put a sand-grouse, inside the sand-grouse put a quail and finally, a sparrow. Then put the camel in a hole in the ground and steam it.

In some of the smaller states for fun at a feast they would enclose a bird in puff-paste, quickly deep fry it, and take the *puri* to the table where the bird would fly out. Paan was a delicacy the recipe for which varied and which was prepared in secret because it contained aphrodisiacs and even gold and pearls. In the past, people had been deliberately poisoned in this way and only trusted cooks were allowed to make it. Those who feared that an enemy might make an underhand attempt on their lives often kept a peacock in the kitchen, for it was believed that if the bird cried in a strange manner it meant that some poison had been smuggled into the room.

Although King Farouk was a glutton, he prided himself on his table manners. Served with his customary twenty or more Southdown chops, he always left one because, he explained, his English governess, Ina Naylor, had drummed it into him as a boy that a gentleman always left something uneaten on his plate. A lover of night life, rarely retiring before the early hours, he therefore had a late breakfast on a tray of thirty boiled eggs, toast and tea. By the time he had eaten half-a-dozen eggs, the rest would be cold, so he had them replaced by freshly boiled ones, and this routine carried on until he felt like a change. Then he would gorge on lobster and chicken, chops and steak, quail and anything else that he might fancy. Such a feast would last the average person the whole day, but it was not so with Farouk. Within a short time, he would complain that he felt famished and start eating again. To quench his thirst, he would gulp down without a pause the entire contents of a bottle of lemonade or orangeade of the effervescent kind. Gluttony was a vice he had inherited from his forebears.

Farouk discovered in his youth that he was sexually deficient and did all that he could to conceal this, especially after a dancer stormed out of his Abdin Palace bedroom deriding the King's puny penis before his attendants. To try and gain virility, he tried various aphrodisiacs, amphetamines, and hashish mixed with honey. He became obsessed with the pursuit of women who excited him, and came to be regarded as a philanderer who would get his procurers to approach attractive women who were seated with friends in restaurants and the like. Although his being so fat made his sexual performance clumsy, he did not cut down on his gormandizing. After all had not his grandfather, Ismail the Magnificent, been both a great trencherman and a lover who had collected three thousand concubines? And so Farouk usually made one nymph a night his aim — sometimes it was two and three and he bedded them all together, or, if more convenient, he would have sex with a girl in her billet and take another back home. According to Michael Stern in his biography of Farouk, it was 'sexual activity rather than intercourse' and in his brief life he had such affairs with some five thousand women. Stern says this was made possible by his setting up 'a ministry for procuring' which made Egypt the only country 'to raise pimping to cabinet level'. Antonio Pulli

Bey was in charge and his department, it was said, was the most efficient of all.

Although Farouk had ten palaces, they proved insufficient for his illicit intimacies and when his first wife, Queen Farida, berated him for smuggling his poppets into the palace at Alexandria, he settled the dispute by having built at Moussa a fine new hospital, which won for him popularity with the public, and where he retained as his erotic eyrie a luxurious penthouse suite of seventeen rooms, with a superb vista over the Mediterranean. In Cairo, a cottage retreat was constructed for him on a hillock by the Pyramids which after his deposition was turned into a café for tourists.

In exile, Farouk resided for a time at the Eden Paradiso in Anacapri where the lift was mainly occupied by waiters carrying food up to him on the third floor. This went on even at night for when he felt any pangs of hunger they had to be soothed at once. His appetite for girls remained just as strong. When attending a display of *haute couture* by Emilio Pucci, the designer, he appeared to be impressed by one of the creations. Delighted, Pucci signalled to the model to show it off from all aspects before a possible royal patron. When this was rewarded with applause from Farouk, Pucci inquired: 'So the dress pleases, your Majesty?'

'The dress? Oh, the dress!' returned the ex-King. 'I was thinking how much better she would look without it.'

In 1944 Farouk's gluttony so affected his health that he had a check-up in a Lausanne clinic and he was advised to diet. When friends visited his hotel during the morning, however, they were amazed to find him seated at a table crowded with dishes bearing every kind of meat available, including poultry and game. 'This is my new diet,' he would tell them. When the doctors discovered how he was tucking in pastries as well on the sly, they insisted on moving him into the clinic so that they could control what he ate. But he proved incorrigible and arranged for his secretaries to bring into his room chocolates and cakes camouflaged as something else. Eventually he left, still overweight. He was clearly too accustomed to having his own way, too self-indulgent to change those habits.

During Farouk's last years, when he went on his nightly wanderings, the *Fonte dei Papi*, a garden bar on the Tiber, was where he liked best to pause for a snack. Its owner, Colombo Magalotti, recollected later: 'His appetite was absolutely fantastic. I have seen him eat twenty bags of potato chips and fifteen sandwiches, and wash them down with a dozen bottles of orange soda. And this before dinner. He just couldn't stop eating.'

In 1965 Farouk died in his forty-seventh year and weighing twenty stone. His last meal consisted of a dozen oysters, lobster Thermidor, a double portion of roast lamb, fried potatoes and French beans. He refused crêpes because they contained alcohol and had instead a large helping of trifle.

The late Aga Khan was more fortunate than Farouk. He was spiritual head of the Muslims of the Ismaili sect, the adherents of which are forbidden to drink alcohol, but an American who sold him 11,000 bottles of wine on the French Riviera, was told that, by a happy dispensation of Allah's, wine turned to milk in his mouth. It was said of him that he looked like a gourmet and ordered like a gourmet. Out of all the Prophet Mahamet's ten wives and fifteen concubines, his favourite was Aylshah, nine years old at their marriage, forty-four years younger than he, and on whose lap he died. She said of him: 'The Prophet liked three things most — women, scent, and eating, but mostly women.' This was probably true of the Aga Kahn, and, as regards women, it was certainly true of his son, Aly, who gained a reputation as a great lover.

One of Aly's biographers, Leonard Slater, estimated that he must have had at the very least a 1,000 love affairs. The pursuit of women became his purpose in life. 'I think only of the woman's pleasure when I'm in love,' he liked to say. Elsa Maxwell's opinion was: 'When he fell in love, it was madly and deeply. The snag, it might last only one night.'

At the races with a woman, who was one of his closest confidants, Aly, as they walked to his box, told her in a low voice: 'See that woman sitting over there. And that one. And that one.' He continued indicating one woman after another. 'He was pointing out his conquests,' this friend disclosed later. 'Practically all the women in that section of the grandstand had been to bed with him.'

Tales that Aly had sex with half-a-dozen beauties a day were dismissed by the cynical as gossip-writers' fantasies. Others claimed that both he and his father achieved this by plunging their elbows into cold water to revitalize themselves. Some frequenters of night clubs alleged that they had witnessed Aly using the ice in champagne buckets to that end. According to Leonard Slater, however, this sexual skill had been gained through Aly's having been sent by his father as a youth for instruction to an old Arab doctor, an hakim, in Cairo, where he has spent six weeks learning *imsák*. As a result, another intimate friend of his, explained: 'No matter how many women Aly went with, he seldom reached a climax himself. He could make love by the hour, but he went the whole way himself not more often than twice a week. . . . Otherwise his life would not have been possible, because he only thought of that every night, and every day, too.' Aly's chauffeur has revealed that he had instructions to drive very slowly through Hyde Park whenever there was a lady friend with his master at the back of the Rolls. This was so that he could have sex with her. He would do this *en route* from one lady's flat to another's.

Russia has never been short of exponents of excess and Grigori Rasputin behaved rather like Peter the Great's mock Pontiff and the members of his 'Most Holy and Most Drunken Synod'. It was a Russian general's wife, Irina Danilova Kubasova, who, when Grigori was aged sixteen, enticed him into her bedroom, and, together with several of her maids, seduced him. This led to his frequenting women of easy virtue in his village, even following his marriage. There was a bizarre religious sect, the Khlist, which believed in redemption through sexual indulgence, that Rasputin now joined and travelled far through his country, taking part in their dissolute rites.

When Rasputin established his ascendancy over the Tsar and Tsarina and held court over women disciples in the flat at St Peterburg, his wife put up with infidelities without a murmur, for he had brainwashed her into believing that they had purpose in God's plan for his life. 'He has enough for all,' she would say. Apart from visiting his imperial patrons and influential people, Grigori was usually to be found in his dining-room known as the 'Holy of Holies', talking to his important women admirers. Those not so fortunate, petitioners for favours, packed the waiting-room where inquisitive eyes and ears worked feverishly every time the door opened. Their imaginations then took flight embroidering on what they had glimpsed and overheard. What could 'You believe that I pollute you — I do not pollute you, I rather purify you' mean, which he had said as he ate fish and cheese. Why had he leered, saying: 'The first word of the Saviour was "Repent". How can we repent if we have not sinned first?' And he seemed to be drinking glass after glass of Russian Madeira, a very potent, fortified wine. Once while doing this, he had been noticed stroking the hair of a girl on his knees and telling her: 'If God sends a temptation, we must yield to it voluntarily and without resistance, so then we may afterwards do penance in utter contrition.'

This religious rake did not care whether other people knew how he behaved in his 'Holy of Holies'. He made no attempt to conceal or to change his mode of life. The unkempt man's attraction for society women can be explained by what the French call *nostalgie de la boue*. They enjoyed it when he dipped his dirty fingers into a jar of jam and told an elegant lady: 'Humble yourself. Lick it clean.' And she would dutifully do so in public. On another occasion, reminiscing about his childhood, he described how as a boy he had first witnessed sex in action

— between horses in a stable. With a coarse air, he suddenly seized a court lady and muttered: 'Let me mount you, my lovely mare.'

Many women were proud to boast that they had slept with the holy satyr. When a newcomer to the choice circle repulsed him, a married disciple, who doted on him, was astounded and questioned: 'Why don't you want to be his? How can one refuse anything to a saint?' To which the young woman retorted: 'Does a saint need sinful love? What sort of saintliness is that?'

'Grigori makes everything near him holy,' was the reply.

'And would you be ready to accede to his desires?'

'Of course. I have already been his and I am proud and happy to have done so.'

'But what does your husband say?'

'He considers it a very great honour. If Grigori desires a woman, we all think it a blessing and an honour — both our husbands and ourselves.'

Rasputin loved dancing to gipsy music at the cabaret called the Villa Rode in St Petersburg and would hold drinking parties at the Donon, and in Moscow at the Yar. These at times turned into orgies. When reports of them reached the Tsarina, she would dismiss them as either 'calumniation of the holy man' by his enemies or traps set by Satan from which he would certainly escape. Tales of his having been seen embracing married women she would spurn, claiming they were only brotherly kisses like those of the Apostles.

There was, of course, a tradition of uninhibited behaviour in the country going back to the times of Peter the Great and Catherine, so the police ignored it as long as it was confined to private houses, but they did make attempts to prevent Rasputin from disgracing himself in public such as persuading the management of the Villa Rode to keep a private room well away from the public for his entertainment. But it was not possible to curb his wild antics and his indiscretions when intoxicated. In March 1915, after a day spent in prayer at a certain tomb in fulfilment of a vow, he descended on the Yar in Moscow accompanied by sycophants and newspapermen and embarked on some hard drinking with singing gypsies. Becoming garrulous, he bragged about his intimate relations with the Tsarina. Attracted by the noise of the roistering, a gate-crasher from the main restaurant shouted that he believed him to be an imposter and not Rasputin. 'I'll prove it,' he returned and unbuttoning his trousers exposed his huge instrument — destined to be hacked off when he was murdered and kept by a maid who in 1968 produced it to a journalist in Paris — preserved in a box and looking 'like a blackened, over-ripe banana, about a foot long'.

Of all modern politicians, Mussolini probably indulged most in promiscuous sex. From the age of sixteen he had intercourse anywhere and at any time usually without troubling to remove his clothes. No girl or woman was safe alone with him, unless she was skinny for he preferred them plump. There was no finesse about the way he tackled them and no consideration was shown for their comfort. It took place immediately against a tree or his desk or on the floor — and quickly for he was a busy man. It was said that he did not want to sleep with them in bed for fear that they were amused by the nightshirt he wore instead of pyjamas. Nevertheless, despite his roughness and the ferocity of his thrusting, he could afterwards, if only for a short while assume the part of a romantic lover uttering with feeling tender words and even playing appropriate strains on his violin.

Despite his philandering, Mussolini was happily married and Rachele, his wife, was aware of it, admitting knowledge of some twenty mistresses. She excused such behaviour on the grounds that it was customary with highly-sexed men and in any case he was devoted to his children.

Many musicians seem to need a good mixed diet sex-wise to stimulate their art. Leopold Stokowski made this clear to his second wife, heiress Evangeline Johnson, when in his forties he married her after a brief courtship of less than a month. Being a broad-minded modern, she agreed to allow him the freedom to roam around. In Philadelphia he had slept with so many students of its top music school, the Curtis Institute, that it was called the Coitus Club. When not doing this he would be slipping in and out of the beds of his admirers in high society, as well as actresses and maids, undeterred as to whether they had husbands or not. 'I have a date with one of my nurses,' he would say, 'an angel of mercy who will rejuvenate me.' His profusion of amorous adventures and achievements fascinated the public. They regarded him as a sort of male Brigitte Bardot. The peak came in 1937 when he had his affair with Greta Garbo and she revealed: 'I felt the electricity going through me from head to toe.' After ten months together in Italy, the couple suddenly parted. It was the end, too, of Stokowski's second marriage. Evangeline had endured far more of her husband's extra-marital relations than she was willing to tolerate any longer.

The divorced Lothario for the next seven years haunted the boudoirs and billets of those who fascinated him, and then at the age of sixty-three, he wed at Reno millionairess Gloria Vanderbilt, forty years his junior. This much discussed marriage finally crumbled in 1962. Although now in his eighties, Stokowski was still able to prove that he had a youthful virility. The intervals only between each twilight romance lengthened until he died in his ninety-sixth year.

Some practitioners of another art, were equally amorously accomplished. Toulouse-Lautrec has already been mentioned. More recently, there was Picasso. A close friend has written that when Pablo reached sixty 'his sexual gluttony became obsessive'. Candidates for his couch had to be both young and beautiful, because after an affair they invariably became models. 'For me,' he said once, 'there are only two kinds of women — goddesses and doormats.' A graphologist studying his handwriting thought it showed that he 'loves intensely and kills the thing he loves'. This is borne out by his reaction when his first marriage to Olga Koklova was breaking up through her becoming more and more possessive and hysterical causing him to paint a number of female monsters with withered breasts and distorted sexual organs. The misery of his marriage found expression in this manner, but when his mistress, Marie-Thérèse, gave birth to a daughter, the breasts he then painted were full and ripe, the lips turned up at the corners, and the bodies though still twisted radiated sensual satisfaction. Pierre Cabannel believed that stimulation from sex provided the basic motive for Picasso's 'lyrical flights' and gave them force. 'Desire, with him, was violence, dismemberment, tumult, indignation, excess.'

Out of all those who earn their living from entertaining the public, those in the performing arts are subject to the most strain and it is not surprising that some seek relief in various forms of excess. Alcohol and drugs were to destroy Edith Piaf in France, as they did in America with Judy Garland, John Barrymore and others.

Dr Samuel Hirschfield of Los Angeles who was Barrymore's physician for several years has recorded that his patient since the age of seventeen was 'more or less a chronic drunkard'. Two years earlier, John had been debauched by his nymphomaniac grandmother and it is likely that the traumatic experience led to his uncontrollable addiction to alcohol. Later, he was to say: 'It's slander to say my troubles come from chasing women. They begin when I catch them. . . . The way to fight a women is with your hat. Grab it and run. . . . When they find the arms of Venus di Milo, they will discover boxing gloves on the hands.'

Such was Barrymore's charisma that although he broke his promises to reform time after time there were always producers willing to take a chance and risk giving him a major role. For example, when Irving Thalberg was casting his film of *Romeo and Juliet*, despite the fact that John was drink-sodden and unpredictable, he agreed to let him play Mercutio on condition that he lived in a sanatorium near the studios in a male nurse's charge. In addition, he was coached for the part by Margaret Carrington. During the first few weeks his behaviour proved impeccable. Then he suddenly absconded and it was only after a hectic hunt that he was discovered in a drinking den and taken back to the studios, where Margaret Carrington kept a close eye on him for the rest of the filming. She expressed her feelings thus: 'If only drink would finally kill the Barrymores, what a better world this would be!'

Ironically enough, it was John's alcoholism that was to contribute largely to one of his greatest stage successes. In 1937 he was persuaded by his third wife, Elaine Barrie, to take the leading part of an elderly, ham actor in *My Dear Children* so that she could establish herself in the theatre by playing the role of Allan Manville's daughter, Cordelia. It was a feeble comedy and Barrington's well-wishers were dismayed that he planned to return to Broadway in such a vehicle after an absence of fifteen years. To make matters worse, his excesses had ruined his memory and during the dress rehearsal he could hardly remember any of his lines. On the first night of the try-out at the McCarter Theatre of Princeton, he overcame this problem by ad libbing, and, thanks to his brilliant timing, the audience reacted with appreciative, loud laughter. So for the rest of the tour, he ad libbed more and more, combining this with inspired foolery and thus injecting new blood into a lifeless farce which now became an unexpected box office draw.

By the time *My Dear Children* had reached Chicago, wrote John Kobler, 'it was a sideshow with John the main exhibit, a mad circus, a carnival of lunacy in which he exploited his own weaknesses for laughs, his intemperance, his profligacy, his womanizing, a spiritual striptease with himself as a kind of Gypsy Rose John'. For example, one evening when a fire engine shrieked past outside the theatre, he shouted: 'My wife!' Then the next time the same thing occurred, succeeded by the backfiring of a truck, he went on: 'And she's got her mother with her!'

None of this endeared Barrymore to the rest of the cast for, receiving few cues from him, it was exceedingly difficult for them to follow on when he deviated from the text. His bad habits backstage also upset them. He would hover in the wings, bottle in hand, telling tap-room tales, laughing boisterously and making vulgar noises so as to confuse the actors before the footlights. As for the actresses, he never ceased enticing them to have sex with him, although the touring manager had gone to the trouble of recruiting three attractive girls willing to respond to all overtures.

My Dear Children was a smash-hit at the Selwyn Theatre and the city's upper crust vied with one another to have John as an honoured guest at their parties. But he never received a second invitation for he misbehaved outrageously. At last on 31 January 1940, the play had its first night at the Belasco, New York, before a sympathetic audience of socialites that greeted Barrymore's first appearance with a standing ovation lasting five minutes. At first, he was somewhat put off by this and gave an almost straight performance. From the second night, however, he hammed and ad-libbed in the manner the customers expected. They applauded wildly when he drank a tumbler filled with tea masquerading as whisky, then held it out to them and grimaced: 'God, how I wish that was the real stuff!' Soon after the final curtain fell on the third evening, he fainted from exhaustion and the theatre went dark for the rest of that week. Four months later, the run ended earlier than it needed to have done for Barrymore had had enough. The public loved the show; the critics detested it. One wrote: 'If there is everything repellent in a man's capitalizing on his own degradation, then there is something even more repellent in the public's coming to snicker at it.'

According to an estimate made by a physician who tried

in vain to cure Barrymore of his alcoholism he must have drunk at least sixty-four barrels of the hard stuff in the last forty years of his life. He was not a glutton as regards food, though on one occasion to celebrate his having played *Hamlet* on Broadway for a hundred and one performances, thus beating Edwin Booth's record, Barrymore played truant from a matinée and spent some six hours eating and drinking with Feodor Chaliapin, the celebrated bass, who had to sing at the Metropolitan that night. John asked him how after such a feast, he could do so.

'I thought for a moment,' Barrymore recalled, 'that the lusty Feodor would explode. He laughed until the dishes on the speak-easy tables rocked. Then he yelled in Russian: "I can eat and drink like a big horse before singing because I am such a damned fine actor.!" '

In another kind of excess Barrymore would probably have also held his own with Chaliapin. In December 1934, when aged fifty-two, he paid the madam of a brothel $1,200 for his exclusive use of its facilities. 'It was an extraordinary place with a madam who looked like Moll Flanders,' Barrymore later disclosed:

> There were numerous girls all Eurasians. They had astoundingly happy dispositions. The most interesting character in the place, however, was madam's Greek lover, Dmitri. His name sounded Russian, but he was a Greek. Dmitri seemed a rather tragic figure in that his whole soul longed for expression in cooking whereas he was condemned in a manner of speaking to the patchoulied prison of madam's affections. My coming seemed to hearten him. I, too, was interested in cooking, although I am an eccentric actor. We would sit up late in the kitchen, trying out recipes. His knowledge of the French cookery school was vast. He detested curries, said they reminded him of the madam and her insistence that he remain faithful to her. In fact, she would call out to him, right when we were engaged in some special bit of cooking, and

demand that he come at once to her room. I managed eventually to talk her out of this disrupting action, and Dmitri seemed grateful. What a sad fate for a virtuoso of the cuisine to find himself irrevocably transplanted to another field of art! Sometimes tears would come to his eyes as he looked at the pots and pans. He confessed that the jealous madam even had burned a cook-book sent by one of his wives whom he referred to as 'the Salonika one'.

Barrymore, married four times, once told an audience in Omaha that marriage was mankind's greatest calamity. 'It is merely a bad tooth that could and should be extracted whenever the pain prompts a visit to the dentist.' He also defined love as 'the delightful interval between meeting a beautiful girl and discovering that she looked like a haddock'. He liked to relate how he had behaved like a modern Romeo or rather a human fly by crawling along the tenth-storey cornice which ornamented the exterior of the St Francis Hotel in San Francisco. It was the only way he could reach the window and get into the bedroom of 'a glacial blonde' who made him feel at the time 'like an explorer who had just conquered the North West Passage'. Whenever he repeated this yarn, Barrymore varied the name of the hotel according to where he happened to be.

Gene Fowler, in *Good Night, Sweet Prince*, tells how, after a drunken fracas in a Hollywood restaurant, he brought back the actor to the Fowler home. 'My daughter had no pleasant welcome for either Mr Barrymore or myself . . . she was at this time a strict prohibitionist,' he states.

'Will you serve us one small drink?' Fowler asked. 'We've just had a trying experience?'

Jane glared at them, then said: 'I'll get you something. I'll get you *both* something special.'

While the fifteen-year-old girl was on her way to the kitchen, Barrymore remarked: 'Spirit! Great spirit! It is written in her eye.' The sound of bottles and other glassware from the direction of the kitchen caused him to say reverently: 'The Angelus!'

They did not know, of course, that Jane was mixing for them a potion of Worcestershire Sauce, spirits of ammonia, onion essence, and a dash of peppermint.

'She has such a gentle manner,' said the actor.

'Yes,' Gene admitted, 'she is an especially sweet child.'

Jane returned with two whisky glasses filled to the brims. She set them before Barrymore and her father who thanked her for behaving so hospitably and tolerantly. While Gene was lifting his own glass, John tossed off his drink with delicacy but with speed. 'Then his eyes opened wide,' Fowler wrote. 'He began to make desperate, swimming motions, first the breast-stroke, then the trudgen, and finally a frantic Australian crawl. When his windpipe lost some of its paralysis, he rose to his feet and gasped: "My God! I'm in the house of the Borgias!" '

When, after Errol Flynn's death, there was litigation over his estate in London's High Court, Mr Justice McGary commented that, as a sexual athlete, the star might truly be regarded as having attained Olympic standards. 'In his career, in his three marriages, in his friendships, in his quarrels and in bed with the many women he took there, he lived with zest and irregularity. . . . Hollywood has never been deficient in what was then, as always, one of Errol's great interests in life — namely a generous pool of available pulchritude.'

Flynn had affairs from an early age and when he first arrived in New York on his way to the celluloid city, he slept with a Russian princess, sadistically inclined, who battered his back with a steel-bristled brush, making it bleed. In California, a fiery film acress, Lili Damita, eight years older than he, became his regular mistress. Bed became a lively arena for amorous wrestling with 'Tiger Lil'. But that soon proved insufficient exercise for him and he was off mounting fillies wherever he could catch those that excited him. Brandy was becoming his favourite tipple of which he would toss off large quantities as though it were beer.

Errol's yacht, the *Sirocco*, now became the centre for his love life. His chums co-operated by bringing along girls of whom he had first pick. They would be given drinks laced with some aphrodisiac and bunked. If they went down well with their partners, Flynn would ask them to stay on for some cruising. Rejects were motored back home. His closest friend was David Niven with whom he shared a cottage on the beach they called 'Cirrhosis-by-the-sea'.

In 1942 Flynn was charged with the rape of two girls under age. A sharp lawyer, however, succeeded in discrediting their evidence and the Los Angeles jury acquitted him. But this narrow escape did not make him more careful. His next affair was with Norah Edington, barely aged eighteen, whom he made pregnant and married when she would not have an abortion. To add to his embarrassment, a twenty-year-old blonde claimed that he had fathered her two-year-old daughter. All this did not deter him from having a series of brief affairs in New York. He was drinking more heavily than ever. It possibly affected his sexual performance and there were tales that he sprinkled cocaine on the tip of his penis to improve this. When a close friend suggested that far from his having raped girls, it was they who had tried to rape him, he replied: 'I must admit I never had to rape anyone.'

Flynn would drink all night, then turn up at the studios completely sozzled. Directors despaired of getting him to finish a picture. He would promise not to drink in the studios, then do so surreptitiously by bribing the boys serving him with black coffee to lace it with cognac. He kept vodka in flower vases in his dressing-room and had a crate of oranges delivered there into all of which he had injected vodka with a hypodermic syringe. At the end of a day on the set, shooting *The Adventures of Don Juan*, Flynn, about to disappear into his dressing-room, pointed at two girls, clearly tarts, he had brought back after lunch and invited the director, Vincent Sherman, to come inside and make a foursome for sex.

'How can you spend all day working and then tackle them?' Sherman inquired.

'Oh, it's easy,' Flynn retorted. 'I just lie there reading the trade papers while they work on me.'

After Errol and Norah had divorced, he married in 1950 Patrice Wymore, aged twenty-one, who wore glasses and whom he described as 'a square'. But even the reception was spoilt by his being served a writ charging him with having raped one Denise Duvivier on his yacht, the *Zaca*, a year earlier. However, he was able to prove his innocence in this instance.

For the next two years it looked as if he might be settling down as a family man when a daughter was born but the idyll did not last and the marriage ended. His own end came in October 1959, when, after a week-long drinking crawl round Hollywood, he collapsed in his bedroom, shot some stuff into his veins with a hypo, gulped down a dose or two of vodka and passed out. Not long after this he had a massive heart attack and, taken to hospital, did not recover.

Sexologists have claimed that drunkards destroy all desire in themselves and lose the power to get erections. For example, F. R. Sturgis wrote in *Sexual Debility in Man*: 'a chronic alcoholic is eight times out of ten, sexually speaking, a eunuch'. Certainly, as far as actors are concerned, Errol Flynn and John Barrymore were two of those exceptions to such a rule.

Mae West believed that everybody was fascinated by sex. John Mason Brown wrote of her: 'She makes passion palatable to a puritan public by making even its intensity ludicrous.' At the start of her career, she felt that to achieve success she needed an outrageous novelty. This she found and exploited to the full with sustained bravura.

No woman's sayings have been quoted more frequently than Mae's, except possibly Dorothy Parker's, and through her wisecracks she made the masses accept her as the

Queen of Sex obsessed with snaring men. For example:
'Come up and see me some time. Come up Wednesday.
That's amateur night.'
'I used to be Snow White, but I drifted.'
'When I'm good, I'm very good, but when I'm bad,
I'm better.'
'Too much of a good thing can be wonderful.'
'I'm a girl who works at Paramount all day
and Fox's all night.'
'An orgasm a day, keeps the doctor away.'

Mae practised what she preached, enjoying stallions,
such as Patsy Perroni, whom she recalled climaxed every
hour in the twenty-four hours they were together in her
bed, which had a mirrored ceiling above it so that she
could watch all the love play. The total number of times
came in fact to twenty-six, she added, certain of the count,
having kept a note of the number of protectors taken out
of her bedside safe.

When Mae was playing Catherine the Great at Philadelphia in 1944, every one knew what men in the large
cast had slept with her because after the event they bought
themselves smart new suits. A sensation was caused in Las
Vegas, eleven years later, when she opened in a new show
supported by eight husky musclemen. She began singing
I'd Like to Do All Day What I Do All Night and ended with
What a Night as she distributed keys to her suite to the
body-builders, saying: 'Don't crowd me, boys. There's
enough for everybody.' The big scene came with the men
in evening cloaks, and apparently nude underneath,
standing in a row with their backs to the audience. As Mae
walked along upstage of them, each man in turn would
open his cloak for her inspection, and, with her gaze fixed
upon private parts, she would quip:
'I'm glad to meet you — face to face.'
'I feel like a million tonight. But — one at a time.'
'This muscleman is an all-round guy. He won the broad
jump, too.'
'Take it easy, boys and last a long time.'

Joel Friend, the dancer, had to teach a new recruit his routine when a muscleman left. This happened quite frequently because it was then believed that every orgasm diminished an athlete's vigour, and Mae expected them to perform in her bedroom as well as to go through the motions on the stage, to which some objected, including a 21-year-old Adonis who confided to Friend that he could not cope with Miss West's nightly demands. He hardly got any sleep and felt that he was heading for a nervous breakdown. The dancer advised the youth to tell the switchboard operator not to put through any calls to his room. However, Mae got a maid to knock on his door and give him a note in which the Queen of Sex insisted on his coming to her suite or quit the show.

Mae would interview all applicants herself. Friend wondered how she went about it and eventually a candidate disclosed that she had begun by asking him to take off his trousers. He stammered that he couldn't as he wore no underwear. To which she had replied: 'That's OK. If you had, I'd ask you to pull them off, too.' Whether the fellow was engaged or not, it seems depended on how much he appealed to her sexually. The public got a male striptease show — the first in America — and she provided herself with a stud of picked partners.

When the theatre critic, George Nathan, saw a picture of Mae West representing her as a sort of Statue of Liberty liberating her fellow Americans from the shackles confining their sexual urges, he commented wryly: 'She looks to me more like the Statue of Libido.' If such a monument were ever erected to her, a suitable site might be West Point — then guides to that military academy might tell tourists that it was named after her because so many cadets 'passed out' after a night in her arms.

A century ago most artists tried to conceal their promiscuity, but now it has become the fashion not only to brag about sexual exploits but to exaggerate for publicity purposes.

None of the excesses of film stars in their public and

private lives can have exceeded those that took place during the production of *Caligula*. Over 300 women seeking parts were required by the director, Tinto Brass, to undergo screen tests when they had to actually demonstrate their sexual skills and how convincingly they could express rapture during intercourse. He was delighted when a man seeking work as an extra revealed that he had two penises. This prodigy was immediately engaged. Brass was determined that the orgy to end all orgies aboard ship should come over as authentic in every way so he took two days over shooting it, and nothing was faked. Tinto directed with zest, having oral sex with a *Penthouse* Pet on the set to demonstrate to an actor the most cinematically effective way of doing it. When questioned by the Press as to how she reacted to this, Mrs Brass said that her husband was just being his normal 'extroverted self'. Peter O'Toole as the Emperor Tiberius entered into the spirit of the show with such vigour and so stabbed a Roman guard for failing in a drinking contest that the actor had to be rushed to hospital.

According to Pier-Nico Solinas in his book, *Ultimato Porno*, *Penthouse*, which was financing the film, wanted it to be 'a soft-core soft-focus copy of the magazine', whereas Tinto Brass's intention was to make 'a kind of anarchist, hard-core slapstick comedy'. It was only after shooting had ended that *Penthouse* discovered that this was how the picture had turned out. One editor after another was employed by them for three years before *Caligula* reached the cinemas in a form of which they approved.

XIX

ABNORMAL APPETITES
AND APHRODISIACS

We have traversed the centuries and we have seen how homo sapiens is ever thirsty and ever hungry for food and for sex, and how with some it becomes an obsession. A few have also developed abnormal appetites, eating anything from old boots to razor blades. Sir John Franklin, the explorer, was alarmed to see an Eskimo youth consume at a single sitting not one tallow candle but 14 lb. of them. Evelyn's diary entry for 2 January 1684, reads: 'I dined at Sir Stephen Fox's; after dinner came a fellow who ate live charcoal, glowingly ignited, quenching them in his mouth, and then champing and swallowing them down.' There was a human ostrich who, if invited out to dinner, would eat not only the food but the plates, glasses, cutlery, finishing up with the table-cloth as well for dessert.

Robert Southey in his *Common-place Book* relates how there was a mad fashion among riotous drinkers about 1792 of eating the wine glass, biting pieces out of it, grinding them with the teeth, and actually swallowing the fragments — 'the enjoyment being to see how an aspirant cut his mouth!' Southey adds: 'I never saw this, but R. L. had done it. Mortimer, the artist, did it, and is said never to have recovered from the consequences.'

In France, a servant girl would eat a broomstick for

lunch, while a nineteenth-century American poet found that he composed his best poems when chewing shavings and strips of wood. Entering the study of a London friend in his absence, he sat on a chair facing its back and, taking out a whittling-knife, attacked the top rail. This sharpened his appetite and he was starting to eat another portion of polished birch when the owner of the mutilated chair came in. He behaved magnanimously and quipped: 'My dear fellow, why have you fed yourself such hard and indigestible fare, when that sofa pillow, stuffed with down was available?'

In 1754 there died at Wittenberg an eighty-year-old gardener, named Kahle, who first attracted notice as a boy by devouring a basket, and who, once, alone in a room, bit the leather coverings off the chairs and ate them, then he fed on an inkstand and the quill pens — all seasoned to his taste. Grenadier Joseph Kelliker began swallowing stones following a meal at the age of three and continued doing so after joining the army, as well as consuming 25 lb. of beef a day. Eventually, a bullet penetrating his stomach hit the collection of stones and he died as a result of the shock caused by the concussion.

Most of those addicted to abnormal provender do not suffer from indigestion. Topham Beauclerk, however, in his reminiscences describes how an acquaintance of his doted on buttered muffins but could not eat them because they disagreed with his stomach, so he decided to shoot himself and then ate several buttered muffins for breakfast before doing this 'knowing that he would never again be troubled with indigestion'.

To ordinary folk, the tastes of some gourmets may also seem odd. Harold Nicolson knew a millionaire whom he described as 'inordinately greedy, inordinately rich' and who would prepare every day his favourite soup in a silver cauldron before his privileged guests. Balinese spices went in, together with Ithaean olives, a shelled and shattered lobster, bottles of Veuve Clicquot and amontillado. According to Nicolson, this tasted of 'very hot cough mixture drunk with shrimp sauce'. Not so long ago, the *Tatler*'s tit-bits of gossip included the news that Countess Mestenburg's 'little weakness is budgerigar casserole' and that her regular guests included Princess Michael of Kent and Raine Spencer. And a new book revealed that gastronome Willie Mark recommended for a special treat lips of chimpanzee, bear's paw stew, and boiled elephant trunk, whilst Pierre Troisgras believed one would die happy after washing down Iranian caviar with iced vodka aged in pearwood casks and chilled to a temperature of 35° F. More catholic in her tastes and a frequent visitor to London, Lucienne Goldberg of New York, asks: 'Why don't Harrods rent out sleeping bags in the Food Hall? Wouldn't that be a heavenly place to wake up in?'

Of course, to be fair, people react differently to various foods. What is distasteful and harmful to one may be enjoyed and safely eaten by another. As Reay Tannahill has pointed out, if one heeds all the warnings of diet pundits, almost anything can kill you. Too much sugar can cause obesity and salt is even more dangerous — just 1 oz. daily can shorten a man's life by as much as thirty years, and ⅓ oz. a day of caffeine is like taking a deadly poison. Nutmeg and avocado pears are also toxic, onions can make one anaemic, the oxalic acid in spinach and rhubarb build kidney stones, cabbage can bring on goitre, and cyclamates used as slimming sweeteners are worse than sugar for they can lead to cancer of the bladder. Even liquorice is blamed for high blood pressure, and as for bitter almonds they are the equivalent of taking prussic acid in solid form.

Those who crave sex and lack potency have turned to aphrodisiacs. Brillat-Savarin relates how the Sultan Saladin wishing to find out how chaste his pious dervishes were, imprisoned two in his palace, and, for a time, had them fed exclusively on meat. Soon all traces of their past severe regime vanished. Their skins filled out again and they grew sleek. Then two odalisques of rare loveliness were introduced as their companions, but all the wiles of these sirens failed to seduce the holy men. The Sultan, however, now changed their diet to one entirely of fish, and when a week had passed he exposed them once more to the blandishments of the concubines. This time, the dervishes succumbed.

Oysters are reputed to be aphrodisiacs, but that was not why Charles Dickens's colourful character, Dando, craved them. He used to go into oyster shops without a farthing, and then stand at the counter eating natives until the man who opened them grew pale, threw down his knife, staggered backward, struck his white forehead with his open hand, and gasped, 'You are Dando!!!'

Dickens continues:

> He had been known to eat twenty dozen at one sitting, and would have eaten forty, if the truth had not flashed upon the shopkeeper. For these offences, he was constantly committed to the House of Correction. During his last imprisonment, he was taken ill, got worse and worse, and at last began knocking violent double knocks at Death's door. The doctor stood beside his bed, with his finger on his pulse. 'He is going,' says the doctor. 'I see it in his eye. There is only one thing that would keep life in him for another hour, and that is — oysters.' They were immediately brought. Dando swallowed eight, and feebly took a ninth. He held it in his mouth and looked round the bed strangely. 'Not a bad one, is it?' says the doctor. The patient shook his head, rubbed his trembling hand upon his stomach, bolted the oyster, and fell back — dead. They buried him in the prison-yard, and paved his grave with oyster shells.

On the tombstone of another lover of oysters this was engraved:

> Tom, whom today no noise stirs,
> Lies buried in these cloisters;
> If, at the last trump,

He does not quickly jump,
Only cry 'Oysters'.

Dickens as well as Thackeray and other well-known personalities once made their way to an oyster saloon in Drury Lane to observe a musical mollusc which had become the talk of the day for gastronomes. This stimulated sales for the astute proprietor as the curious stuffed themselves with the other oysters. He had discovered that the unique specimen had a small hole in its upper shell and when water was forced through the opening a loud whistling sound was produced. On such excessive interest in trivialities does the prosperity of businesses sometimes depend!

Down the ages and in many countries people have become obsessed with oysters. Cicero believed that plenty of them made his oratory more effective and King Louis XI of France treated the faculty at the Sorbonne annually to a sumptuous repast of them 'lest their scholarship should become deficient'. Later, one of Bonaparte's brightest marshals attributed his military skill to starting his breakfast with a 100 of them.

Casanova became notorious for the oyster orgy when he entertained two nuns to a feast of them and champagne, having first so overheated the room that the young women were forced to discard their outer clothes. Unaccustomed to alcohol, it was not long before they became tipsy, enabling him to coax them into taking part in a game of sucking oysters out of each other's mouth including his. Then he began letting oysters slip down between the nuns' breasts and retrieving them with his lips. Next, he pretended that oysters had become trapped inside their corsets which the girls were teased into removing. Now, he insisted that some slippery morsels had disappeared lower down and made much play of comparing the dimensions of his dupes' legs. In his extensive memoirs, Casanova gives details of his amorous adventures claiming to have had sex with over 132 women, including twelve sets of two women at once, and to have deflowered thirty-one virgins.

Professor McCary, the American sexologist, was of the opinion that a gourmet meal with choice wines in a glamorous setting was the surest way whereby a Don Juan could persuade a woman to join him in bed. McCary describes a pudding he has served his dinner guests which many of them have called 'very sexy'. It consists of slices of pears and strawberries soaked in Cointreau and drenched in a fragrant sauce of beaten egg yolks, confectioner's sugar, cloves and cinnamon.

McCary adds: 'The dessert is smooth, rich and creamy in texture — qualities we subconsciously equate with sexuality. In addition, its redolence (cloves, cinnamon, liqueur) is "exotic", another word we tend, however vicariously, to identify with sexual concepts.'

In this article, *Aphrodisiacs and Anaphrodisiacs*, in the *Encyclopaedia of Sexual Behaviour*, the same writer also draws attention to basic physical analogies between various forms of food and both male and female genitalia. In other words, not only does eating equal intercourse, but also food equals penis, vulva. 'Although little known even to specialists, the making and eating of phallic foods (the representation of certain foods, usually bread, cakes and other pastries, in the form of sexual organs) is a custom that has been practised for centuries in many civilizations throughout the world as a significant religious rite.'

Norman Douglas in *Paneros* gave an entertainingly comprehensive guide to the subject. He lists many of the foods excessively active amorists have devoured for stimulation, such as pigeons, partridges and turtle-doves, in the hope that their reputed amorous qualities would be transmitted to those who ate them. In the East, a much-recommended preparation consisted of tiger's testicles crushed and mixed with arack of rice. For vegetarians, a wide selection of aids to vigour were available — pistachio nuts, marjoram, parsley, roots of chervil and of fern, radish, lotus, sandix, carrot, cummin, thyme, sage borage, celery, calamint, saw-wort, penny royal, walnuts, almonds, dates, quinces, mint, onions, musk, carraway, sage, vanilla, origan, ginger truffles, asparagus, swallows' nests from China, and chestnuts which, wrote the Elizabethan, Buttes, in his *Dyets Dry Dinner*, in appearance 'much resembleth *Testes*, the instrument of lust'. In Paris, street-sellers did a brisk trade shouting: 'Artichokes! Artichokes! Heats the body and the spirit. Heats the genitals!' A sweetmeat in the sixteenth century popular with lovers, coated with sugar or candied, was the eringo, sea holly roots. Highly regarded, too, was the sorceress Circe's plant, the mandrake. It was some of these that Leah ate before sleeping with the promiscuous Jacob. They proved most effective and she bore him a fifth son (Genesis 30: 14-16). Mandrake, it was said, could infect with a fury of passion even an elephant.

Onions are the erotic stimulants that were most often taken by the ancient Greeks. Ovid says in his *Amaroriae*: 'Some mingle pepper with the seed of the boiling nettle, and yellow camomile ground up in old urine; but the goddess . . . will not thus be driven to her joys. Let white onions . . . be eaten.' In Rome in Pliny's day, both partners or only the reluctant one would often take an erotic cocktail of garlic ground up with coriander in white wine before attempting sex.

The tomato and the datura have also been regarded as having qualities exciting desire. A plant of the same family, bhuta-kohali, a recipe prescribes, 'having exposed its juice to the sun till dried, mix it with ghee, sugar candy, and honey and you will find that it gives you the strength of ten men'.

Those seeking a sexual boost and fond of fish have in the past eaten sucking-fish, star-fish, cuttle-fish, the roes of sturgeon or smoked or salted mullet, anchovies, turtle, prawns, shrimps, cray-fish, the fins of sharks, buttered crab, sea-urchins, whelks, and mussels. Some claimed from experience that shell-fish would 'raise Venus from the sea'.

Ambergris is still considered to be a powerful aphrodisiac in parts of the East today and coffee is drunk out of a cup with a piece fixed in a hollow drilled in the bottom. In seventeenth-century Europe, a tincture of it would often be added to both coffee and tea. A commoner form of stimulant given to those just married in Persia was sheep's trotters soaked in vinegar.

In ancient China, according to what a scholar living in that century, Wang Chieh, wrote in his *Kuang-tz'û-hsü*, excess potency was possessed by beavers, deers, seals, and lizards, so their genitals were used as stimulants. The *Tung-hsüan-tzû*, a collection of sex recipes from the early days of the Ming dynasty, contains one for 'The Bald Chicken Potion' which was reputed to cure 'a man's five sufferings and seven aches and preserve him from impotence'. Lii Ta-ching, Prefect of Sku, tried this when aged seventy and, thanks to it, had three sons, but it had unfortunate consequences for his wife. He had such excessive intercourse with her that she could neither sit nor lie down, so he threw what he had left of the concoction into the yard where a cock swallowed it. The effect was startling. The fowl sprang on to a hen and copulated without stopping for several days, picking the hen's head until it was completely bald.

The recipe for this goes: 'Powderize and sieve 3 gramme each of jou-tsung-jung (*Boschniakia glabra*), wu-wei-tzû (*Schizardra sinensis*), t'u-szû (*Cuscuta japonica*), yüan-chih (*Polygala japonica*), and 4 grammes of shê-ch'uang-tzû (*Cridium japonicum*). Take this daily on an empty stomach in a spoonful of wine. If taken for sixty days a man will be able to copulate with forty women. The powder may also be mixed with wax and rolled into pills as small as *wu-t'ung* seeds. Start by taking these regularly for between five and nine days, thereafter as required.'

Master Tung-Hsuan includes in his collection of recipes one for enlarging the penis. To make this, one first powderizes and sieves 3 grammes of a fungus, jou-tsung-jung, (*Boschniakia glabra*) and 2 of hai-tsao (sea grass). Mix with liver extract from a white dog killed during the first moon and apply to the penis as an ointment three times.

Then wash off with fresh water taken from the well early in the morning. This would lengthen the organ to three times its original size.

The aphrodisiac with the worst reputation is cantharides which probably originated in the Orient and was introduced into western Europe by returning Crusaders. It consists of dried and powdered blister beetles, commonly known as Spanish flies, which through inflaming the gastro-intestinal system excites the genitals. In 1758, the notorious Marquis de Sade procured a number of prostitutes in Marseilles and made them take part in mutual whipping and have intercourse with him and his valet Latour. They were offered and greedily consumed delicious bonbons containing cantharides and as a result their urge for sex became uncontrollable and they abandoned themselves to every kind of excess. Nearly two centuries previously, Cabrol, a pupil of the great surgeon, Ambroise Paré, wrote how in 1572 they went to see a man in Provence originally suffering from a quartan fever.

> To cure it he had consulted an old sorceress, who made him a potion composed of an ounce and a half of nettles and two drams of cantharides, which made him so ardent in the venereal act that his wife swore to us that he had been astride her, during two nights, eighty-seven times without thinking it more than ten, and even while we were there, the poor man ejaculated thrice in our presence, embracing the foot of the bed and moving against it as if it were his wife.

Madame de Pompadour when she feared King Louis XV's love for her was waning obtained a tincture of cantharides, but fortunately for her, before she could take any, the bottle was found by the Duchess de Brancas who recognizing the smell of the liquid destroyed it, and the Pompadour resorted instead to a milder but safer ardour-encouraging diet of celery soup and *chocolat à triple vanille*. Had she been a Greek or Roman courtesan she might have tried pepper, myrrh and equal quantities of two scents called Cyprus and Egyptian. According to Pliny, glands of animals, too, were used, and in particular those of the pig, the stag, the horse and the hyena.

An anonymous English poet gave in verse form in 1597 his recommended diet for male lovers whose heat needed stoking up:

> Good sir, if you lack the strength on you back
> And would have a Remediado
> Take Eryngo rootes and Marylebone tartes
> Redde wine and riche Potato
>
> An oyster pie and a Lobster's thighe
> Hard eggs well drest in Marow
> This will ease your backes disease
> And make you good Cocksparrowe. . . .

Red wine mixed with powdered partridge brain is good for sex, according to the thirteenth-century theologian, Albertus Magnus. Four hundred years later, a popular 'cocktail' for such purposes consisted of ants, cinnamon and wine, whilst in orgies bees' semen, blood, and the genitals of all kinds of fowls and animals would be added. A less outrageous aid to love made a great deal of money for an impudent quack of a clergyman, Dr Graham, who in the last decade of the eighteenth century, invited those in need of sexual stimulation to patronize the Temple of Health and Hymen he had opened in London's Pall Mall and for a charge of £100 to lie all night in his splendidly ornamented 'Celestial Bed for Superior Beings' on a mattress stuffed with stallion's hair and other ingredients guaranteed to possess aphrodisiac powers — and reinforced with 1,500 magnets. Further assistance came from burning incense and music. Most of his clientèle were roués of rank seeking novel distractions.

There have been those who have tired of being oversexed such as the eighteenth-century musician who complained to his physician that his playing was deteriorating through his being racked every few hours by erotic desires. The medico tried a variety of remedies — bleeding, sedatives, fasting — but none helped, so he told him to marry and the patient made a lusty country girl his bride. At the start, this appeared to cure his neuroticism, but he wore his wife out and she became so ill that intercourse had to cease and his satyriasis flared up again. In desperation, he sadly came to the conclusion that castration was the only solution. Then, at the eleventh hour, a friend advised him to try a course of saltpetre which to his astonishment so reduced his ruttishness that he could hardly cope with the occasional approaches of his enfeebled spouse.

XX

THE NEW PERMISSIVENESS

In *Passion and Prudery*, published in 1971, Wilton Rugoff discusses the new permissiveness as recommended by its advocates in the previous decade. He mentions the New York psychologist, Albert Ellis, who in *Sex and the Single Man* denounced premarital chastity as masochism and give it as his firm belief that the more sexually active a person is the happier and healthier he will be. Dr David R. Reuben agreed in his best-seller, *Everything You Always Wanted to Know About Sex . . . But Were Afraid to Ask*, stressing that every organ must be exercised regularly. 'Use it or lose it,' he warns. Rugoff comments that whereas the Victorian physician warned against indulgence, the Space Age one warns against abstinence. 'One has a vision of millions of readers coming away with a desperate feeling that they must copulate constantly or face atrophy.'

The theme of *The Sensuous Woman* by 'J' was bigger and better orgasms, stimulation by mouth, group sex with exchange of partners, threesomes, and a dozen varieties of masturbation, including the use of an electric vibrator. Mr Rugoff comments that in a society where every process is being mechanized, this book by a woman author offered a formula for ecstasy in which a machine replaced the phallus. 'American technology can hardly go further.'

Dr Wm. H. Masters and Mrs Virginia E. Johnson's *Human Sexual Response*, was characterized by Malcolm Muggeridge as 'the apogee of the orgasm'. In it, the authors arranged for nearly 700 men and women of all ages to allow themselves to be studied and photographed while engaged in coitus and masturbating. In their next book, *Human Sexual Inadequacy*, Masters and Johnson stressed the laboratory approach to sex. All these details, studied and graded by machines, would guide couples to the recommended goal of the maximum sexual activity achievable. According to these writers, as Milton Rugoff underlined, 'the machines demonstrated, among other things, that masturbation with a mechanical dildo gave women the most sexual pleasure'. A machine was more satisfying to them than intercourse with men.

Rugoff also pointed out that the licence to dwell upon the sensual act without restraint poses a new problem for the novelist, who, by describing it so often and in such detail, had turned it into a set piece that either bores us stiff or must be read in the same way as one listens to a soprano doing a familiar aria.

It is perhaps not surprising that Germaine Greer, who championed Women's Lib with her 1969 book, *The Female Eunuch*, and who admits to many lovers and abortions, has become bored by sex and advocates abstinence as a better form of Birth Control than the Pill. Interviewed by *Woman's Own* in November 1985, she said: 'Sex has become so recreational and trivial. Everybody's read all the sex books, so everybody knows what to do, but nobody knows what to say.' Women had become too accessible. 'It never occurred to anybody that if men got the opportunity they wouldn't be able to do it. So now we've got sex clinics treating men for lack of interest. . . . No wonder women are drinking and queuing up for tranquilizers from their G.P.s.'

The latest statistics certainly give cause for concern as regards drink. The number of women diagnosed as addicts has trebled in the last five years. Alcohol is killing more women than ever before; six times as many die of cirrhosis of the liver as did twenty years ago.

The *Sunday Mirror* found a new scapegoat for Britain's industrial decline when in January 1986, it announced that office love affairs were losing the country billions of pounds each year. 'As the love bug reaches epidemic proportions, industry is suffering. Valuable man hours are spent flirting behind the files and trysting in the typing pool.' This had been revealed in a new study by the Strathclyde Business School. Sex went on in store cupboards, washrooms and mattresses in delivery vans. Industrial psychologist, Cary Cooper, was calling for extra training to cope with the crisis. There should be a permanent Agony Aunt in every office and factory. American companies were already aware of the problems and employed counsellors to deal with emotional problems.

What would be the effect on workers, one wonders of listening to Dr Ruth Westheimer, whose arrival from New York was reported in the same issue of the *Sunday Mirror*. She had earned over a million dollars on American TV advising people to live out their sexual fantasies and her video *Terrific Sex* and book *Guide to Good Sex* were best sellers in the States. 'Men are just not capable of expressing their sexual desires,' she said. 'If they want covering head to toe with cold cream, they should tell their partners.' Sex was OK for the over sixties as long as they did not attempt acrobatic positions.

The most disturbing aspect of permissiveness today is the growth of the blue video market and its harmful effects on children. Unity Hall in the *News of the World* for 29 December 1985, claimed that they were turning young couples to group sex in Britain's 'once staid suburbs'. After talking to 349 husbands and wives, aged twenty to thirty-nine, in the suburbs of London, Birmingham, Manchester, Liverpool, and Glasgow, it was found that more than a fifth of young couples held or went to parties where blue videos were shown. London led the way in group sex after watching them.

When one excess becomes too common, snobs can be expected to turn to something else. A recent raid resulted in the finding of an amazing letter from a titled lady high up in London society. In it, she rebuked her son for dabbling in pornography and she added: 'Why don't you get yourself involved in something more stylish like cocaine?' A frightening attitude that might have come in former times from a Caligula or a Borgia. *Plus ça change, plus c'est la même chose*. The road to ruin is not a straight one, but goes round and round in circles.

SELECT BIBLIOGRAPHY

ATHENAEUS: *The Deipnosophists*
BALSDON, J. P. V. D.: *Life and Leisure in Ancient Rome*
BENSON, E. F.: *King Edward VII*
BERTEAUT, SIMONE: Edith Piaf
BLOCH, IWAN: *Sexual Life in England, past and present*
    The Sexual Life of Our Times
BRASSAI: *The Secret Paris of the 1930s*
BRILLAT-SAVARIN, J. A.: *The Physiology of Taste*
BRITTAIN, A.: *Roman Woman*
BROTHWELL, D. R.: *Food in Antiquity*
BURNETT, JOHN: *Plenty and Want*
BURNS, DAWSON: *The History of Temperance*
BUTTES, HENRY: *Dyetts Dry Dinner*
BYNG, JOHN: *The Torrington Diaries, 1734-8*
CARCOPINO, J.: *Daily Life in Ancient Rome*
CAREME, M. A.: *French Cooking*
CHAFETZ, M. E.: *Liquor, the Servant of Man*
CLEUGH, JAMES: *Oriental Orgies*
COUGHLAN, R.: *Elizabeth and Catherine*
CRAFTS, W. F.: *Intoxicants*
CREEVEY, THOMAS: *The Creevey Papers,*
    ed. Sir Herbert Maxwell
CUTNER, H.: *A Short History of Sex Worship*

DANIELSON, B.: *Love in the South Seas*

DAY, LILLIAN: *Ninon de Lenclos*

DILL, S.: *Roman Society from Nero to Marcus Aurelius*

DIODORUS SICULUS: *The Bibliotheca Historica*

DOUGLAS, G. N.: *Paneros*

DUTTON, J. P.: *The good fare and cheer of old England*

ELLS, G. and MUSGROVE, S.: *Mae West, the Lies, the Legend, the Truth*

EPTON, NINA: *Love and the French*

EPULARIO: *The Italian Banquet*

EVANS, JOAN: *Life in Mediaeval France*
   The Victorians

EVELYN, JOHN: *Diary*

FAEFF, M.: *Catherine the Great*

FERMIGIER, ANDRÉ: *Henri de Toulouse-Lautrec*

FLYNN, ERROL: *My wicked, wicked ways*

FOWLER, GENE: *Good Night, Sweet Prince*

FRENCH, RICHARD: *Nineteen Centuries of Drink in England*

FURNAS, J. C.: *The Life and Times of the late Demon Drink*

GRAHAM, STEPHEN: *Peter the Great*

GRANT, MICHAEL: *The Climax of Rome*
   The Ancient Mediterranean
   Julius Caesar
   Nero

GRAY, IAN: *Peter the Great*

GREENWALD, HAROLD: *The Prostitute in Literature*

GRIMLEY, GORDON: *Wicked Victorians*

HANSON, L. & E. M.: *The Life of Toulouse-Lautrec*

HARRIS, FRANK: *My Life and Loves*

HAYWARD, ABRAHAM: *The Art of Dining*

HEYMAN, DAVID: *Poor Little Rich Girl*

HIBBERT, CHRISTOPHER: *Benito Mussolini*

HICKEY, WILLIAM: *Memoirs*, ed. Peter Quennell

HOLINSHED: *Chronicles*

HUKERS, W.: *The Romance of Tea*

HURWOOD, B. J.: *The Golden Age of Erotica*

JACOBS, H. E.: *The Saga of Coffee*

JEAFFRESON, JOHN: *A Book About The Table*

JUVENAL: *The Sixteen Satires*

KIEFER, OTTO: *Sexual life in ancient Rome*

KINGSMILL, HUGH: *After Puritanism*

KIRWAN, A. W.: *Host and Guest*

LONGMATE, N. R.: *The Waterdrinker*

LONGWORTH, PHILIP: *Three Empresses*

MACLEAN BAIRD, I. and HOWARD, ALAN: *Obesity*

McCARY, JAMES LESLIE: *Encyclopaedia of Sexual Behaviour*

McLEAVE, HUGH: *The Last Pharaoh*

MANNIX, DANIEL: *The Hell-Fire Club*

MARCUS, STEVEN: *The Other Victorians*

MAY, ROBERT: *The Accomplisht Cook*

MAYHEW, HENRY: *Selections from London Labour and London Poor*

MEAD, WILLIAM EDWARD: *The English Mediaeval Feast The Grand Tour in the Eighteenth Century*

MELIK, W. D.: *Sex on the Campus*

MINNEY, R. J.: *The Edwardian Age Rasputin*

MISSON, H.: *M. Misson's memoirs and observations in his travels over England*

MOATS, ALICE LEONE: *The Million Dollar Studs*

MORITZ, CARL: *Travels through various parts of England, in 1782*

NEVILL, R. H.: *The Gay Victorians*

OLDENBOURG, ZOE: *Catherine the Great*

OTERO, CAROLINE: *My story*

OUDARD, G.: *Peter the Great*

PARES, SIR BERNARD: *A History of Russia*

PARTRIDGE, BURGO: *A History of Orgies*

PETRONIUS ARBITER: *Cena Trimalchionis*

PRIESTLEY, J. B.: *The Edwardians*

RENNER, H. D.: *The Origin of Food Habits*

RHEIMS, MAURICE: *The Glorious Obsession*

RITZ, MARIE: *César Ritz, Host to the World*

RONSELL, MARY C.: *Ninon de Lenclos*

RUGOFF, MILTON: *Prudery and Passion*

RYLEY-SCOTT, G.: *Encyclopaedia of Sex*

Phallic Worship
Far Eastern Sex Life
RYAN, MICHAEL: *Prostitution in London*
SAMUELSON, J.: *The History of Drink*
SANGER, W.: *The History of Prostitution*
SLATER, LEONARD: *Aly*
SOYER, ALEXIS: *The Pantropheon*
STARKEY, THOMAS: *England in the reign of Henry VIII*
STERN, MICHAEL: *Farouk*
SUETONIUS TRANQUILLUS: *The Twelve Caesars*
TACITUS, PUBLIUS CORNELIUS: *The Annals of Ancient Rome*
TEONGE, HENRY: *Diaries, 1675-9*
TSCHUMI, GABRIEL: *Royal Chef*
TURNER, E. S.: *Roads to Ruin*
Taking the Cure
VAN GULIK, R. H.: *Sexual Life in Ancient China*
WALISZEWSKI, K.: *Peter the Great*
Catherine II
WILSON, COLIN: *Rasputin*
WOODFORDE, JAMES: *The Diary of A Country Parson (1758-82)*
WYDEN, PETER: *The Overweight Society*

INDEX

Accomplished Cook, The..., (May) 58
Acropolis (bordello), 10-11
Addison, Joseph, 168
Adler, Polly (madam), 190-1
Aga Khan, 203
Agrippina (wife of Claudius), 16
Albemarle, George, 3rd Earl of, 76
Albert, Prince of Monaco, 159
Albertus Magnus, 229
Alcobaça, Abbot of, 103
Aleppo (Syria), 123
Alexander I (Tsar), 120
Alexandra, Queen, consort of Edward
    VII, 173
Alexis I Mikhailovich (Tsar), 112
Alfonso XIII (King of Spain), 160
Alfred, Duke of Edinburgh, 178
Aline (model), 162
Allais, Alphonse (barman), 131
Alvanley, Lord, 175
Amaroriae (Ovid), 226
Amour au 18 ème siècle, Les sociétés d',
    108
Amusements de Spa (Polluitz), 128
Anastasia, Grand Duchess, 179
Anatomy of Melancholy (Burton), 46
Andalusia (Spain), 102
Anecdotes (Piozzi), 95
Anne (Queen of England), 72, 81
Anne of Austria (Queen of France),
    48
Annunzio, Gabriele d', 151

Antony, Mark, 13-14
Aphrodite, Temple of, 11
Aphrodite (Paris bordello), 108-9
Aphrodite (Louÿs), 28
Apicius, M. Gavius, 12
Apollinaris (water), 175-6
Apraxin, Theodor M. (Admiral), 115
Argenson, Marc R., Marquis d', 107
Arthur (British King), 41
Artois, Robert, Comte d', 38
Ascot Races, 148-9
Astarteion, Temple of, 28-30
Astor, Mrs W. M. junior, 189
Athenaeum, The (periodical), 188
Athenaeus (Greek anecdotist), 12, 28
Atlantic City, 188
Augier, Emile (playwright), 157
Augustus (Roman Emperor), 14
Avantageuse (amatory aid), 108

Babylonia, 28
Bacchanalia, 12, 122, 188
Bach, J. S., 68
Bagenal, Beauchamp, 84-5
Ball, Dr John (pathologist), 154-5
'Balsamic Corroborant', 101
Balzac, Honoré de, 139
Bardot, Brigitte, 208
Barrymore, John, 192, 209-14, 216
Barucci, Giulia (whore), 172
Bath (Somerset), 70-1

Bath, or the Western Lass, The (Durfey), 71
Beatty, Warren (film star), 193
Beauclerk, Topham (writer), 221
Béchamel, Louis de, 105-6, 141
Beckford, William, 103-4
Bede, The Venerable, 33
Beefsteak Club, 135
Berkeley, Theresa (whore), 101-2
Bernier, Francis (traveller), 121
Black, Kitty, 199
Blair Castle (Scotland), 185-90
Blayney, Lord, 84
Bleak House (Dickens), 152
Bloch, Iwan (writer), 151
Blois, Marie Anne de, 50
Boerhaave, Herman (physician), 128
Boleyn, Anne (Queen), 43
Boniface (Archibishop), 33
Booth, Lawrence (Archibishop), 39
Borgia family, 39-40, 234
Borsage, M. du (architect), 108
Boswell, James, 87, 89-96
Boutourlin, Peter I., 115-16
Brady, 'Diamond' Jim, 176-7
Brass, Tinto (film director), 219
Bretonne, Restif de la, 109
Briand, Aristide, 160
Brillat-Savarin, Anthelme, 103, 125-6, 137, 222
Brooke, Fulke, 5th Baron, 60
Brown, John Mason, 216
Bruce (Russian General), 115
Bryer, Emma (journalist), 155
Buckingham Committee (1834), 152
Buckingham Palace, 170
Burchard (Bishop of Ostia), 39
Burghley, Wm. Cecil, 1st Baron, 44
Burnet, Gilbert (historian), 51, 52
Burton, Robert (writer), 46
Buttes, Henry (writer), 226
Byng, Colonel John, 84

Cabannal, Pierre, 209
Cabrol (pupil of Paré), 228
Caesar, Gaius Julius — *see* Julius Gaius (Caesar)
California, 188
Caligula (Roman Emperor), 15-16, 234
Caligula (film), 219
Cambacérès, J. J. R. de, 141
Cambis (King of Lydia), 22

Camden, William (historian), 43
Canterbury Tales (Chaucer), 35
Cantibaris (Persian gourmand), 22
Canute (English King), 7
Capri (island), 14-15
Caracalla, M. Aurelius (Emperor), 20
Cardigan, George Wm., Earl of, 174
Carême, Marie-Antoine (chef), 135-7, 140
Carlisle House, Soho, 99
Carlton Hotel, Cannes, 160
Carlton House, 132, 134
Carrington, Margaret, 210
Carroll, Earl, 191
Carteret, Sir George, 81
Casanova, Giovanni, 224-5
Cassini, Oleg (couturier), 196-7
Castiglione, Contessa di, 172
Castlemaine, Lady — *see* Villiers, Barbara
Castlerosse, Lord (Irish Peer), 198-9
Cathcart, Vera, Countess of, 191
Catherine I (Empress of Russia), 113
Catherine II (The Great), 117-19, 206
Cathrine of Braganza, Queen, consort of Charles II, 127
Cato, the Elder, 22
Catullus, G. Valerius (poet), 15
Chaliapin, Feodor, 212
Chapman, Thomas D. D., 73
Charles V (Emperor of Germany), 45
Charles II (King of England), 45, 51-4, 57, 99, 108, 124-5, 127
Chatsworth (Derbyshire), 173
Chaucer, Geoffrey, 35
Chesterfield, Philip, 4th Earl, 72-3
Chevalier, Maurice, 196
Christian IV (King of Denmark), 45-6
Christina (Queen of Sweden), 49
Churchill, Charles (poet), 86
Cicero, M. Tullius, 13, 224
City Feast (Ward), 66
Clarence, George, Duke of, 7
Clarence, William, Duke of, 135
Clarissa Harlowe (Richardson), 88
Claudel, Paul, 130
Claudius (Roman Emperor), 16, 17
Cleland, John (writer), 100
Cleopatra (Queen of Egypt), 13-14
'Cock Ale' (early cocktail), 130
Coetlogen, Marquise de, 127
Coffee Drink, The Virtue of (Rosee), 123-4
Colette (writer), 160

Colette's (Florida bordello), 191
Coli Paco (dancer), 158
Collins (Tsar Alexei's doctor), 112
Common-place Book (Southey), 220
Compleat Housewife (Smith), 130
Confoute, Joe (ponce), 192-3
Connors, Babe (madam), 192
Cook, Captain James, 99
Cooper, Cary (psychologist), 233
Corbett, Jim ('Gentleman'), 192
Corinth, 11
Cornelys, 'Mrs' (madam), 99
Cornwall, C. W. (Speaker), 84
Cornwall, Richard, Earl of, 39
Corrigan, Laura (hostess), 126
Cox, Richard, 154
Cramm, Gottfried von, 198
Crazy Years, The (Wiser), 172
Creevey, Thomas (diarist), 164
Crusades, 40
Crystal Palace, 169
Curio, G. Scribonius, 13
Curmonsky (epicure), 131
Cuthbert (Archibishop of York), 33

Damita, Lili, 214
Darlington Church register, 56
Dashwood, Sir Francis, 86
Davenport, Edward L., 133
Dead Souls (Gogol), 184
Dean, James, 198
de Comminges (French Ambassador), 52
de Rochefort, Jorevin, 56
Defoe, Daniel, 60, 77, 87-8, 102
Delphi, 10
Denison, J. E. (Viscount Ossington), 170
Description of England (Harrison), 44
Desmoulins, Camille, 8
de Vere, Marthe, 156
Devonshire, Elizabeth, Duchess of, 111
Diamond, Jack (gangster), 190
Diarium Romanum (Burchard), 39
Dickens, Charles, 152, 223, 224
Diet and Pleasure (Reboux), 130
Diocletian (Roman Emperor), 20
Diogenes, 168
Dionysus (Greek god of wine), 12
Dirga-Kali (goddess; wife of Siva), 121
Dixon, William H., 188
Dodds, E. C., 168

Domitian (Roman Emperor), 19
Don Juan, Adventures of (film), 215
Doryphorus (Nero's 'husband'), 17
Douglas, Norman, 225
Drink and Drinking (Mendelssohn), 131
Drunkard's Delight (Juniper), 84
'Drunken Parliament', 51
du Barry, Marie, Comtesse, 110
Dubois, Mme (Comédie Française), 100
Duff, Dr Alexander, 122
Dufferin, James, 2nd Baron, 84
Dumas, Alexandre (père), 138-9
Dunstan (Archbishop), 33
Durfey, Thomas (playwright), 71
Duval, Alexandre (dramatist), 157
Duvivier, Denise, 216
Dyets Dry Dinner (Buttes), 226

East Indies (Hamilton), 120
Edgar (English King), 33
Edinburgh University, 155
Edward IV (King of England), 7
Edward VII, 7, 160, 165, 170, 171-2
Edwardians, The (Priestley), 174
Edwards, Daniel (merchant), 123
Eldon, John, 1st Earl of, 84
Ellington, George, 188
Ellis, Albert (psychologist), 231
Eldon, John, 1st Earl of, 84
Elizabeth I (Queen of England), 43-4, 45
Elizabeth Petrovna (Tsarina), 117
England, A Foreign View of (De Saussure), 82
Eon de Beaumont, G. d', Chevalier, 117
Erotica (books), 149-51
Estoile, Pierre de l' (diarist), 45
Evelyn, John (diarist), 52, 54, 220
'Everlasting Club', 51
Everleigh M. *and* A. (sisters), 191-3
Everything You Always Wanted to Know About Sex .... (Reuben), 231
Exhibition, The Great (1851), 169

Falsification of Food (Mitchell), 124
Fanny Hill (Cleland), 100
Farida, Queen, consort of Farouk, 102
Farouk (King of Egypt), 8, 200-3
Farr, James (publican), 124
Farting Club, 61

241

Fay, Larry (gangster), 190
Female Eunuch, The (Greer), 232
Festus, S. Pompeius (historian), 42
Fielding, Henry, 78
Fields, David (writer), 197-8
'Finishes' (London dives), 145-6
Fitzboodle's Confessions (Thackeray), 140-3
'Five Hundred' (US society), 189
Flanner, Janet, 193-4
Flaubert, Gustave, 30, 139-40
Fletcher, Andrew (of Saltoun), 56
Florists Club, 61-2
Flynn, Errol 8, 214-16
Folkestone, Lord, 133
Foote, Dr Edward B., 188
Fordyce, Dr George, 74-5
Fortnum and Mason, 190
Fowler, Gene, 213
Fowler, Sir Robert, 166-7
Fox, Charles James, 134
Francis I (King of France), 49-50
Francis, Sir Philip, 83
Franklin, Sir John, 220
Friend, Joe (dancer), 218
Froissart, Jean (chronicler), 38
Frundsberg, Georg von, 68

Galanterie Parisienne, La (Vèze), 111
Galba (Roman Emperor), 18-19, 21
Gambetta, Léon, 176
Gamel, Achmed el (merchant), 177
Garbo, Greta, 208
Gargantua (Rabelais), 42
Garland, Judy, 209
Garrick, David, 93
Garway, Thomas, 127
Gastronomy as an Art (Brillat-Savarin), 126
Gauguin, Paul (painter), 144
Gautier, Théophile, 140
Gawain (knight), 41
Geduyn, Abbé, 49
George I (King of England), 72
George III (King of England), 132
George IV (King of England), 132-5
Geta, Septimus, 10
Gin Act (1736), 78
Glyn, Elinor, 174
Goadby, 'Mrs' (madam), 99
Godalming (Surrey), 117
Gododin, The (Celtic poem), 32
Gogol, Nikolai, 184

Goldberg, Lucienne, 222
Golden Palace (of Nero), 17
Good Night, Sweet Prince (Fowler), 213
Gopalsami (phallic god), 120
Gough, John O., 154
Grafton, Augustus, 3rd Duke of, 83
Graham, Dr James (quack), 229
Grant, Cary, 197
Gray, Thomas, 73
Great Eaters of Kent (Taylor), 46-7
Greer, Germaine, 232
Griffs, W. E., 122
Gronow, Rees Howell, 84
Grunstein (lover of Empress Elizabeth), 117
Guide to Good Sex (Westerheimer), 233
Guildhall (London), 164-6
Gustavus II (Adolphus), King of Sweden, 68

Hall, Unity, 233
Hamilton, Captain (traveller), 120
Hamilton, 'Mrs General', 133
Hamlet (Shakespeare), 212
Handel, G. F., 68
Hanson, L. *and* E. M., 162
Hanway, Jonas, 128-9
Hardecanute (English King), 7
Harley, Robert, 1st Earl of Oxford, 81
Harrington, Sir John, 45
Harris, Frank, 165
Harrison, William (antiquarian), 44-5
Hartington, Spencer, Marquess of, 173
Hastings, Battle of, 34
Haynes, Charlotte (madam), 99
Hayward, Abraham, 171
Hebrides, Tour to the (Boswell), 92
Heinkel, Count Guido, 157
Heliogabalus (Roman Emperor), 19-20, 141
Hengist (Saxon chieftain), 32
Henry I (King of England), 7
Henry VIII (King of England), 43
Henry IV (King of France), 38-9, 48
Henry, Prince of Prussia, 192
Herbert, Victor (song-writer), 189
Hercules, 10
Hermes (god of roads), 12
Hermitage (St Petersburg), 119
Herodotus, 28
Hertford, Richard, 4th Marquess of, 172

Hervé, Jean, 108-9
Heyman, David (writer), 196
'Hickey, William', 98-9
Hints... for the Healthy (Kneipp), 125
Hirschfield, Dr Samuel, 209
Hirtius, Aulus, 13
Hogarth, William, 77
Holinshed, Raphael (chronicler), 40
Hood, Thomas (poet), 166
Hook, Theodore E., 81
Horace (Q. Horatius Flaccus, Roman poet), 23
Horsham (Sussex), 164
Hortensius, Q. (orator), 21
Host to the World (Ritz), 176
Howley, Joyce, 191
Human Sexual Inadequacy and ... *Response* (Masters & Johnson), 232
Hutton, Barbara, 7, 194-8

I Want What I Want... (Herbert), 189
Interns' Ball (Paris), 172
Ismail (the Magnificent, Khedive of Egypt), 159, 201
Italians and debauchery, 102
Ivan the Terrible (Tsar), 116

'J' (writer), 231
Jackson, Michael (pop star), 199
Jacob (son of Isaac), 226
Jacob's coffee shop, 123
James I (King of England), 45-6
James I (King of Scotland), 44
Japan, The Religions of (Griffs), 122
Jay Singh (Maharajah), 200
Jefferson, Thomas (President), 76
Jerome, Leonard K., 188
John (King of England), 7
Johnson, Dr Samuel, 91-8
Johnson, Virginia E., 232
Jong, Erica, 194
Journals (Walpole), 75
Juggernaut (Hindu god), 121
Julia (wife of Tiberius), 16-17
Julius III (Pope), 40
Julius, Gaius (Caesar), 13
Juniper, William, 84
Juvenal (D. Junius Juvenalis, satirist), 16, 27, 42

Kahle (German gardener), 221
Kelliker, Joseph, 221
Kéroual, Louise de, Duchess of Portsmouth, 54
Kipling, Rudyard, 171
Kneipp, Sebastian, 125-6
Knes-papa (mock Pontiff), 113-16
Knyveton, John, 74, 96-7, 134
Kobler, John, 210
Korda, Sir Alexander, 8
Koklova, Olga (Picasso), 209
Kotiki (Japanese sacred book), 122
Krishna (Hindu god), 121
Kuang-tz'û-hsü (Chieh), 227
Kubasova, Irina D., 204
Kuprin, Alexandre, 179-84

Lancet, The (periodical), 144, 155
Langrishe, Sir Hercules, 81
Langtry, Lily, 160, 172
Lasalle (courtesan, La Paiva's victim), 157
La Sourde, Berthe, 161
Latour (de Sade's valet), 228
Leah (Jacob's wife), 226
Lecky, W. E. H. (historian), 56
Lenclos, Ninon de, 48-9
Lender, Marcelle (actress), 162
Leopold II (King of Belgium), 159
Lépic, Baron, 158
Lettres Persanes (Montesquieu), 109
Lewis, Sir Watkin, 98
Lii-Ta-ching (Prefect), 227
Linklater, Eric, 84
Livingstone, Belle, 190-1
Lockhart, R. H. Bruce, 178-9
London Spy, The (periodical), 61
Louis XI (King of France), 224
Louis XIV (King of France), 50, 74, 107, 110-11
Louis XVI (King of France), 8
Louis XVIII (King of France), 137, 140, 141
Louvre (Paris), 137
Louÿs, Pierre (novelist), 28-9, 30
Lucullus, L. Licinius, 12-13
Lust (d'Annunzio) 151
Luther, Martin, 68

Macaulay, Thomas, Lord, 45
McCary, J. L. (sexologist), 225
McCormick, Mary, 196

McGary, Mr Justice, 214
Macrobius, 28
Magalotti, Colombo, 203
Magdalen Society (US), 187
Magna Carta, 7
Malory, Sir Thomas, 41
Mann, Sir Horace, 79
Mansfield, Jayne, 197
Mansion, The (speakeasy), 190
Mantua, Isabella, Duchess of, 37
Mariage, Physiologie du (Balzac), 139
Mark, Willie, 222
Market Women's Club, 64-6
Marriage Bed (Defoe), 102
Marriage of Figaro (Beaumarchais), 139
Marriott, Charlotte, Lady, 167
Marriott, Sir William, 166
Mary I (Queen of England), 44
Masters, Dr Wm. H., 232
Maugham, W. Somerset, 8, 176
Maxwell, Elsa, 203
May, Robert (chef), 58
Mazarin, Duchess of, 54
Mdvani, Alexis ('Prince'), 196
Mdvani, Serge, 196
Medmenham (Bucks), 86
Memoirs of a British Agent (Bruce Lockhart), 78
Menager (chef), 171
Mendelssohn, Oscar, 131
Menshikov, Alex. D., Prince, 115
Mercurius Politicus (periodical), 127
Messalina, Valeria (wife of Claudius), 16
Mestenburg, Countess, 222
Methodist Episcopal Church, 153, 187
Metternich, Clemens, Prince, 120
Middlesex Hospital Journal, 168
Milan (King of Serbia), 176
Milan, Beatrice, Duchess of, 37
Miller, Gilbert (impresario), 199
Milo of Crotona, 10
Mirapoix, Duc de, 76
Mirielle (model), 161
Mitchell, John, 126
Mitra, Rájendralála, 121
Mittira (goddess of love), 28
Mnester, M. Lepidus, 15
Mogul Empire, Travels in the (Bernier), 121
Molière, J. B. P., 49
Moll Flanders (Defoe), 87
Monroe, Marilyn, 97

Montagu, Lady Mary W., 86
Montaigne, Michel de, 138
Montbazon, Duchesse de, 197
Monte Carlo, 158, 160
Montesquieu, Charles de, Baron, 109
Montezuma II (Aztec Emperor), 126
Moore, Thomas (poet), 134
Morny, Duc de, 156
Morris, Revd Charles, 153
Moscow, 178
Moulin Galant (Paris), 11
Moulin Rouge (Paris), 161
Muggeridge, Malcolm, 232
Murat, Prince Achille N., 156
Mussolini, Benito, 207
Mussolini, Rachele, 207
Mustang Ranch (bordello), 193
My Dear Children (play), 210-11
My Life and Loves (Harris), 165
Mysteries of the Court (Reynolds), 132

Nadajinsky (confessor), 113
Napoleon I (Emperor), 141
Napoleon III (Emperor), 172
Nash, Thomas (poet), 43
Natanson, Thadée, 162
Nathan, George (critic), 218
Naturales Questiones (Seneca), 21
Naylor, Ina (governess), 200
Nero (Roman Emperor), 17-18
Nevill, George (Archbishop), 39
New America (periodical), 188
New York, 187-8, 193
New Atlantis, The, 100
News of the World (newspaper), 233
Nicholas I (Tsar), 135
Nicholas II (Tsar), 158
Nicholas, Prince of Montenegro, 159
Nicolson, Sir Harold, 221
Nicomedes (King of Bithynia), 13
Nihongi (Japanese sacred book), 122
Niven, David, 215
Norfolk, Charles 11th Duke of, 134-5

Oberea (Queen of Tahiti), 99
Obesity, 68
Odéon, Grand Bal de l', 137
Odyssey (Homer), 10
Ogle, Sir Thomas, 55
Oldfield (satirized by Pope), 68-9
Olearius (traveller), 112
Orgies, History of (Partridge), 41

Orissa, Antiquities of (Mitra), 121
Orleans, Henrietta, Duchess of, 124
Ostrowman, Count, 119
Otero, Caroline ('La Belle Otero'),
    158-60
Othello (Shakespeare), 43
Otho (Roman Emperor), 19
O'Toole, Peter (actor), 219
Ovid (P. Ovidius Naso), 226
Owen, Robert Dale, 187

Paderewski, Ignaz J., 192
Paiva, George, Marques de, 157
Paiva, Therese (La Paiva), 157-8
Palm Beach (Fields), 198
Palmerston, Henry, 3rd Viscount, 170
Paneros (Douglas), 225
Panmure, 1st Baron, 84
Pantagruel (Rabelais), 42
Pantheon (London bordello), 99, 100
Paoli, Pasquale de, General, 96
Paré, Amboise, 228
Paris (pantomimist), 19
Parker, Dorothy, 216
Partridge, Burgo, 41, 193
Pashkof, Anna, 114
Passion and Prudery (Rugoff), 231
Patiala, Maharajah of, 199
Pearl, Cora (courtesan), 156
'Pederasts, Sacred Fraternity of', 108
Penthouse (periodical), 219
Pepys, Samuel, 53-5
*Perfect School of Instruction for Officers of
    the Mouth* (Rose), 57-8
Peron, Evita, 197
Perroni, Patsy, 217
Persia, Shah of, 159
Peter the Great (Tsar), 113-15, 204,
    206
Peter the Hermit, 40
Petronius, Gaius (satirist), 23
Phillips, George, 129
Physiologie du Gout, La (Brillat-
    Savarin), 125
Piaf, Edith, 209
Picasso, Pablo, 208-9
Pierlone, Cardinal, 39
Pike, 'Parson' (of Kirkby Mallory), 72
Pindar, 10
Piozzi, Hester Lynch (Mrs Thrale), 95
Plato's Retreat (bordello), 193
Platter, Thomas, 45
Plautus, T. Maccius, 42

Plea for Nineveh (Reeve), 51
Pliny, the Younger, 21, 229
'Plon-Plon', Prince (Napoleon Joseph
    Bonaparte), 156
Plutarch, 28
Poet's Pub (Linklater), 84
Polluitz, Baron von, 128
Pompadour, Jeanne, Marquise de,
    110
Pompeia (Caesar's wife), 13
Pompey, the Great (Gnaeus Pompeius
    Magnus), 13
Pontchartrain (France), 157
Pope, Alexander, 68-9, 124
Portsmouth, Duchess of — *see*
    Kéroual, Louise de
Potemkin, Grigory, Prince, 118
Priapus (god of fertility), 12
Priestley, J. B., 174
Procopius (historian), 17·
Prohibition (US), 190
Procurers, 147-8
Promenades dans Londres (Tristan), 144
Prostitution, History of (La Croix), 100
Prostitution in London (Ryan), 144
Prostitution, London Society for
    Prevention of Juvenile, 144, 147
Protasoff, Mlle (lady-in-waiting), 118
Public Advertiser (periodical), 127
Pucci, Emilio (designer), 202
Puccini, Giacomo, 7
Pulli Bey, Antonio, 201-2
Pulteney, Wm. 1st Earl of Bath, 81
Puranas (Hindu legends), 122
Puri, Great Temple of, 122
Pyrallis (Roman prostitute), 15

Quatz' Arts, Bal des (Paris), 173, 198

Rabelais, François, 42-3
Rambler (Johnson), 93
Rape of the Lock (Pope), 124
Rasputin, Grigori, 204-7
Rathaus (Berlin), 152
Reboux, Paul, 130-1
Rector's (restaurant), 176
Reeve, John, 51
Regent, Prince — *see* George IV
Religions of Eastern Asia, The
    (Underwood), 122
Rennie, Michael (actor), 198
Reuben, Dr David, 231

Reventlow, Count Ernst zu, 196
Reynolds, G. W. M., 132-3
Richard II (King of England), 38
Richardson, Samuel, 88
Ritz, César (restaurateur), 175
Ritz, Marie-Louise, 176, 196
Rivoli, Duc de, 156
Robbers (Fielding), 78
Rochefoucauld, Duc de la, 82
Rochemont, Valentine de, 105
Rochester, John Wilmot, Earl of, 53
Romeo and Juliet (film), 210
Rose, Giles (chef), 57
Rosebery, Archibald, 5th Earl of, 171
Rosee, Pasqua, 123
Rothschild, Alfred de, 130
Roxana (Defoe), 88
Royal Pavillion, Brighton, 135
Rubirosa, Porfiro, 197
Rudd, Daniel (interior decorator), 198
Rugoff, Wilton, 231-2
Rullus, Servilius, 21
Russell, Edward (Admiral), 60
Russian Journals (Wheeler), 119
Ryan, Dr Michael, 144

Sabinus, Asellius, 14
Sachs, Hans, 68
Sackville, Charles, Earl of Dorset, 55
Sade, D. A. F., Marquis de, 228
Saint-Evremond, Charles, Seigneur
    de, 49
St James's Park, 88-91
Saint-Pierre, Abbaye de, 39
Saladin, Sultan, 222-3
Salammbô (Flaubert), 30-2
Salisbury, Robert Cecil, Earl of, 45
Sandwich, John, 4th Earl of, 86
Satyricon (Petronius), 23-7
Saussure, Horace de, 82
Savarin — *see* Brillat-Savarin
Scandal, The Age of (White), 101
Scarron, Paul, 49
Schroeden-Dervient, Wilhelmina, 151
Schutz, Dutch (gangster), 190
Schwab, Charles M., 189
Scott, Sam, 62-4
*Second Discourse on the Affairs of
    Scotland* (Fletcher), 56-7
Second Satire of Horace (Pope), 68
Secret History of Clubs (Ward), 61
Sedley, Sir Charles, 55
Seneca, M. Annaeus, 21, 23

Sensuous Woman, The ('J'), 231
Servilia (Caesar's mistress), 13
Sévigné, Marie de, 127
Sex and the Single Man (Ellis), 231
Sexual Behaviour (McCary), 225
Sexual Debility in Men (Sturgis), 216
Sexual Life in England (Bloch), 151
Shakespeare, William, 43
Shand, Morton, 8
Shaw, Artie (band leader), 193
Sherek, Henry (impresario), 199
Sheridan, Richard B., 134
Sherman, Vincent, 216
Shield of Minerva (dish), 19
Shirley, Sir Anthony, 123
Simenon, Georges, 7
Simon, André, 103, 155
Simpson, Matthew (bishop), 187
Sirocco (yacht), 215
Siva (Hindu god), 121
Slater, Leonard, 203-4
Smart, Lord (Irish peer), 85
Smokers' Club, 62-4
Smollett, Tobias, 77
Sodom; or...Debauchery (Rochester), 53
Solinas, Pier Nico, 219
Song of the Shirt, The (Hood), 166
Soubise, Prince de, 105
Southey, Robert, 220
Soyer, Alexis (chef), 168-9
Spa (Belgium), 128
Sparks (Nevada), 192
Speakeasies, 190
Spectator, The, 168
Sporus (Nero's 'Empress'), 17
Stair, Lord, 86
Step to the Bath, A (Ward), 70
Stern, Michael, 201
Stokowski, Leopold, 207-8
Stowell, William, 1st Baron, 84
Strachan, John (bishop), 98
Strathclyde Business School, 233
Sturgis, F. R., 216
Suetonius, Gaius, 14-15, 17, 18
Sunday Express (newspaper), 155
Sunday Mirror (newspaper), 131, 199,
    233
Swift, Jonathan (Dean), 85
Synod, Most Holy and Most Drunken,
    204

Tahiti, 99, 187
Tacitus, P. Cornelius, 18, 21

Talleyrand, Charles M., Prince, 120
Tannahill, Reay, 222
Tany, François, 140
Tasmanian aboriginals, 8
Tatler, The (periodical), 177, 222
Taylor, John ('water-poet'), 46-7
Taylor, Revd William, 153
Tea, Essay on (Hanway), 129
Teonge, Revd Henry, 57
Terrific Sex (Westerheimer), 233
Thackeray, William M., 129, 140-3, 224
Thalberg, Irving, 209-10
Theobalds (Cheshunt), 45
Theodora (wife of Justinian I), 17
Thicknesse, Philip, 101
Thirty Years War, 68
Thrale, Henry, 95
Thrale, Hester Lynch (Mrs Piozzi), 95
Three Weeks (Glyn), 174-5
Tiberius (Roman Emperor), 14, 15-16
Tigellinus, Ofonius, 18
Timbs, John, 166
Titus (Roman Emperor), 19
Tolstoy, Leo, 151
Torrington, George, 4th Viscount, 83
Toulouse-Lautrec, Henri de, 161-2, 208
Town Topics (periodical), 171
Townshend, Charles, 2nd Viscount, 86
Travel Diaries (Beckford), 103
Tristan, Flora, 144-9
Troisgras, Pierre, 222
Tschumi, Gabriel (chef), 175
Tukoji Rao, Maharajah, 199-200
Tung-Hsüan-tzû (sex recipes), 227

Ultimate Porno (Solinas), 219
Underwood, H. G., 123
Urban-Dubois (chef), 140

Valois, Marguerite de, 48
Vanderbilt, Cornelius, 188
Vanderbilt, Gloria, 208
Vauxhall Gardens, 53
Versailles, 107
Vespasian (Roman Emperor), 19
Véze, Raoul, 111
Victoria (Queen of England), 144, 170, 189
Villarceaux, Marquis de, 48

Villiers, Barbara, Lady Castlemaine, 54
Virro (low-born upstart), 27
Vishnu (Hindu god), 121
Vitellius (Roman Emperor), 19
Vitzthum, Count, 115
Vocacitas, Temple to, 20
Voluptarian Cabinet (Wilson), 99-100
von Cramm, Gottfried, 198
Vortigern (British King), 32
Voyages (Olearius) 112

Waliszewski, K., 116
Walpole, Horace, 4th Earl of Orford, 74-6, 79, 87
Walpole, Sir Robert, 85-6
Walsingham, Thomas (chronicler), 38
Wang Chieh (Chinese scholar), 227
Ward, Edward (Ned), 61, 64, 66, 70-71
Wardlow, Henry (Bishop), 44
Warwick, Richard Neville, Earl of, 36
Wary Widow, The (play), 56
Wellington, Arthur, Duke of, 133
Wesley, John, 128
West, Mae, 216-18
Westheimer, Dr Ruth, 233
Westminster Hall, 136
Westminster Magazine, 100
Wheeler, Catherine *and* Martha, 119-20
Whisperer, The (periodical), 99
White, T. E., 101
White Ship, 7
Whorehouse Directory' (McDowell), 187
Widener, 'Fifi', 189
Wiser, William, 172
William II (King of England), 38
William III (King of England), 60
William IV (King of England), 136
William II (Kaiser), 160
William, Prince of Orange, 156
Willoughby, Francis, 102
Wilmot, John, 2nd Earl of Rochester, 53
Wilson, Mary (madam), 99
Wolsey, Thomas (Cardinal), 43
Woman's Own (perodical), 232
Women of New York (Ellington), 188
Wood, Nicholas, 46-7
Woodforde, Revd James, 69-70, 128
Woods, Josie (madam), 188

Yama the Pit (Kuprin), 179-84
York, 168

Zotof (*Knes-papa*), 113-15